Books by Sally Edwards...

•The Big Book of Running, Rockport Press, with Carl Foster, 2010

• Heart Zones Cycling, Velo Press, 2006 with Sally Reed

• Fit and Fat, Alpha Publishing with Lorraine Brown, 2003

• Health in a Heart Beat, a 6 Week Emotional Fitness Training Program with Dan Rudd, Ph.D., 2004

• The Heart Rate Monitor Book for Cyclists Velo Press, 2000 with Sally Reed.

• The Heart Rate Monitor Workbook for Cyclists Velo Press, 2001 with Sally Reed.

• Middle Schools Healthy Heart in the Zones Human Kinetics, 2001 with Deve Swaim.

• High Schools Healthy Heart in the Zones Human Kinetics, 2001 with Deve Swaim.

• The Heart Rate Monitor Guidebook, Heart Zones Publishing, 1997, 2002, 2005, Revised 2010

• Caterpillars to Butterflies, Heart Zones, 1997

• Heart Zone Training, Adams Media, 1996

• Snowshoeing, Human Kinetics, 1995

• The Heart Rate Monitor Book, Polar Electro Oy, 1993

• The Complete Book of Triathlons, Prima/Random House, 2001

• Triathlons for Women, Velo Press, 1992, 2002, Revised 2010

• Triathlons for Kids, Triathlete Magazine, 1992

• Triathlons for Fun, Triathlete Magazine, 1992

• The Equilibrium Plan: Balancing Diet and Exercise for Lifetime Fitness, Arbor House, 1987

• Triathlon Training and Racing Book, Contemporary Books, 1985

• Triathlon: A Triple Fitness Sport, Contemporary Books, 1982

Library of Congress Cataloging-in-Publication Data

Edwards, Sally 1947-
The Heart Rate Monitor Guidebook by Sally Edwards.

Includes bibliographical reference (p.) and index.
Self-Help. 2. Sports 3. Health. 4. Fitness. 5. Psychology 6. Heart Rate Monitor

ISBN 0-9700130-2-7

Table of Contents

The Forward to Heart Zones Training
Introduction by Carl Foster, Ph.D.

The Forward to Heart Zones Training

by Sally Edwards

Thanks for selecting The Heart Rate Monitor Guidebook and opening up your new path to fitness and personal fulfilment.

Heart Zones Training is a new training system and it works. It doesn't matter if you've started exercise programs and quit a hundred times. It doesn't matter if you've started just as many diets and been frustrated time and again by the "yo-yo" effect. The promise here is a reality.

A reliable, accessible fitness program has been a long time coming. Since 1968, when Dr. Ken Cooper wrote his pivotal exercise book, Aerobics, the idea of fitness through exercise has been in the air. Cooper sent millions into motion, and it was an excellent first step, a great kick-off to the movement. He was followed by hundreds more best-selling/worst-delivering fitness authors, video-exercise queens, and equipment gadgeteers who promised the dream and delivered only short-term results.

They and we have failed. One of the reasons for this failure is the basic premise (maybe it'd be more accurate to call it a "conceit," since wasn't that what those effortlessly fit diet and exercise gurus always seemed, a bit conceited?): that what works for one person, who just happens to be an athlete, works for us all. In fact, as you well know, it didn't work, and the net effect is what we see today: people getting more sedentary, less fit, and with little or no hope that they can get fit, ever.

We've been through the "you-only-have-to-diet" plan and the "you-only-have-to-exercise" plan. Both of these became monsters on the loose in the hearts and minds of men, women, and even children, succeeding in chewing up the thing we could least afford to lose: our hope.

There's no mystery to this sad process - when you don't get results, you lose hope, and losing hope keeps you from trying again in the future. None of us want to get fooled again.

I'd like to offer you, my readers, an honest program that makes sense, a dose of hope for the weary and cynical. I still believe that everyone can become who they want to be physically, emotionally and spiritually. Why? Because I've seen Heart Zones Training work. Now, I don't believe that it's going to work for those who are too cynical (or lazy!) to even try to help themselves, but I do believe I can show you the common sense of this program and give those sincere folks who have lost their hope another chance.

Heart Zones Training works. Guaranteed. It's so much guaranteed that if you can't follow the book or find that it doesn't deliver on its promise, I'll give you a no-questions-asked 100% refund. It's that solid a program.

What this program offers are the tools, the instructions, the data, and the support for you to make and reach your personal goals using your most important muscle in your body, your heart.

We've done our best to make this journey easy for you. Through the use of icons that appear in the margin, information of special interest-such as losing weight, getting healthier, aerobic fitness, or high performances training is highlighted so you can skip from key point to key point as best fits your needs. Or, of course, you can sit down and read The Heart Rate Monitor GUIDEBOOK to Heart Zones Training all the way through.

You can consider Heart Zones Training to be one more vehicle on the information superhighway, but this isn't any plodding bus filled with an uneven mix of passengers coming from and going to who knows where, whose final destination is at the whim of some distant corporation or uninterested driver. Heart Zones Training© is a brand new, high-speed electric train, whose cars split off at the rider's request, becoming personal vehicles which conduct you to within feet of your goal, not miles.

We swim in the midst of a flood of fitness information these days, but the key to avoiding being swept away by it is to remember that if it doesn't fit, if it's not tailored to your personal needs, then it's not going to take you where you want to go.

Consider The Heart Rate Monitor Guidebook your personal rescue vehicle, set on the course of your lifetime fitness. Bon Voyage.

Sally Edwards, Exercise Physiologist, MA, MBA

*CEO, The Sally Edwards Company - www.TheSallyEdwardsCompany.com
Author*

Professional Athlete

Founder, Heart Zones USA

Founder, FLEET FEET SPORTS retail stores

Introduction
by Carl Foster, Ph. D.

There is a reason to read a book like this and it's bigger than it seems at first glance. For some of you it might be that it finally time, time to get back to fitness training or to shed some pounds or to improve on a sports performance. For many, this is a book to devour because it is a matter of your life and health; it is a book your doctor should require for you to read. Or, still other's of you may be suffering from AOA, Adult Onset of Athleticism. This is a condition that occurs as you progress through the years and you connect, you discover, the athlete that is inside every single one of us. For me, The Heart Rate Zones Guidebook is one of my most precious and essential books I have ever read to help folks get fitter and fittest. That is what I want and I hope you do too. But, there is a more important reason to read Edwards' book.

The real reason to read this book is best told in the story of Milo of Crotona. Milo was the young farm boy who lifted a newly born calf every day as it grew. Everyday the bull calf added weight and everyday Milo became stronger as he used the baby calf as his weight training. Eventually, the calf grew into a fully-grown bull and in the process of this daily routine, Milo became the strongest man on earth. Because of his newly gained strength, he became one of the ancient Olympic champions.

The point of the story, of course, is that humans adapt very well to exercise so long as it is gained over time and is difficult enough to provoke adaptation, but not so hard that every day is a maximal effort. The problem for contemporary exercisers, whether fitness walker or elite athlete, is that training for sport is a little more complicated than lifting the local bullock. What one needs, is a way of gauging how much exercise is enough; a method that allows one to understand the interplay of Frequency-

Intensity-Time relative to producing fitness gains.

Too much exercise, or too frequent exercise at too high of an intensity, can lead to over training syndrome in serious athletes. Too intense exercise can lead to discomfort, or even danger, to the beginning exerciser. At the other end of the street, strategies for monitoring exercise training can make sticking to a plan much more likely to succeed.

Thanks to the wonders of technology, you can monitor almost anything you want during exercise these days. Everything from heart rate, to oxygen uptake, to oxygen saturation in the muscles can be measured not only in the laboratory, but also in the field. However, these same wonders of technology can make the process of trying to monitor exercise so complicated that no one, not even the Ph.D.'s that make their living with this kind of stuff, really understand what it's all about.

What the normal person really needs is a translator, a person who can boil down the academic bomfog that the Ph.D.'s create into strategies that are simple enough for a normal person to understand, and practical to use. The author of this book, Sally Edwards, is that translator. And, she is brilliant at it.

I've known Sally for nearly a decade. My first meeting with her started with an argument about how to monitor exercise. I barely escaped with my life. She's used her training knowledge to win races from a mile to a 100-miles. She knows the literature well enough to challenge the Ph.D.'s on their own turf. At the same time, I recognized that here was a person who could serve the essential role of translator for the technoweenie stuff that I loved to pontificate about, but which I could never seem to make normal people understand, a person who understood not only academically but as an elite athlete, an aging American, and as the occasionally injured. In other words, Edwards is someone with both perspective and communication skills. One of her first books, was a classic, as if not more important than classics like Aerobics and The Complete Book of Running. It opened the door for the widespread use of heart rate monitors by presenting a simple but effective approach that could be used by everyone from fitness walker to athlete.

The Heart Zones Guidebook is her best book to date. It is much more developed, but no less simple and practical than any of the 17 sports and fitness books she has written. The concepts Sally first presented two decades ago have been culled and refined, pushed and tweaked. The things that worked well have been expanded. The things that were harder to deal with have been refined. For the person who wants to get the most out of their exercise program, at whatever level, this is the first, the very first book that you should read. It may be the only thing you ever need to read.

Carl Foster, Ph.D.
Past President, American College of Sports Medicine
Professor of Exercise and Sport Science, University of Wisconsin-La Crosse
Chairman of Sports Science, U.S. Speedskating
Author, Physiological Assessment of Human Fitness

Co-Author, The Big Book of Running, 2010 with Sally Edwards

Adi Adi, Sally's 11-year old Australian Shepherd, pound dog, and running partner, donning a Timex heart rate monitor, Yes, heart rate monitors can be used with animals to assess their current level of fitness and to help them train properly.

Chapter 1

Your First Seven Steps

Physical activity is one of life's most individual pursuits. Regardless of whether you exercise in a group or by yourself, working out is still ultimately about you being motivated by your own personal reasons to be physically active. You might want to get healthy, you might want to stay fit, or you might want to get still fitter. Still, many people have found they work out better with others - a running group, a personal trainer, a team and/or coach, an exercise physiologist - so they can get on-the-spot feedback and motivation for their fitness efforts.

This is where using a heart rate watch (some prefer to call it a "heart rate monitor") can be so important. When you've got a heart rate monitor, it doesn't matter if you are working out alone or with a group, you now have an extremely reliable, precise source of feedback. With a heart rate monitor, you can be your own best motivator, your own personal trainer, your own exercise physiologist! People around the world are discovering that a heart rate monitor is the best workout partner they've ever had.

> *"You only need two pieces of gear to workout: a good pair of athletic shoes and a heart rate monitor."*
> - Sally Edwards

The heart rate monitor provides a seamless link between your body and your mind. No more wracking your brain as you try to guess your exercise intensity, no more stopping in the middle of an aerobic session to search desperately for your pulse, hoping to get a reasonably close count before your heart rate starts to plummet. For years professional athletes have had access to this kind of information, but now this potent training tool is available to everyone. You, too, now have real training power.

So, whether you are in training with a clear-cut fitness goal, or are exercising for your health or the pure joy of sport, having a heart rate monitor means you can do so more simply and efficiently. Training with your watch will help you better enjoy your exercise or more quickly reach your goal. And when you add to your new tool the information on heart zones training, you are on your way to enjoying each and every moment of physical activity, stretching your body to new places and, in turn, stretching your mind.

Heart Zones Training with your mind-body link – the heart rate monitor - may seem confusing at first. You'll be learning and discovering new ways of looking at the effort you put out, new ways of understanding fitness that you were never taught in your physical education classes at school. A lot has happened in the world of fitness in just the last ten years, and with your heart rate monitor and heart zones training, you are ready to reap the benefits.

The first step to take with your heart rate monitor is easy: strap it on!

STEP 1. TAKE THE 24-HOUR EXPERIENCE

To start, simply wear your heart rate monitor continuously for 24 hours so that you can learn to use it as a feedback monitor. See that heart flashing in the face of the watch? That's your heart actually beating. Stare at the face of the monitor for a couple of minutes. Check to see that every beat at rest is evenly spaced, the heart icon that flashes does so with complete regularity.

Wear your heart rate monitor when you first wake up in the morning and note the number it shows. This is your heart rate at rest or your "resting heart rate." Notice how your heart rate changes from when you are lying in bed to when you are sitting up and walking around. Check out your heart rate when you are in the middle of your day, sedentary and relaxed. That's your ambient heart rate. Note what happens if you get excited or stressed – emotionally, not physically. Does your heart rate change?

Watch as you move around doing different tasks. Do your regular workout and just observe the movement of the numbers. Get an idea of what the highest reading is during your workout. Is it over 100 beats per minute (bpm) or under? If you made it over 100 bpm, note how long it takes for you to break 100 bpm going back down, by resting after you quit exercising. That's a measure of how good your recovery heart rate is. After a day of this, you'll definitely find that your heart rate will increase and decrease as you increase and decrease your efforts or training load.

"Training Load" is a key idea. It is, by definition, the amount of F.I.T. you do. What does F.I.T. mean? That acronym stands for frequency, intensity, time, and when all three are put together it's called training load. Frequency is how often you are exercising. Intensity means how hard you are training (or, as you'll see, in what heart zones). And time refers to how long you are exercising.

Here's a bulletin: scientific research now says that it doesn't matter how long or how frequently you exercise. What most matters is the quality of your workouts, their intensity. The additional good news is that we now know that harder intensity isn't always better; rather the opposite is often true. Depending on your goals, the easier you go, the more results you may get. In addition, the easier you go at first, the

> *"Depending on your goals, the easier you go, the more results you may get."*
> - Sally Edwards

better the odds that you'll still be exercising on a regular basis after an extended period of time. Those who quit training programs most frequently are those who push themselves into too high a training load. They work out too hard, too long, too often. That's called burnout. So, go easy and use your heart rate watch to keep you in the lower heart rate ranges when you first start out.

That's it. You've passed your first experience - 24 hours of continuously using your heart rate monitor. After your first 24 hours of cardiac monitoring, you have probably learned a lot about how your heart responds to your different daily activities. You may have also found that your heart rate watch is not only a source of feedback on your physical activities but is also a source of emotional feedback. Did you get angry in traffic or at the television or thrilled by a phone call from a long-missed friend? If so, you may have noticed the effects of emotional stress on your heart rate. In fact, long-time users of heart rate watches often praise these tools just as much for their ability to remind the wearer to stay emotionally calm as for the monitors ability to motivate users to put out their best fitness efforts!

STEP 2. LEARN TO PROGRAM YOUR HEART RATE MONITOR

Every heart rate monitor works differently, with the functional details dependent on the model. The first step for all users, though, might be to understand the difference between a heart rate monitors and a heart rate watch. While all heart rate watches are heart rate monitors, not all heart rate monitors are heart rate watches. The difference is easy to see. Does your monitor include a readout with the time of day? If it does, then it's a heart rate watch. That's why people talk about heart rate watches and monitors as if they were the same thing – they're not, and now you know why. (For our purposes in this book a heart rate watch and a rate monitor will be considered the same thing.)

So, your heart rate monitor just replaced your time of day watch by giving you both the time and your heart rate in one convenient place. The first thing to do then is to set the correct time of day on your new tool (or your new *toy*, as a lot of people think of it!). This may take you as little as one minute or as many as thirty, but spending the time right now with your instruction booklet and watch is your best investment. You want your heart rate monitor to become your best friend, and it can only be that if you learn how to get comfortable with programming it. This means sharing some of your time with the instruction booklet packaged with most monitors.

Along with setting the time, you'll see that most heart rate monitors also work as stop watches. Try starting and stopping it a few times until you feel confident, since this is a handy feature for measuring the length of your workouts.

Now that you know how to start and stop your stop watch and how to set your time of day, it's time to understand the heart-oriented functions of your watch. Heart rate monitor features are designed around the concept of heart zones. That's a new term and you might want to jump to the sidebar at the end of this chapter for definitions or go to Step #3 to learn more. For now, know that the key purpose of the heart rate functions is to provide you with a range (or "zone") of heart beats in which you exercise. The upper limit of this range is called your ceiling and your lower limit is the floor. Learn how to set your upper ceiling and the lower floor of your heart zone by reading the instruction manual. Memorize this procedure.

Next, learn how to turn on and off the alarm feature. The alarm sounds when you are above your ceiling or below the floor of your zone. If you work out too hard and your heart rate exceeds the top number or upper limit of your zone, an alarm will sound to let you know. Likewise, if you exercise too gently and drop below your floor, the same alarm will sound and tell you that.

Some models have additional and important features. First, your watch might have a back lighting feature which allows you to see the face of the monitor easily when it's dark. You may also have a countdown timer; you can have your watch count backwards for up to three hours and set off a beeper when it reaches zero. The heart monitor part of your tool/toy also might have two new features: heart rate memory and heart rate recall.

Heart rate memory is important because it measures your "time in zone." Your goal is to set the ceiling and floors of your heart rate zone and stay within those boundaries for the workout. But if you go outside the zone limits, above or below, it is going to remember how much time you spent out of zone. Heart rate recall is your download function. After the workout or timed event, you can push the recall button and the heart watch will give you the time spent above your zone, within your selected heart zone, and below it.

All of this is done within 99% of the accuracy of a full EKG machine - the kind you see for cardiac monitoring in a medical environment - without the hassle of being laid out on a table and strapped to a large, immobile machine, and without the incredible expense. Now you know that for every workout from here on in, your first step will be to program your heart zones for that workout and turn on your alarm. If you follow this discipline you can train less time, with more precision and gain the benefit from training in zones.

STEP 3. USE THE FIVE TRAINING ZONES

Before reading this book, you may have already heard about something called a target heart zone. Well, I'm here to tell you that the single, set, target heart zone doesn't exist. There is no one zone, no one range of heart rates, that is best for everyone. Each of our bodies are different and each of our fitness/training goals are different, so there are multiple, different, zones. And in each of these different zones you get different benefits; or, as some say, multiple zones beget multiple benefits.

			WELLNESS HEART ZONE CHART
Zone Number	**Zone Name**	**% Maximum Heart Rate**	**Benefit of Zone**
#1	Health Zone	50%-65%	For getting fit
#2	Fitness Zone	65%-80%	For staying fit
#3	Performance Zone	80%-100%	For getting your fittest

Each of the zones is named for the benefits that you get from exercising within them.

The heart zones chart shows us a few important things. One, as mentioned above, there are multiple zones. Two, each of the heart zones is determined by a percentage of your maximum heart rate. Three, by working out in different zones you receive different benefits.

TRAINING HEART ZONE CHART

Zone Number	Zone Name	% Maximum Heart Rate	Benefit of Zone
Z 1	Healthy Heart Zone	50%-60%	For getting fit
Z 2	Temperate Zone	60%-70%	For staying fit
Z 3	Aerobic Zone	70%-80%	For getting fitter
Z 4	Threshold Zone	80%-90%	For getting even more fit
Z 5	Red Line Zone	90%-100%	For getting fittest

STEP 4. KNOW YOUR MAXIMUM HEART RATE

You may already have noticed the next key idea: your maximum heart rate. So what is it? Your maximum heart rate by definition is the greatest number of times your heart can make within a one-minute period. Your heart will only contract so fast and not one beat faster – that's why it's called your maximum heart rate. Your maximum heart rate is also a fixed number, and you should know that everyone's maximum heart rate is different. Two individuals who are both fifty years old could have a difference as high as 40 beats between their maximum heart rates.

There are a couple of ways of testing to determine your true maximum heart rate. The one I use most often is just to find the highest number you ever observe on your monitor when exercising and call that number your maximum. Others like to use the "talk test," which is to exercise until you find talking uncomfortable and then add 30-40 bpm to that number, resulting in a guesstimate of your maximum.

FORMULA TO CALCULATE MAXIMUM HEART RATE

There is no formula accurate enough to calculate your maximum heart rate. Period. For decades exercise scientists have attempted to find and have popularized different formulas to estimate maximum heart rate. The amount of error in each of these formula's is too large to make them valid. Rather than attempting to use a short cut, a formula, to estimate your maximum heart rate simply do a few sub-max tests to determine this valuable heart rate number. According to Carl Foster, Ph. D. "The formula's like 220 minus age is useless. There is no scientific validation for it - it was fabricated." There are a half dozen sub-max tests that you can take that provide you with a more accurate assessment than a formula. Those tests are found in Chapter 5. Heart Rate Assessments. You can skip ahead and take them now if you choose. Each sub-max test last no longer than 10 minutes so they are short and easy. That's why they are called "sub-max" tests because they are below, usually far below, your maximum heart rate number. (Robergs, Robert A. and Landwehr, Roberto. Prediction of Maximal Heart Rate. Journal of Exercise Physiology. Volume 5 Number 2 May 2002.)

Knowing your maximum heart rate is important, so try the method that is most comfortable for you and use that number to set your zones. As you gain more experience, you'll get a more accurate estimation of your maximum, so be flexible and patient for now and allow that determining your maximum heart rate can be a challenge. Still, now that you have an approximate maximum, you are ready for the next step.

STEP 5. SET YOUR TRAINING HEART ZONES

Now that you have an idea of your maximum heart rate, you need to calculate your five heart zones using your maximum heart rate as the anchor point for them. To help you with these calculations, the Heart Zones Training chart below provides you with these numbers easily.

THE 5 STEPS TO BETTER FITNESS AND PERFORMANCE

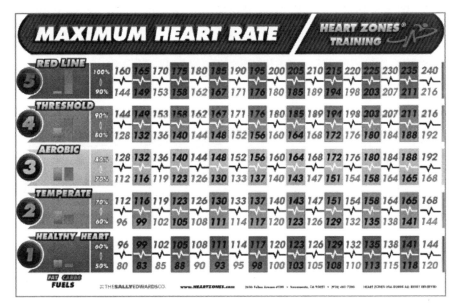

1. *Choose a heart zones: Select one of the five different training zones based on the exercise goals for your workout.*

2. *Set your Maximum Heart Rate: Find your maximum heart rate along the top horizontal row of numbers.*

3. *Determine your Training Zone: The box where your selected training zone and maximum heart rate column intersect is your heart rate training zone.*

4. *Set the Zone: The lower heart rate number in this box is the floor of your training zone and the upper number is the ceiling.*

5. *Stay in Zone: During each workout, maintain your heart rate between your zone floor and ceiling (excluding warm up and cool down).*

HOW TO USE THE MAXIMUM HEART RATE CHART

1. Find your maximum heart rate across the top, horizontal row of the chart on the previous page.

2. Follow the column down from you maximum heart rate to the point that it intersects with the zone of your choice.

3. Read the column that corresponds with this range under Training Zone.

Now that you have toured through your Heart Zones Training Chart, take charge of these five sets of zone numbers. They are yours. You should note the ceiling and floor of each of these zones, as those are the numbers that you are going to be using when you program your monitor. Your maximum doesn't change with age if you continue to be fit so you won't ever have to readjust your zones – they are yours for a near-lifetime.

STEP 6. START YOUR HEART ZONES TRAINING SYSTEM

You are ready. You have everything you need to start your program:a heart rate watch, a maximum heart rate, and your three to five heart zones. You can go out today and start exercising. But there are a few final tidbits of information which will help. First, it helps to know your time in zone. Keep track of how many minutes you train in which zones. If you are just beginning, start with 100% of your workout time in zone one, Healthy Heart. Stay in that zone for at least 2 to 4 weeks before you spend one single minute in zone two. Then, when zone one becomes easy and you are ready for the challenge, start with 10%-25% of your total training time in zone two. For example, if you are training four days a week for 20 minutes, then once a week put your zone two upper and lower limits in your monitor and train there. That would be three days in zone one and one day (that's 25%) in zone two. It's simple.

Next, all workout sessions should have the same general layout. You need to warm up by doing the specific activity slowly and gently until you have started to raise your heart rate level above your ambient numbers. For example, before I start a run, I always spend 10% of my total training time walking, as my warm up, and another 10% for my cool down, by walking again. I don't start by running during my first few minutes.

A typical workout of any length of time looks like the following:

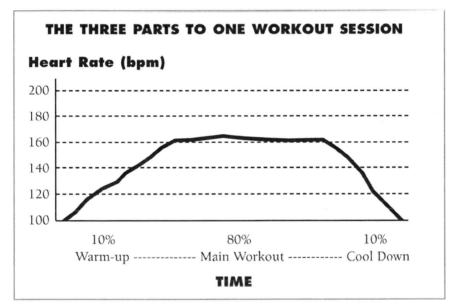

THE THREE PARTS TO ONE WORKOUT SESSION

Heart Rate (bpm)

200 — 180 — 160 — 140 — 120 — 100

10%   80%   10%

Warm-up -------------- Main Workout ------------ Cool Down

TIME

STEP 7. LOG YOUR WORKOUTS

It can help to motivate you and keep you on track to write down your workout. This is called keeping a training log, and you can create one of your own or use the one you'll find later in this book. One of the important features of a log is that it gives you a place to record how much time you spent within your zone and how much time was above or below your training heart zone. Your goal is to stay in zone, remember, so if you hear that alarm sound because you are going too hard or easy just think of it as my voice, your heart zones training coach, telling you to slow down or to pick it up.

Another good reason to keep a log is to monitor your progress. There is a maxim that we follow as athletes and professionals:

That's what is so great about a heart rate watch. It is really your coach, your friend, your indicator of progress, your motivator – the most

> *You can manage best what you can measure and monitor.*

important piece of exercise equipment that you have ever used. Your new heart rate monitor is your management tool. It can measure your workouts, and it can monitor them while you are conducting them.

Everybody, including fitness folks, athletes, personal trainers, coaches - everybody consider personal heart rate monitoring technology a powerful gift. It's changed our lives, and it can change yours. Use the power to make a difference in your life. Use the power to achieve your goals. Use the power to save you time. You've just made one of the most important purchases in your arsenal of power tools – now use it for every workout, as a biofeedback device, as your link between your mind and your heart. I do.

Heart Rate Terms

Ambient Heart Rate— The number of beats per minute your heart contracts when you awake but in a sedentary and stationary position.

Anticipatory Heart Rate — The cardiac response awaiting an event such as heart rate waiting for the start of a race.

ANT+ — A low power transmission protocol developed by Dynastream allowing interoperability between heart rate monitors or other devices.

Average Heart Rate — The average of all of the beats per minute during a period of time.

Cardiac — Pertaining to the heart.

Cardiac Drift — The slow usually steady rise in heart rate during exercise that occurs as a result of loss of blood volume, principally caused by dehydration.

Cardiovascular (CV)— Pertaining to the circulatory and blood vessels systems of the cardiac system.

Ceiling of the Zone -- The top of a heart zone, also called limit.

Criss Cross Workout - A workout that ranges up and down a range of heart beats

Delta Heart Rate - Difference between heart rate measured in a prone or lying down position and that heart rate taken after standing for two-minutes.

Exercise Heart Rate— The heart rate during your exercise activity.

Floor of the Zone —The bottom of a heart zone. The heart rate number at the bottom of a zone is known as the floor heart rate or the limit.

Intensity — The degree of energy, difficulty, or strength, as relates to a workout.

Heart Rate —The number of beats or contraction cycles your heart makes per minute, measured by the electrical impulses (EKG waves) emitted by the heart during this process.

Heart Rate Monitor — An electronic device which measures the electrical activity of the heart and displays it.

Heart Rate Point — A single heart rate number that is the marker such as a midpoint or a threshold heart rate point.

Heart Rate Zone — The same as a heart zone. A predetermined range that your heart rate is present in. There are five heart rate zones numbered one through five, with five being the highest heart rate.

Heart Zones Training — aka HZT, a proprietary and branded CVT (cardio-vascular training system) developed by Sally Edwards which is foundation or core cardio-training.

Maximum Heart Rate - the greatest number of beats per minute possible for your heart; this number is highly individualized and varies with fitness, age, gender, and other factors.

Maximum Sustainable Heart Rate — The highest steady state heart rate that can be sustained or held over an extended period of time.

Mid-point Heart Rate — That heart rate number which is in the middle of a heart zones and lies 5% below and 5% above a ceiling or a floor.

Minimum Heart Rate — The lowest heart rate during the activity. Some heart rate monitors store this number for latter retrieval.

Peak Heart Rate — the highest heart rate number in beats per minute during any single period of time.

Percent of Maximum Heart Rate — The relative heart rate number. The absolute heart rate number divided by maximum heart rate number. Example: current heart rate (absolute) is 140 beats per minute. Individuals maximum heart rate is 200 bpm. The percent of maximum heart rate is 140/200 or the relative heart rate number of 70% of maximum heart rate.

Pairing — Connecting a transmitter with a receiver in order for the two to communicate and transfer data between themselves or other device. Used with digital heart rate monitors that pair using a unique digital code for transmission.

Pulse — The regular throbbing felt in the arteries caused by the contractions of the heart. This is not the same as electrically measured heart rate.

Recovery Heart Rate — The rest time between interval sets. The difference in the heart rate after an exercise session and after rest and commonly measured two minutes after stopping or slowing exercise. There are two types:

- **Total recovery:** a rest period in which you stop moving completely.

- **Active recovery:** continue to move but at a very low effort.

Resting Heart Rate—The number of heart beats per minute when the body is at complete rest.

Steady State Heart Rate —A heart rate or training rate that is sub-maximal and maintained at a constant intensity, speed or rate of work.

Sub-Maximal —exercise intensity below maximum heart rate.

Threshold Heart Rate—The heart rate number at the cross over point between aerobic and non-aerobic exercise intensity.

Time in Zone (TIZ) —The sum of all time within a *single or multiple* heart zones. Can be used to calculate Heart Zones Training Points, load.

VO₂ Max Heart Rate — The heart rate number at your aerobic capacity also known as VO₂ max. VO₂ max is a quantitative measurement expressed in millilitres of oxygen consumed per kilogram of body weight, per minute (ml x kg-1 x min-1).

Zone—a range of heart beats that is fixed percentage of an anchor point such as 10% of maximum heart rate or 5% of threshold heart rate.

Zone Weight—The value associated with a training intensity that is used in the calculation of training load. Example: Zone 3 has a zone weight of 3 points.

For more Heart Zones Training resources and more on Sally Edwards, the legendary athlete, best-selling author, motivational speaker, and small business entrepreneur- please visit www.TheSallyEdwardsCompany.com

Chapter 2
The Five Basic Principles

Every fitness plan has the holy ground of principle: "Thou shalt not allow a cookie to cross thine lips"…"Thou shalt run 'til thou drop"…"Thou shalt suffer pain, then gain." Heart Zones Training, too, has its principles, but there are only five of them, and they're decidedly user friendly.

1. Your sneakers are fitted; your training should be, too.

One size doesn't fit all. Yet we pick up books and magazines or turn on the television, and we see prepackaged programs that are guaranteed to work for everyone, from waif-like super models to gargantuan body-builders. And you, too. What's wrong with this picture?

And what about group exercise - all those aerobic classes or mass bicycle rides? Group exercise, historically, has always been the gold standard. Fill a swimming pool, a workout studio, a stadium or a gym with a group of exercisers and have them follow the leaders. Take an aerobics class - and we all have. Ever notice how the class breaks down into two groups? The ones at the front in the newest outfits - the fittest - compete with the instructor for the crispest move and least body fat; in the back are the ones struggling and just trying to survive. They're drooling from overwork, sweating like crazy, doing a harder workout because their training load is greater, struggling to catch up.

In-between these two groups are the poor folks who reluctantly got pushed forward from the back of the class or former front-of-the-classers who were forced back by absenteeism. All too frequently, before anyone gets out of the back or moves up to the front, she or he quits the exercise program. On the average, most last no more than 6 weeks in a group exercise class. Only a few do really well, and the rest just hang on.

Heart Zones Training, HZT, is individualized training. Success is built around you and your abilities, interests, personality, and other important characteristics, such as body type, genetic makeup, mental stamina, and muscle structure.

What works for someone else may not work as well for you. What we want to do is to make Heart Zones Training fit your abilities and goals, because if we don't, success will always be just out of reach. Each of us is a whole person, with likes and dislikes, with limitations on our time.

Heart Zones Training is a program that is based on your individual fitness levels, your individual interests, your individual history, goals, needs, etc. It's totally about you. It allows you to move at your pace, and to get fit at your rate. Whether you want to accelerate that pace or keep the cruise control set, it's up to you, not the group leader.

The outcomes of individualized training are real and noticeable. Your benefits are based on goals you set and realize. The *doer* in you does what you enjoy, stimulating your interests. You start at whatever fitness level you're on and watch yourself improve, because you'll be seeing, feeling, touching, watching the metamorphosis of your body lead to your increased personal power.

As for time one of the greatest benefits of Heart Zones Training is that you'll get more fitness in less time. You can train as little as ten minutes a day and see measurable benefits. Now that's revolutionary!

2. Multiple zones give multiple benefits.

Remember all those charts on the walls of aerobics or weight rooms, charts listing our "target heart rate zone"? Good. Now forget them. If we want the individualized benefits of Heart Zones Training, we're going to forget about that single, set zone and concentrate instead on several smaller, more specific zones. Why? Because what we want from our training plan are multiple benefits - to be not only leaner, but stronger and healthier.

It's great to fit into your clothes comfortably, to hear "hey, you look trim," to feel the inner satisfaction of accomplishing something as simple as running up a flight of stairs without breathing hard, to be able to keep up with your friends, and then give them that Cheshire smile that says it was easy.

Further more, despite what we might want, we live in a world of constrained time. We've all felt the frustration that comes from seeing people who don't have our time problems giving us advice on health and fitness. The simple fact is that few of us have unlimited time for exercise.

The only way to get the multiple benefits we desire in a realistic, *doable* amount of time is through an understanding of the multiple zones our hearts work through.

Heart Zones Training provides us with multiple benefits because, during the training, we will be exposing ourselves to multiple stimuli. One of the wonders of the human body is its uncanny ability to adapt to whatever stresses we throw at it. This is, of course, a two-edged sword. If the stresses we expose our bodies to are watching television and eating chips, we become very good at spectating and getting fat! But, if we expose the muscular system to resistance training, it adapts into this stronger model.

Back to those aerobic room charts. We told you to forget the "target heart rate zone" (which will be discussed) because there are, in fact, *five* training zones, each providing its unique benefits:

Numbering Your Heart Zones

Percentage of Max Heart Rate	Zone Name	Zone Number
90%-100%	Red Line Zone	Z 5
80%-90%	Threshold Zone	Z 4
70%-80%	Aerobic Zone	Z 3
60%-70%	Temperate Zone	Z 2
50%-60%	Healthy Heart Zone	Z 1

Within each training zone, different physiological activities - different stimuli to the body - occur. For example, if you want to get the health benefits of lower cholesterol and lower blood pressure, you need to train in the Healthy Heart zone, because those are the principle benefits of that zone. If you want to get faster as an athlete, you'll be spending at least some time in the Red Line zone, an area that fitness folks rarely touch. When you're spending time in each of these different zones, you're accumulating the benefits of each one. These physiological and psycho-biological benefits include the metabolizing of different fuels (i.e. burning fat and carbohydrates), strengthening sport specific muscles, cardiovascularly conditioning different oxygen delivery systems, and training kinesthetic pacing skills.

The best part of it is *you* get to choose what benefits *you* want, and *when*!

3. You manage best what you can measure and monitor.

This simple statement has become a mantra for American business over the last few years, and it needs to be a personal mantra for every one of us. Why? Think about it; many of our so-called "failures" in diets and exercise programs stem from our inability to accurately monitor the changes we hope are taking place. The classic example, of course, is starting a training program to build muscle and using only our bathroom scales as the yardstick of success or failure. Muscle mass weighs more than fat, so even though the program may be succeeding - our clothing getting looser and looser, our bodies feeling stronger and stronger - our monitoring device tells us to "forget it"!

Given the number of things in our lives that are neither controllable nor measurable, it's surprising that Heart Zones Training is both. You control it and you measure it.

The preferred tool for measuring and monitoring progress in Heart Zones Training is the heart rate monitor. With the use of this wireless device, you can continuously and instantaneously have information about your performance and your results. With this information and the intelligent interpretation of the information (which we will quickly teach you here), you can have a level of control that just a few years ago was available to only the most elite athletes. A heart rate monitor-based program measures and monitors your ongoing exercise experiences. A heart rate monitor is, quite simply, *the most powerful fitness and health tool available on the market today.* It's your personal power tool.

Can you do Heart Zones Training without a heart rate monitor? Yes, you can, although it will be considerably more difficult - and subject to more error. If you don't have a heart rate monitor, watch closely for the hints and directions on manual monitoring and on other forms of heart rate testing we've included to guide you along the way.

The heart rate data that you're monitoring and measuring are the contractions of your heart muscle, measured in beats per minute. There are several important heart rate numbers, such as resting heart rate, ambient heart rate (also known as sitting heart rate) and maximum heart rate.

And, unlike the pronouncements of those old-fashioned heart rate charts, your maximum heart rate point does *not* necessarily decrease with age. This myth and other discredited beliefs are coming up - hold on because HZT is a new way to cardio-train.

4. Wellness is a continuum.

The great science fiction writer Ray Bradbury once wrote about, "the naming of names," the all-too-human urge to make sure everything has a handle for us to hold on to. We in the fitness industry are no different. In fact, think about the word "fitness." What does it mean, really? At its most basic, it can refer to cardiovascular fitness, muscular fitness, overall physical fitness or even mental fitness. A great word, but a little hard to tie down.

We have the same problem with "wellness," which is certainly more than the absence of disease. For our purposes, let's break wellness down into three areas, which when taken together form a continuum of good health and a critical aspect of Heart Zones Training.

The first component of wellness is one's basic (but not so basic when it's lacking!) health. For most of us, this is the key training area, because here we achieve the most essential health outcomes, such as weight management, lower cholesterol levels, and lower blood pressure. Training in the health area is usually at an easier activity level, where more fat as a percentage of total calories is burned. This is also the training area for those recovering from cardiovascular problems and undertaking cardiac rehabilitation. The two primary training zones in this area are the Temperate zone and the Healthy Heart zone.

for your information:
Of those who practice an exercise program as part of their cardiac rehabilitation, the reduction in the risk of death as a result is 20%.

The second component of aerobic wellness is fitness. When you're in this area, you're maintaining and improving your fitness, but this is measured by different parameters than it was in the health area. Aerobic fitness is measured as cardiovascular fitness, which is improved aerobic and non-oxidative capacity. The exercise physiologists have lots of more precise terms for the fitness area: lactate tolerance enhancement, increased VO_2 capacity, improved threshold heart rate, etc, etc. You can go to the back of this book for definitions of these terms - "Glossary of Heart Rate Terms". It suffices to say you can exercise harder or with more intensity than you could in the health area. Training in the fitness zone is strenuous but fun, challenging yet comfortable, and you can see body changes quicker than changes in the more basic health outcomes.

The third component in our wellness continuum is performance. This is where the athletes hang out, exercising with *high* heart rate numbers – all the way up to their max. The feeling is much different; you breathe hard and fast, you feel the burn in the sport-specific muscles, you see the blood vessels emerging to release heat, sometimes you even have a faint metal taste in your mouth from the anaerobic metabolic processes spewing out with high concentrations of lactates.

There are three different Wellness Zones within the heart zones training system which are a part of the five different zones. In the following chart, you can see how the health zone is within the bottom zones while the fitness zone is in the middle and the performance zones for athletes and competitors are the hotter and higher zones.

When you begin your individualized Heart Zones Training, you select

WELLNESS ZONES

Heart Zones Training Chart

Percentage of Max Heart Rate	Zone Name	Wellness Zone
90%-100%	Red Line Zone	Performance Zone
80%-90%	Threshold Zone	Performance Zone
70%-80%	Aerobic Zone	Fitness Zone
60%-70%	Temperate Zone	Health Zone
50%-60%	Healthy Heart Zone	Health Zone

which of these wellness areas you want to work in on any given day. That depends on the goal of your exercise regimen.

Do you want:

• *to improve your health, by lowering blood pressure and cholesterol levels and seeing weight loss or stability?*

• *to improve your fitness, as measured by improving your cardiovascular capacity?*

• *to improve your athletic performance, by raising your threshold as close as possible to your maximum heart rate?*

Once you pick the one that suits you, then you know where you are going to spend time in the heart zones.

5. Heart Zones Training is a system.

The KISS Principle (Keep It Simple, Stupid) isn't easy when we're talking about all the parts of the whole, then integrating that whole into our lifestyle. Yes, we guarantee that Heart Zones Training will work for you, but maybe we'd better throw another old saying into the mix: "There's no such thing as a free lunch." You are going to have to work the plan to make the plan work for you.

But don't forget that you have a "secret weapon" on your side - a proven methodology hooked to a modern training tool, the heart rate monitor, which together produce results. As your body and mind link with the accurate and reliable information from your monitor, you're able to achieve the small and the big goals that you want.

This system permits you to effectively integrate the different parts of your lifestyle. Without drifting into metaphysics, Heart Zones Training encourages you to see yourself as a whole person and act accordingly; it's as much about the mind as it is about the body. You can fret endlessly about which controls which, or you can just watch the two work in unison when the mind and body sides of the fitness equation are in balance.

Balance - that is the secret of HZT, Heart Zones Training. With these five points, you can make Heart Zones Training a fitness lifestyle. The lifestyle offered here can take you to new levels of health, fitness, and performance. For those of us who live the lifestyle, it offers a deep feeling of fulfillment and happiness.

Workout #1:

The Z1 Heart Healthy Zone Workout

Introduction. Each zone deserves its own example of a workout. Breaking through the aerobic floor is meaningful but you want to do so gently and allow your body to adjust to fitness. Start out with 10 minutes six days a week or 20 minutes three days a week for this workout is your choice. The body equates them as similar but not exact.

Workout Plan. Start by putting on a pair of walking shoes that are comfortable and wear some baggy street clothes. Choose a time of day which is most predictable so there are no distractions or competitions for your time. For most people, this is in the morning when there aren't opportunities throughout the day for planning another activity for that same time. Determine your specific numerical values for the Healthy Heart zone using the chart on page 19.

Workout. Stretch for a couple of minutes. Then start walking slowly and a minute later pick up the pace. It should take you about 60 seconds to break through the heart rate point which marks the floor or lower limit of the Z1 Healthy Heart zone. About every minute or two you need to take a quick glance at your monitor to make sure you are within the zone. For the last two minutes try to stay in the upper half of Zone 1. At the end of the two minutes slow down for about 60 seconds and let heart rate drop below your Zone 1 floor.

Comment. Ten minutes, that's all. Hang out here for several weeks and you'll begin to get fit. To get fitter you need to move up to the Z3 Aerobic zone and to get improved performance you need to exercise at least 25% of your time in the top two zones – Z5 Red Line and Z4 Threshold.

There are three ways to attend a HZT Seminar, Workshop, Certification, Showcase, or Conference: live, online-streaming, or DVD. Advanced training and certifications are offered for teachers, personal trainers, cycling and group exercise instructors, metabolic specialists, individual fitness enthusiasts, and athletes.

Chapter 3

The Heart Muscle and Its Monitor

Before we get into the dynamics of Heart Zones Training, we need to take a look at a couple of machines that are key to Heart Zones Training success. One is electronic - the heart rate monitor - the other, organic - the heart.

YOUR CARDIAC MUSCLE

Everyone loves to use the heart to describe their own personal delight or despair. Poets talk about black hearts, bleeding hearts, and heart aches. Journalists use the heart to describe the cruel - heartless - and therapists want us to feel our emotions by getting connected to our inner heart. Doctors think of it as a plumber might-as a pump that sends liquids through pipes.

The heart is deeply tied to the rhythms of our lives as reflected in our language.

heart of the matter	change of heart
broken heart	in one's heart of hearts
steal one's heart	heart throb
halfheartedly	heavy heart
burning heart	heartless
purple heart	heartfelt
heart-rending	heart strings
heart-to-heart	after one's own heart

For now, we want to understand the very personal communication between the heart muscle and the heart monitor.

Each time your heart "beats" what it's really doing is going through one cycle of contraction and relaxation. The heart tells itself to do this by sending itself an electrical message. As the heartbeat begins, a positive electric charge spreads across the cell membranes. Then, there's a sudden change – the heart sends itself a negative charge that makes it contract. The heart's electrical change from the positive to the negative state is one heartbeat, and this electrical activity is what both heart rate monitors and electrocardiographs measure, allowing them to record your heart-beats very accurately.

for your information:

Don't confuse "pulse meters" with heart rate monitors - they are not the same thing! Heart rate monitors record your heart's electrical impulses, giving very accurate readings of your heart rate. Pulse meters, however, rely on light waves passing through the blood vessels (in your fingertip or earlobe, for example) for heart rate detection. Pulse meters are only fairly accurate when indoors and seated (like on an exercise bike) or at rest, and they are sensitive to changes in light in any situation. Compared to heart rate monitors, pulse meters simply aren't reliable or accurate enough - they're old technology.

YOUR HEART RATE MONITOR

As a sport snowshoe racer, some of my favorite moments have been spent standing in a warming hut out in the snowy back country. It's *cold* out there, shuffling along for miles on snowshoes. One day, standing in one such hut, the fire was just starting to warm me when I noticed my hut-mate, almost indistinguishable and certainly unidentifiable, covered head to toe in winter gear. "You're Sally Edwards," the voice said, "and I read your book. I win all of my races because I use the heart rate monitor like a weapon, and my competition doesn't because I read your books."

"I know," I answered honestly knowing that "I win because of HZT, the Heart Zones Training system too."

A heart rate monitor is a powerful tool. It reminds me of one of those plastic "Transformers" kids play with - I'm always finding new ways of using it. It can motivate you to do better, coach you or allow you to train yourself, sound off with cheeps and chirps to slow you down or pick you up, act as a testing device and even be your confidant and friend. Download your monitor into your personal computer to view your physical performance minute by minute, or use it in a race to challenge you not to get your heart rate too high or too low. Sometimes my heart rate monitor reads my mind, reflecting my emotional state in the rising and falling numbers on its face.

There are many different brands of heart rate monitors, each of which has many different models. Be advised that there are lots of choices and lots of options - microchips seem to trigger some sort of deep-seated "features-and-functions" urge in engineers. Everything is getting techier with smaller monitors, cosmetically correct chest straps, all sorts of bells and whistles. What follows is a quick once-over of the basics.

THE PARTS OF A HEART RATE MONITOR

Heart rate monitors were in the realm of sci-fi not so very long ago. Researchers started checking heart rates around 1912, using water buckets as counterweights in the first laboratory model. The first electronic heart-monitoring tool, the electrocardiograph, was originally the size of a room, and even today you would certainly not want to carry one around (even if you could afford one). Thankfully, today we have the personal heart rate monitor. It may not do everything the electrocardiograph in your doctor's office does, but it does very nicely fill the needs for anyone who wants to accurately measure their heart rate. Today's heart rate monitors are the size of a wrist watch at the price of a pair of top athletic shoes. Tomorrow, the heart rate monitor's computer electronics may integrate into a small fashion-smart watch with no electrode-bearing chest strap.

The names "heart rate monitor" and "heart rate watch" are synonymous. Most, but not all, monitors are watches. The monitor receives and collects the data transmitted from the chest strap and processes it through a computer chip to calculate a heart rate number. This number is updated every 3-5 seconds (or in real time with some monitors). The first few numbers that appear on your watch should be tossed out, because the software inside the computer needs enough sample heart rates to accurately calculate a value. Likewise, if you quickly accelerate or decelerate, your heart rate values will always be lagging behind your real heart rate number.

Attached to the elastic chest strap is the transmitter unit. The transmitter *receives* (okay, that's a little odd, but hang with us here) the data from our heart through its electrodes, processes it, then *transmits* it to the monitor.

for your information:
For more on heart rate monitors, jump to Appendix III in the back of the book and read on...

When I ran the Houston Marathon, my plan was to hold my heart rate at 162 bpm (beats per minute). Proving that Murphy's Law dares to operate even in Texas, my transmitter died at mile ten. Luckily, it wasn't one of those long, slow, agonizing deaths – it just dropped dead at the 10 mile marker. At first I was devastated, running without my coach and without constant information. Then I passed through denial and depression, until the monitor miraculously came back to life.

I was joyous, but worried - the monitor now read 182. Then it struck me - the fickle thing was picking up signals transmitted by the chest belt on the runner next to me! Boy, was he in trouble, but I needed that data to qualify for the Olympic marathon trials. So I did the only logical thing - I asked if he would let me run with his transmitter - loan it to me. He did. I set a PR and we became friends.

Strange readings are not the monitor's fault every time. What happened to my friend Heidi is a classic example. She called long distance recently in a stew. She perceived she was running at the same effort as always, but her heart rate was ten beats higher than usual. She thought the monitor had gone coo-coo and wanted me to tell her how to fix the watch.

for your information:

Edwards' Hint: If there are two people wearing transmitters within receiving distance of one another, the monitors may pick up both signals and add them together, or pick up your neighbor's signal, giving you a weird reading. Don't worry, you're not having some kind of coronary episode – just move away from your pal, or move your watch to your outside wrist. This is called "Cross Talk".

On my end, I was happy with the news, because that told me that her Heart Zones Training program was working. "Congratulations," I replied. "The readings might mean you're getting in shape, but let's do a test to be sure." I asked her to go run that favorite course of hers at that new heart rate and time herself. She phoned me back - this time thrilled. She ran her course five minutes faster, ten beats higher, but it didn't feel any more difficult. She was getting fitter. Her heart rate watch was her coach, and it helped her achieve her individual goal - getting faster.

HOW TO CHOOSE A HEART RATE MONITOR

It's a training tool that isn't an option for those who want the most from their CVT, cardiovascular training. This popular and near-essential device is inexpensive, accurate, and tons of fun. Yes it is a motivation monitor, a fat-burning monitor, and a performance monitor. Its a personal coach, but even more, it is the most important tool that you can use to stay in the zone. On our Heart Zones website, I have provided you with both an article on how to select the right monitor to fit your needs as well as a Buyer's Guide. Use this to make your next purchase - and if you don't have one - get it today.

WHAT IS NEW IN HEART RATE MONITOR TECHNOLOGY

Technology is swift and changing at warp speed. To avoid getting dated here, there are a few new and exciting developments in heart rate and other devices like power meters, metabolic meters, speed-and-distance (use GPS or accelerometers) monitors that you might want to know about:

Interoperable-- With the development of the ANT+ standard, different devices can now talk or communicate with each other. You can ride with a power meter from one manufacturer that transmits the data to your handlebars dashboard made by a different company that uses a heart rate transmitter belt from a third and different company. ANT+ sounds like it is spelled - ant plus and it was first developed by a Canadian company, Dynastream. It stands for "a tiny network" and the plus symbol stands for all of the devices that use this protocol can talk or connect with each other. Even your body fat scale can transmit using ANT+ to your computer to provide you with per cent body fat, lean body weight, metabolic age, even the weight of your bones.

Digital vs Analog -- Check your transmitter belt to learn what type of transmission your monitor uses. Digital is your best but digital does not transmit, work, under water if you are a swimmer.

Smart Fabrics -- Look at your transmitter belt's underbelly - the side that you put against your skin. On each side of the plastic shaped transmitter "small box" there are two different electrode flat pads that are part of the transmitter belt. Using fabric woven to include the sensors integrated into them, new apparel is being produced that eliminates the need for the elastic belt not the transmitter. The development of new sensors that can measure and transmit data such as skin temperature, body position, location, and hydration level, are just now being developed.

MBAN -- This stands for mobile body area network which is a new convergent technology using sensors, cell phone applications, and other technologies. MBAN fuses together heart rate monitor, accelerometers, GPS satellite navigation, impact, blood glucose meters all in one device transmitting the data in real time to you on a wrist-top computer or cardio-equipped dashboard as well as to a web-site for latter review.

APPs -- Mobile phone and device applications are one of the hottest new technologies with smart phones that incorporate receivers that are bluetooth and ANT+ enabled. These apps can incorporate music, steps per minute, speed-distance, location, heart rate (even as an EKG wave), and other bio-physiological measurements. With the development of Web 3.0 as an app friendly ecosystem, apps are the future direction for data collection, storage, retrieval, communication, and analysis.

Workout #2:

30-MINUTE WORKOUT FOR ANY SPORT

Introduction. The ratio of training load to rest or recovery is important in your training because it provides you with a way to progressively and systematically change the regimen by adding intensity which leads to training improvements. Unfortunately, many athletes quantify the training load in broad, inexact simple terms like hard and easy. Your training will be more effective if you quantify the ratio of training load and rest in terms of training zones or even a specific heart rate point.

Purpose. To raise your threshold heart rate using long intervals at specific heart rate points.

Workout Plan. To do this 30-minute interval training session you must know your maximum heart rate and threshold heart rate. For this example we will use a maximum heart rate of 200 bpm and threshold heart rate of 175 bpm. The workout involves four-minute segments at 180 bpm or 90 percent maximum heart rate (formerly known as "hard") and two-minute segments at 120 bpm or 60 percent maximum heart rate (formerly known as "easy").

The Workout. After warming up adequately doing some form of cardiovascular exercise, accelerate quickly and steadily to 180 bpm and then hold this rate during the remaining portion of the four-minute period. At the end of four minutes, quickly decelerate to 120 bpm and stay at that level for the remaining portion of the two minutes. Do five sets of four minutes at 180 bpm training load and two minutes at 120 bpm recovery for a total of 30 minutes. Finish with a warm down.

If you have a programmable heart rate monitor you can set the alarms at two minutes, a high heart rate limit of 180 bpm and a lower heart rate limit of 120 bpm. Using the stop watch and alarm functions, accelerate until you hear the upper limit alarm and then maintain until the four-minute mark, then slow down until reaching the lower limit alarm and hold until the two-minute mark.

Outcome. What you have accomplished is a long interval workout at or above the threshold of most individuals. If you are in training to race, this workout plan should be a weekly regular. You can replace distance for time if you prefer to run by distance. You can also expand the duration progressively from 30 minutes to 36, 42 and 48 minutes.

Chapter 4
Trapped under a paradigm

Much of how we relate to exercise and lifestyle changes is tied to our preconceived - and too often mistaken - notions, or paradigms, of how the body works. The heart rate monitor is the tool we use to shift our paradigms about exercise, about losing weight, about training. Like my friend Heidi, once we get objective information, we're able to change these notions.

PERCEPTION AND REALITY

What color is a can of that famous cola? Red, of course. Everybody knows that. But let's say you scuba dive to about 60 feet to look at that same cola can underwater. What color is it now? If you said, "Still red," you're wrong. The color we call "red" is a specific wavelength of light that bounces off objects painted or tinted to reflect that color. As it happens, this particular wavelength of light can't penetrate very deeply into water. The cola can isn't "red" when you see it lying in deep water because there is no red light that deep. But an interesting thing happens when divers do the above experiment – they *still* tend to see a red can. Our brains fill in the missing color because we *know* that cola cans are red.

That's an example of the power of paradigms to determine how we look at the world. And, by the way, a paradigm can be as harmless as "all cola cans are red," or it can be as problematic as "no pain, no gain," or "no pain, no brain."

Our views of training are colored by a set of accepted paradigms - the target heart rate, for example. "Target heart rate" sounds scientific, doesn't it? But, strangely enough, the target heart rate was never ferreted out by research, or proven by major experiments. It was, rather, a speculation number which, over the years, became accepted as gospel. Recently, the mythical target zone has grown wider and more cumbersome. The American College of Sports Medicine in *Guidelines for Exercise Testing and Prescription* enlarged it to 55%-90% of maximum heart rate. This zone, once considered a window, is now a sliding glass door through which almost any activity can pass, allowing far too much variation for an individual (you!) to perform targeted training within.

ON THE BUS

In the summer of 1994, my troupe of travelling heart rate merrymakers journeyed to 14 cities in the U.S. with a seminar series to spread the word about Heart Zones Training. It reminded me of folk hero and author Ken Kesey when he and his cohorts hopped into their psychedelic-painted bus in the late '60s and traveled across America. The chemistry, of course, has changed. We've moved from the chemicals of the "Electric Koolaid Acid Test" to self-generated endorphins. But one of Kesey's observations has stood the test of time: you're either on the bus or you're off the bus.

Either you get it or you don't. People across the country are struggling with a losing war on weight, looking for some faint glimmer of hope after the endless lack of success with fitness programs. They're beginning to think that fitness programs – like diets - don't work, and there's nothing that can or will.

The whole concept of a single target heart rate zone is tied up in those failures. On one particular stop early that summer, I was struck by the realization that American fitness buffs, those professionals who were our seminar participants, couldn't give up the notion that there wasn't really a single target heart rate zone. This mythical zone was their entire aerobic belief system, their rock of Gibraltar. On this particular evening, I was lecturing at the Cooper's Aerobic Centre in Dallas, which is, in truth, the Mother Church of the whole aerobic movement.

That afternoon I toured the Cooper Center facilities with one of their personal trainers. In the aerobics room, we toured had a target heart rate chart posted on the wall that was based on the formula 220-age = max heart rate It was the *only* chart on the wall - that's how important it was to this aerobics room and to the aerobicisers' knowing their zones.

This wall chart showed age on the bottom axis and heart rate on the vertical axis, and how maximum heart rate and target training zone allegedly decline with age, based on the concept that, with each passing year, we get physiologically worse.

As I started to - politely, mind you - launch into my discourse of, "I want to tear down every one of these posters In every athletic club..." the trainer interrupted me. "Sally, I'm embarrassed that we have these old posters on the wall. They're part of the *old* aerobic movement. We know the posters are wrong," he sheepishly admitted, "but we don't have anything to replace them with."

It made me realize that you can't take an entrenched belief system like the age-adjusted maximum heart rate formula away from someone without replacing it with another belief system. That's the problem with paradigms. Having our existing paradigm disappear hurts and confuses us.

That chart also reminded me of how deeply entrenched the whole notion of age-predicted, maximum heart rates are; how many people have bought into the "220 minus your age" formula for determining their training zones.

This useless equation is a myth, a leftover paradigm from the days when exercise scientists were looking for something simple rather than right. Fitness professionals and participants bought into it because it was universally preached to them, passed down from book to book, graduate to undergraduate, as if it were carved in stone. The sad part is that not only do these old systems not work, they leave people misguided well and sometimes in too high, dangerous and in other cases too low a zone to gain much benefit.

I went to leading researcher at the time Frank Katch, Ed. D., Professor of Exercise Science at the University of Massachusetts, in search of the origin of the mythical single training zone. Katch had asked me to stop by and teach his graduate students a seminar on heart rate monitors since my work with HZT and monitors was both revolutionary and exciting to him. On the front cover of one edition of his very popular college textbook, *Exercise Physiology*, was the same chart that was on the Cooper's Clinic wall in Dallas. Once again, the chart's importance was reflected in its position on the front of the leading textbook of the time.

I asked where the chart originally came from, and Dr. Katch remarked that he had taken the chart from a textbook written by the professor before him. That professor probably borrowed it from *his* professor's textbook, and so on and so on. Like the Energizer Bunny, it just keeps going and going and going. And, it's a self-fulfilling prophecy that if we tell people their fitness is declining with age, it happens.

Somewhere back in the 1940s, this paradigm came from several respected scientist researchers from the Harvard Fatigue Lab. Without any other research method or data available at the time, they were forced to use statistics from cross-sectional studies of the population at large to predict maximum heart rate. These early exercise scientists compared a group of 20 year-old's' maximum heart rate with a group of 40 year-old's and with a group of 60 year-old's. All the people were inactive. The researchers merely discovered that, in cross-sections of these populations, the maximum heart rate dropped by about one beat per year.

Research is just now leaking out of the fitness labs from the first truly longitudinal research on maximum heart rate. A longitudinal study is one that tracks the same cohorts of individuals over a long period of time, like 10 or 20 years. And what have these studies found? In these studies, maximum heart rate does not decline with age among those who maintain their fitness level. It only declines if they quit exercising.

for your information:
There are no longitudinal studies on changes in Max HR for women.

That's how myths grow. In this case, the entire fitness community believes in and has structured every single exercise program on a concept with no foundation - that there is a single target heart rate zone which is a percentage (typically 70%-85%) of a person's inaccurate, age-predicted, mathematically construed maximum heart rate. Rather, there are multiple zones which give you multiple benefits. If you exercise in multiple zones, you get their benefits.

Time to take down those wall posters charts and get on the bus. Now.

MAXIMUM HEART RATE

Maximum heart rate is the highest number of times per minute your heart can contract. This makes sense, doesn't it? It's the heart rate at the point of exhaustion in an all-out short effort. You can continue to increase your intensity, but when you reach the maximum heart rate point, your heart simply won't beat any faster. (Most researchers believe this genetically determined point is your body's way of protecting itself. If your heart beats too fast, it doesn't have enough time between beats to fill the chambers adequately, to fully contract and effectively pump the volume of blood needed to your body parts.)

There are at least a dozen mathematical equations to predict - guess - your maximum heart rate. Don't use any of them; they're all too inaccurate. Only a formula that uses your specific cardiovascular response can accurately predict your individual maximum heart rate. (And we're going to provide you with several fun tests that can do just this, after more paradigm shifting.)

My search for supportive data on maximum heart rate goes back to my UC Berkeley college notes. I found my class notes on maximum heart rate and target heart rate zone, now on yellowing pages.

As students, we had to take lab work and test each other with everything from underwater weighing to various anthropometric measurements. Sure enough, there were my maximum heart rate test results from 1969 as a 22-year-old coed - Sally Edwards' maximum heart rate: 194 bpm.

Today, at the age of just over 60, my maximum heart rate for running remains 194 bpm, for cycling 183 bpm, and for swimming 170 bpm.

Here's the pregnant "but": this is one woman's 40-year longitudinal study. I have stayed fit and active all my years. If I were to ever use, please don't, the age adjusted formula with my running maximum heart rate (220-60 = 160 bpm) the error would be 33 bpm or more than an entire zone, so the older you get, the greater the error, the worse the prediction formula. The formula is useless.

Where did "220" come from? Sadly to say, it was invented in the early 1970's by scientists Fox, Naughton, and Haskell who never intended it to become the gospel, the foundation for all cardio-training in the world.

In fact, research by Robert Robers and Roberto Landwehr, two Ph. D. scientist has established there is an enormous margin of error for this formula - as great as thirty beats per minute. Quite frankly, that's just

for your information:

Children have smaller heart size and less total blood volume, which results in their having a lower stroke volume than an adult. To compensate, they have a higher heart rate for the same absolute workload.

not accurate enough to work very well for very many people. Certainly it doesn't work for most people, and not at all for very active individuals.

And, the formula is dangerous beyond the fact that there is no scientific research to support it. The equation *overestimates* maximum heart rate for young adults and *underestimates* it in older people - both are dangerous situations.

The bottom line is that this prescription that results in this single zone notion based only on age has failed us, and failed us miserably. Frankly, the ACSM prescription does not address the needs and goals of each individual. A new guideline needs to be set by all fitness organizations based on sub-max testing of individuals.

TRAINING HEART RATE *NOT* TARGET HEART RATE

Busting some myths is harder than others. Busting the target heart rate theory is more difficult than keeping off the twenty pounds from the last diet. Few succeed at keeping the weight off, but we'll take a shot at target heart rates anyway.

The target heart rate zone is generally described as 70%-85% of your maximum heart rate. This is the standard training zone or aerobic

for your information:
Fit women with the same body size have higher heart rates for the same workload as fit men. This is due to women's smaller left ventricle and lower blood volume, the result of males having more testosterone and it's effects on all muscles of the body.

exercise prescription that is recommended by most professionals. The purpose of this one zone is an attempt to use important physiological criteria to set safe, simple, and effective training load dosages of exercise. The problem is having only that one zone. It still doesn't focus on or support benefits of Zone 1 and Zone 2 or Zone 4 and Zone 5.

If I followed the age predicted formula, I wouldn't be able to run, I'd just have to walk to be able to stay at the low 120 bpm edge of the contrived target zone, and I would not get enough exercise for my goals. I would be able to run at 146 bpm, but that pace is so easy for me that it's like being on cruise-control. I would be training too low to meet my racing objectives, and I would be terribly unhappy and unsatisfied. I'd probably quit. The error in all of the formulas is just too great and is simply unacceptable to use any formula.

One of the only times that it is fun to have an inaccurate age-predicted maximum heart rate is when I workout on a cardiovascular machine that is heart rate programmed and presets my zones for me if I give it my age. Because of the huge error in the arithmetic formula, I get to enter my age as 33 years old so it will set my zones correctly for my true maximum heart rate.

When training at an athletic club in a Chicago suburb last year, I was

A Quick Electronic Fountain of Youth

Determining an accurate Max HR is the key factor in setting your individual zones. To prove that let's look at my numbers:

	Max	70%	85%
Age Predicted:	170	119	145
Tested Max HR:	195	135	163
Error:	25	16	18

Heart Zones Training on a cardio-machine called the "Cross Trainer." The woman on the Cross Trainer next to me was in her mid-thirties and her control panel showed a heart rate reading of 195 bpm. She was working hard but not hurting herself. The heart rate number was flashing to indicate she was out of her machine-set target heart rate. I asked her how she felt about that large a heart rate number. She said, with great trepidation, "I am really, really worried that I am training too hard. But this is comfortable for me, and I don't know what else to do but do a workout that feels like I am accomplishing something and ignore the heart rate number." Clearly, she had a high true maximum heart rate, and the age-predicted formula had failed her as it had failed me.

The benefits of exercising below 70% of your maximum heart rate are substantial. It is simple to understand why so few people have been successful at exercising particularly in the one zone - 70%-85% range - they haven't been told the correct information. Being able to get into a zone that is 70-85% maximum heart rate is extremely difficult for the unfit to accomplish. It is too high and too strenuous, so why exercise when you can't do it anyway?

for your information:
A higher Max HR is not better than a lower Max HR.

For people who are fit, the single zone is simply too easy. It may seem odd to people struggling to get into the zone, but one of the most common complaints at health clubs is, "I've been taking aerobics for one year - or two or three - and nothing is happening." It's also a complaint I hear from joggers, who are working hard, but not getting the results they anticipated.

The problem is the same for both groups: *there is no such thing as one target heart rate range.*

Do you want the truth? There are *multiple* zones that provide *multiple* benefits – not one zone for everyone. There are at least five different max zones, and they are clearly identifiable by their physiological frame-work. The five zones are part of a continuum, beginning with the health zones, passing through the middle, fitness zone, and ranging all the way up to the performance zones.

> *Quick tip: a better way of describing "target" Heart rate is to call it a "training" heart rate.*

NEW RATING OF PERCEIVED EXERTION (RPE)

So, why can't you tell yourself how hard you're working? (Hint: this is the next paradigm in need of a good, swift shift!) You ought to be able to do that, right? There's even a chart, called the rating of perceived exertion (RPE), that shows you how to correlate how you feel- your perceived exertion-to your heart rate. This sounds like you can plan to use the money saved on a heart rate monitor to buy frozen yogurt. But you'd better put down that spoon. Guess what? RPE doesn't work.

Here's a myth that fitness professionals have bought into big time, probably because people always think it's simpler to go with the subjective analysis of feelings rather than determine the facts. (This may have been true before the advent of the heart rate monitor, but definitely isn't true anymore!) After all, if you're in touch with your feelings, why bother collecting the data which could show it differently?

The problem is just this - perceived exertion using only your personal perceptions of effort to set your training intensities misses the target. It was quantified by exercise scientist Dr. Gunnar Borg in 1973 when he first based a rating scale on perceived exertion. For a sample of the problems with this paradigm, let me give an example of one of my workouts based on RPE.

I love to train with my dog Adi Adi . She is an eleven-year-old Australian Shepherd pound dog and has her own training style - go hard all of the time, and chase a rabbit if you can. While I usually forego the rabbits, we love to run off-trail for hours. Sometimes, even I - a crown princess of heart rates – throw my heart rate monitor to the wind and just run, using my perceived exertion rating.

I know from years of cardiac monitor training that I get the greatest feeling of well-being running long distances, at sea level, on the flats (that is the description of every workout in my hometown of Sacramento, California), in my favorite easy and narrow heart rate zone of 150-155 bpm, or 77%-80% of my tested maximum heart rate. I've done these runs for years, so I should know how that rate feels...shouldn't I?

I decided one day to test my theory, so I put on my downloadable monitor and took off with Adi Adi for a 12-miler. This time, I put masking tape over the face of the watch so I wouldn't peek at my heart rate. I ran totally subjectively, chasing rabbits in my head, using my perception that I was running at my preferred exertion rate of the low 150s.

Immediately afterwards, I upload the information from my monitor onto the web and to my consternation - but not great surprise - I found that I had done a steady state run at around 140 bpm. Basically, going by RPE left me feeling unhappy and dissatisfied.

Some researchers have found that perceived exertion can be very accurate. Others report it to be unacceptably inaccurate. It's my opinion that if you want to train with clear and accurate information, using the guess method attached to your feelings is probably not the most sound way. Remember Heart Zones Training Principle #3: *You manage best what you can measure and monitor.*

HEART ZONES TRAINING WITH RPE

There are some athletes who are addicted to their monitors. They wear them for every workout and then to work. There are times when it's fun to just go work out and not be conscious of intensity, percentages and zones. Take a break if you're an addict and feel your exertion freely.

FOR HIGH-PERFORMANCE FOLKS

Most of my training friends know what their max VO_2 Many know an inordinate amount of baseball trivia, too. The former is important to your training. Often I read in one of the many popular sports and fitness magazines that a celebrity cyclist is training at a intensity of 85% VO_2 max for a 40K time-trial ride. How amusing. What does any of that mean to anyone who doesn't have a gas analyzer on hand to calculate their oxygen uptake? It doesn't mean anything - it's physio-babble.

The other thing that always gnaws away at me in those same magazines is the suggested lactate threshold training levels. Do they think their readers have the ability to take their own blood samples while they're training, then pass the vials along to some handy lab they pass somewhere along their training course in order to have the lactate concentration analyzed?

To a large extent these ludicrous recommendations are the fault of exercise scientists who are too fond of quoting exercise intensity in terms of their two favorite measurement tools: blood lactate or oxygen consumption. There's a cavernous gap in between them, with their labs chock full of hundreds of thousands of dollars of testing equipment, and us, armed only, if we're lucky, with our heart rate monitors. The bottom line is that there are only three ways to measure your exercise intensity:

• *Direct measurement of maximal oxygen consumption using analysis of expired air samples collected while the individual is exercising. Equipment cost: $10,000-$75,000 and retailers don't stock them.*

• *Blood samples taken during exercise and analyzed for the concentration of lactic acid. Equipment cost: $500-$10,000, plus, a high messiness factor if attempted "on the run." You have to prick a body part like a finger or an ear lobe and draw blood to measure this.*

• *Continuous measurement of heart rate with a wrist top personal heart rate monitor. Equipment cost: $40-$500.*

Now, I am not trying to say that measuring oxygen uptake and lactates isn't worthwhile. Of course it is. These have been the measurement choices of exercise scientists for the last twenty-five years because they are the most accurate ways of measuring energy costs and training load. If you are at all serious about long-term fitness, I thoroughly recommend that at least once every ten years you have a complete physical, with lactates and oxygen consumption as part of the assessment, and that you keep these records and monitor your own aging process. However, it seems clear to me, if not to those magazine editors, that it is only with a heart rate monitor that individuals can measure exercise training loads cheaply, accurately, practically, and on an ongoing basis.

for your information:
VO$_2$ max means the maximum volume of oxygen you can utilize at any one moment. It's measured using a gas analyzer and it changes dramatically with conditioning. A high VO$_2$ max is best because it means you can do a lot of work.

Workout #3:

THE STEP-TRED-ROW-CYCLE HEART ZONES TRAINING WORKOUT

My travel schedule has been hectic lately, plus I have had a debilitating Achilles tendon injury so I have sought a different protocol for exercising until both of those conditions change. I discovered a new one-hour indoor workout that I can do at the gyms in most hotels (which are usually these small rooms with four or five pieces of poorly maintained equipment) or at my athletic club which has kept me in great shape given the circumstances. It's a form of what's called indoor circuit training but it's done on machines rather than circuit stations and it's done by alternating zones. The circuit consists of four different machines, on each of which I do a three zone ladder. The sequence of the cardio-circuit isn't key unless you want to vary between upper body and lower body equipment such as a stepper which is lower body and a rowing machine which is a lot of upper body. The sequence I particularly like is a stepper, a treadmill, a rowing machine and an exercise bike. I like to use three zones in the ladder - Z2 (60%- 70% maximum heart rate, Temperate Zone), Z3 (70%-80% maximum heart rate, the Aerobic Zone), Z4 (80%-90% maximum heart rate, the Zone) each for five minutes. Since I know those zones literally by heart now, I know how to solve the exercise machine problem.   The exercise equipment sets the zone based on my age, they don't let me set the zones.

To overcome the problem, you have to "over-ride the formula," a formula that is preset in each piece of cardio-equipment. Recovery phase of the workout is the time in between the four different machines and I use this time to answer all of its questions like "how much do you weigh," "what type of workout". I always have to override the formulas by saying I am 25 years old on the treadmill (actually I am just over 60) and I want to manually control the workout so I punch in that request.

I start each time in Z2 for the first five minutes and that allows me to comfortably warm the specific muscles that I am using on that machine as well as recover from the circuit before.

For example, after I get off the stepper and start programming in my personal information into the treadmill, I am recovering from the stepper while I start walking at the floor of my Z2 zone which for me is 120 bpm. During that first five minutes, I slowly increase the belt speed so that I get to 130 bpm in about 2.5 minutes. This is the midpoint of my Z2 Temperate Zone and by the end of five minutes I have watched my heart rate increase to the ceiling of my Z2 which is the floor of my Z3 which is 145 bpm. I have to tell you that Z4, which is 80% of my maximum heart rate, is the point that I can feel the intensity; and I hang out a lot in the lower half of my Z4 for that five minutes as it's hot in the upper half, or for me 170-180 bpm, for very long.

At the end of an hour, I feel that glow and good feeling that I get whenever I have a workout where I have maximized my time and gotten the most benefit possible. That's what this workout is all about - incredible cardiovascular benefit from every single minute of workout time.

And remember, that maximum heart rate is sport specific so you have to find out your stepper maximum heart rate, and your rowing max, and so forth. I have discovered and try it for yourself that those adjustments that are sport and equipment specific are approximately as follows:

- Cross Country Skier = maximum heart rate

- Treadmill -- subtract from cross country ski machine 5 bpm

- Rowing ergometer = subtract from cross country ski machine 20 bpm

- Indoor cycling -- subtract from treadmill max 15 bpm

Chapter 5
Heart Rate Assessments

Before we go any further, you've probably got some questions. I'll bet the biggest one is, "How do I determine my maximum heart rate?" That's the basis for the Heart Zones Training system using maximum heart rate, and that's what you need to do next. There's another Heart Zones Training system but you have to wait to Chapter 18 to learn all about that methodology.

Your maximum heart rate is a specific number, the maximum number of contractions per minute that your heart can make. There are a number of basic facts about maximum heart rate for you to know:

• *Maximum heart rate is genetically determined; you're born with it.*

• *Maximum heart rate is a fixed number, unless you become unfit.*

• *Maximum heart rate cannot be increased by training.*

• *Maximum heart rate declines with age only in sedentary individuals.*

• *Maximum heart rate is affected by drugs.*

• *Maximum heart rates that are high do not predict better performance.*

• *Maximum heart rates that are low do not predict worse performance.*

• *Maximum heart rates has variability among people of the same age.*

• *Maximum heart rates for children are often over 200 bpm.*

• *Maximum heart rates cannot be accurately predicted for most people by any formula.*

• *Maximum heart rates does not vary from day to day.*

• Maximum heart rates testing requires the person to be fully rested.

• Maximum heart rate testing needs to be done multiple times to determine the exact number.

For us, there's one more point to remember:

•Maximum heart rate is the anchor point from which you set your individual training zones.

Maximum heart rate is a critical piece of information, since you design your entire Heart Zones Training program around it. It serves as a marker for exercise intensity. There are a number of different approaches to capturing this number. These include taking a maximum heart rate test to determine the true number or doing a sub-max test from which you can predict your maximum heart rate pretty accurately.

GUIDELINES FOR DETERMINING MAXIMUM HEART RATE

The first step is to follow the guidelines that have been prescribed for exercise testing by the American College of Sports Medicine (ACSM). Before taking any tests or following any exercise prescription, you should follow their prudent guidelines.

Apparently healthy men greater than age 40, and apparently healthy women greater than age 50, should have a medical examination and diagnostic exercise test before starting a vigorous exercise program, as should symptomatic men and women of any age. However, these procedures are not essential when such persons begin a moderate intensity exercise regimen.

Here, briefly, is a synopsis of the recommendations: If in doubt, prior to engaging in any vigorous physical activity or exercise test, consult your physician for clearance. It's wise to see your physician on a regular basis regardless, so get a clearance while you are there.

GUIDELINES FOR HEALTHY ADULTS UNDER AGE 65

Basic recommendations from American College of Sports Medicine and American Heart Association updated in 2007:

• *Do moderately intense cardio activity 30 minutes a day, five days a week, or*

• *Do vigorously intense cardio-activity 20 minutes a day, 3 days a week, and*

• *Do eight to 10 strength-training exercises, eight to 12 repetitions of each exercise twice a week.*

Moderate-intensity physical activity means working hard enough to raise your heart rate and break a sweat, yet still being able to carry on a conversation. It should be noted that to lose weight or maintain weight loss, 60 to 90 minutes of physical activity may be necessary. The 30-minute recommendation is for the average healthy adult to maintain health and reduce the risk for chronic disease.

SUB-MAX HEART RATE TESTS

If you aren't in shape and haven't been for awhile, you don't want to take a maximum heart rate test designed to bring you to your actual maximum heart rate. Instead, there are exercise assessments that you can do that estimate your maximum heart rate more accurately than any mathematical formula. These assessments are called "Sub-Max Tests". One of the first steps to getting started training in the zones is to take them. Each of them is below your maximum heart rate so you don't go near your highest number. Each of them requires a bit of calculation so sharpen your pencil, don your monitor, and let's get going.

To score the sub-max tests, you need to decide on your current level of fitness as either low shape, average shape, or excellent shape. This is a subjective assessment but remember, you are only estimating your maximum heart rate not precisely measuring it. There is only one way to precisely measure maximum heart rate - go so fast and so hard that you reach it. I don't want you to do that, rather, I want you to complete the Sub-Max tests because your risk of a cardiac incidence are lower. The following definitions for assessing your current level of fitness are based on your cardio not muscular shape:

- **Low Shape** - if you do not exercise at all, or if you have not exercised recently (last 8 weeks). Remember, you can be thin, have no weight-loss goals, and still be in low shape.

- **Average Shape** - you walk a mile 3 times a week, or participate in any aerobic activity 3 times a week for 20 minutes.

- **Excellent Shape** - you regularly have training sessions that total more than 1 hour a week, or you walk or run at least 5 miles a week.

TAKING YOUR PULSE MANUALLY

Your heart rate and your pulse rate are usually, but not necessarily, equal. "Heart rate" refers to the electrical impulses that cause your heart to beat, but "pulse rate" refers to the movement of blood through your arteries. If you have mitral fibrillation, you have no pulse rate but you have a heart rate. If you have cardiac arrest, you don't have a heart rate but you *do* have a pulse rate (for a short period of time, anyway).

Each time the left ventricle of the heart contracts, a surge of blood is pumped into the aorta and into the peripheral vessels of the arterial system. This stretch and subsequent recoil of the arterial wall during a complete cardiac cycle can be felt manually by applying light pressure over any artery that is near the surface of the skin. This stretch and recoil is what we usually are measuring when we talk about our "pulse."

To manually measure your radial pulse, take two fingers and place

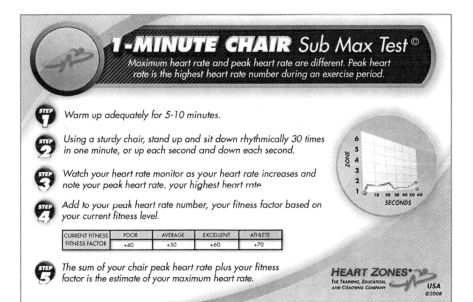

1-MINUTE CHAIR Sub Max Test ©

Maximum heart rate and peak heart rate are different. Peak heart rate is the highest heart rate number during an exercise period.

STEP 1 Warm up adequately for 5-10 minutes.

STEP 2 Using a sturdy chair, stand up and sit down rhythmically 30 times in one minute, or up each second and down each second.

STEP 3 Watch your heart rate monitor as your heart rate increases and note your peak heart rate, your highest heart rate

STEP 4 Add to your peak heart rate number, your fitness factor based on your current fitness level.

CURRENT FITNESS FITNESS FACTOR	POOR	AVERAGE	EXCELLENT	ATHLETE
	+40	+50	+60	+70

STEP 5 The sum of your chair peak heart rate plus your fitness factor is the estimate of your maximum heart rate.

HEART ZONES®
THE TRAINING, EDUCATION, AND COACHING COMPANY
USA
©2008

1-MINUTE CHAIR Sub Max Test ©

Using the table below, add the number that best corresponds to your current fitness level to estimate your maximum heart rate.

CURRENT FITNESS LEVEL	POOR SHAPE	AVERAGE SHAPE	EXCELLENT SHAPE	FIT ATHLETE
FITNESS FACTOR	40 BPM	50 BPM	60 BPM	70 BPM
YOUR PEAK HEART RATE	+ ____ BPM	+ ____ BPM	+ ____ BPM	+ ____ BPM
ESTIMATED MAXIMUM HEART RATE	____ BPM	____ BPM	____ BPM	____ BPM

WWW.HEARTZONES.COM
2636 Fulton Avenue #100 • Sacramento, CA 95821 • (916) 481-7283

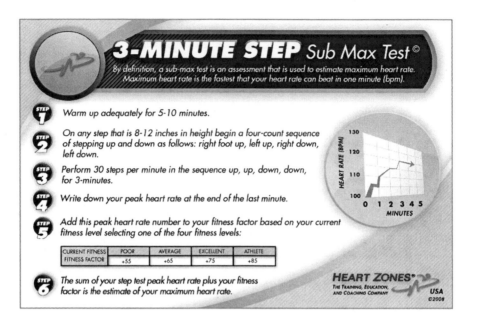

3-MINUTE STEP Sub Max Test©

By definition, a sub-max test is an assessment that is used to estimate maximum heart rate. Maximum heart rate is the fastest that your heart rate can beat in one minute (bpm).

STEP 1 Warm up adequately for 5-10 minutes.

STEP 2 On any step that is 8-12 inches in height begin a four-count sequence of stepping up and down as follows: right foot up, left up, right down, left down.

STEP 3 Perform 30 steps per minute in the sequence up, up, down, down, for 3-minutes.

STEP 4 Write down your peak heart rate at the end of the last minute.

STEP 5 Add this peak heart rate number to your fitness factor based on your current fitness level selecting one of the four fitness levels:

CURRENT FITNESS	POOR	AVERAGE	EXCELLENT	ATHLETE
FITNESS FACTOR	+55	+65	+75	+85

STEP 6 The sum of your step test peak heart rate plus your fitness factor is the estimate of your maximum heart rate.

HEART ZONES®
THE TRAINING, EDUCATION,
AND COACHING COMPANY
USA
©2008

3-MINUTE STEP Sub Max Test©

Using the table below, add the number that best corresponds to your current fitness level.

CURRENT FITNESS LEVEL	POOR SHAPE	AVERAGE SHAPE	EXCELLENT SHAPE	FIT ATHLETE
FITNESS FACTOR	55 BPM	65 BPM	75 BPM	85 BPM
YOUR PEAK HEART RATE	+ ____ BPM	+ ____ BPM	+ ____ BPM	+ ____ BPM
ESTIMATED MAXIMUM HEART RATE	BPM	BPM	BPM	BPM

WWW.HEART ZONES.COM
2636 Fulton Avenue #100 • Sacramento, CA 95821 • (916) 481-7283

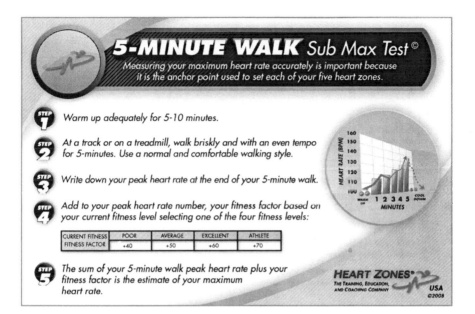

5-MINUTE WALK Sub Max Test©

Measuring your maximum heart rate accurately is important because it is the anchor point used to set each of your five heart zones.

STEP 1 Warm up adequately for 5-10 minutes.

STEP 2 At a track or on a treadmill, walk briskly and with an even tempo for 5-minutes. Use a normal and comfortable walking style.

STEP 3 Write down your peak heart rate at the end of your 5-minute walk.

STEP 4 Add to your peak heart rate number, your fitness factor based on your current fitness level selecting one of the four fitness levels:

CURRENT FITNESS	POOR	AVERAGE	EXCELLENT	ATHLETE
FITNESS FACTOR	+40	+50	+60	+70

STEP 5 The sum of your 5-minute walk peak heart rate plus your fitness factor is the estimate of your maximum heart rate.

HEART ZONES®
The Training, Education, and Coaching Company
USA
©2008

5-MINUTE WALK Sub Max Test©

Using the table below, add the number that best corresponds to your current fitness level.

CURRENT FITNESS LEVEL	POOR SHAPE	AVERAGE SHAPE	EXCELLENT SHAPE	FIT ATHLETE
FITNESS FACTOR	40 BPM	50 BPM	60 BPM	70 BPM
YOUR PEAK HEART RATE	+ ___ BPM	+ ___ BPM	+ ___ BPM	+ ___ BPM
ESTIMATED MAXIMUM HEART RATE	BPM	BPM	BPM	BPM

WWW.HEART ZONES.COM
2636 Fulton Avenue #100 • Sacramento, CA 95821 • (916) 481-7283

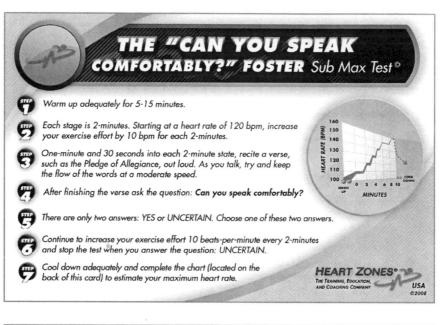

THE "CAN YOU SPEAK COMFORTABLY?" FOSTER Sub Max Test©

STEP 1 Warm up adequately for 5-15 minutes.

STEP 2 Each stage is 2-minutes. Starting at a heart rate of 120 bpm, increase your exercise effort by 10 bpm for each 2-minutes.

STEP 3 One-minute and 30 seconds into each 2-minute state, recite a verse, such as the Pledge of Allegiance, out loud. As you talk, try and keep the flow of the words at a moderate speed.

STEP 4 After finishing the verse ask the question: **Can you speak comfortably?**

STEP 5 There are only two answers: YES or UNCERTAIN. Choose one of these two answers.

STEP 6 Continue to increase your exercise effort 10 beats-per-minute every 2-minutes and stop the test when you answer the question: UNCERTAIN.

STEP 7 Cool down adequately and complete the chart (located on the back of this card) to estimate your maximum heart rate.

HEART ZONES®
THE TRAINING, EDUCATION, AND COACHING COMPANY
USA
©2008

SCORING THE "CAN YOU SPEAK COMFORTABLY?" FOSTER Sub Max Test©

Your estimated maximum heart rate is your heart rate when you first feel "Uncertain" saying aloud the Pledge of Allegiance. To that number add the "Math Factor":

- If you are in Poor Shape add **50 bpm**.
- If you are in Average Shape add **40 bpm**.
- If you are in Excellent Shape add **30 bpm**.
- If you are in Fit-Cardio or Competitive Athlete Shape add **20 bpm**.

CALCULATION

HEART RATE AT "UNCERTAIN"	_____ BPM
ADD THE MATH FACTOR	➕ _____
ESTIMATED MAXIMUM HEART RATE	_____ BPM

WWW.HEART ZONES.COM
2636 Fulton Avenue #100 • Sacramento, CA 95821 • (916) 481-7283

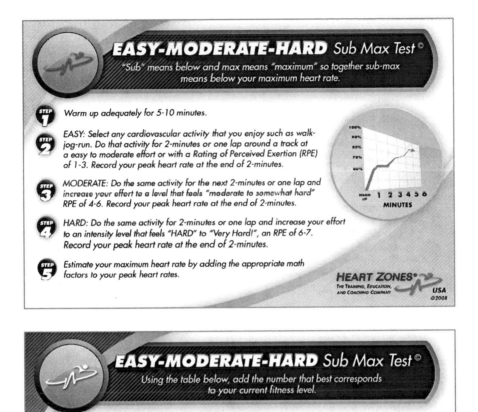

EASY-MODERATE-HARD *Sub Max Test* ©

"Sub" means below and max means "maximum" so together sub-max means below your maximum heart rate.

STEP 1 Warm up adequately for 5-10 minutes.

STEP 2 EASY: Select any cardiovascular activity that you enjoy such as walk-jog-run. Do that activity for 2-minutes or one lap around a track at a easy to moderate effort or with a Rating of Perceived Exertion (RPE) of 1-3. Record your peak heart rate at the end of 2-minutes.

STEP 3 MODERATE: Do the same activity for the next 2-minutes or one lap and increase your effort to a level that feels "moderate to somewhat hard" RPE of 4-6. Record your peak heart rate at the end of 2-minutes.

STEP 4 HARD: Do the same activity for 2-minutes or one lap and increase your effort to an intensity level that feels "HARD" to "Very Hard!", an RPE of 6-7. Record your peak heart rate at the end of 2-minutes.

STEP 5 Estimate your maximum heart rate by adding the appropriate math factors to your peak heart rates.

HEART ZONES®
The Training, Education, and Coaching Company
USA ©2008

EASY-MODERATE-HARD *Sub Max Test* ©

Using the table below, add the number that best corresponds to your current fitness level.

RPE*	DESCRIPTION OF FEELING OF EFFORT
0	Rest
1	Really Easy
2	Easy
3	Moderate
4	Sort of Hard
5	Hard
6	HARD
7	Very Hard!
8	At My Limit!
9	Past My Limit!
10	Destroyed

CURRENT EFFORT LEVEL	EASY	MODERATE	HARD
ADD THE MATH FACTOR	60 BPM	40 BPM	20 BPM
YOUR PEAK HEART RATE	+ ____ BPM	+ ____ BPM	+ ____ BPM
ESTIMATED MAXIMUM HEART RATE	____ BPM	____ BPM	____ BPM

WWW.HEARTZONES.COM
2636 Fulton Avenue #100 • Sacramento, CA 95821 • (916) 481-7283

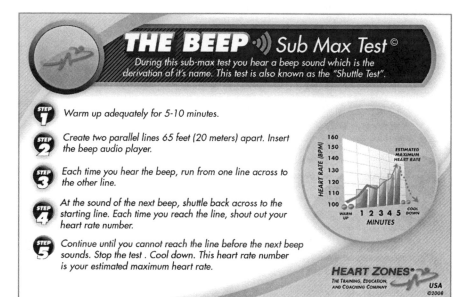

THE BEEP ·))) Sub Max Test©

During this sub-max test you hear a beep sound which is the derivation of it's name. This test is also known as the "Shuttle Test".

STEP 1 Warm up adequately for 5-10 minutes.

STEP 2 Create two parallel lines 65 feet (20 meters) apart. Insert the beep audio player.

STEP 3 Each time you hear the beep, run from one line across to the other line.

STEP 4 At the sound of the next beep, shuttle back across to the starting line. Each time you reach the line, shout out your heart rate number.

STEP 5 Continue until you cannot reach the line before the next beep sounds. Stop the test . Cool down. This heart rate number is your estimated maximum heart rate.

HEART ZONES®
The Training, Education, and Coaching Company   USA
©2008

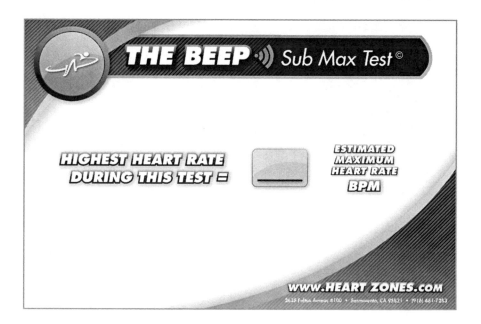

THE BEEP ·))) Sub Max Test©

HIGHEST HEART RATE DURING THIS TEST = _____   **ESTIMATED MAXIMUM HEART RATE BPM**

WWW.HEART ZONES.COM
2636 Fulton Avenue #100 • Sacramento, CA 95821 • (916) 481-7283

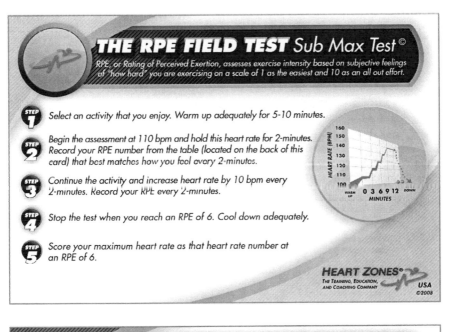

THE RPE FIELD TEST Sub Max Test©

RPE, or Rating of Perceived Exertion, assesses exercise intensity based on subjective feelings of "how hard" you are exercising on a scale of 1 as the easiest and 10 as an all out effort.

STEP 1 Select an activity that you enjoy. Warm up adequately for 5-10 minutes.

STEP 2 Begin the assessment at 110 bpm and hold this heart rate for 2-minutes. Record your RPE number from the table (located on the back of this card) that best matches how you feel every 2-minutes.

STEP 3 Continue the activity and increase heart rate by 10 bpm every 2-minutes. Record your RPE every 2-minutes.

STEP 4 Stop the test when you reach an RPE of 6. Cool down adequately.

STEP 5 Score your maximum heart rate as that heart rate number at an RPE of 6.

HEART ZONES®
The Training, Education, and Coaching Company
USA
©2008

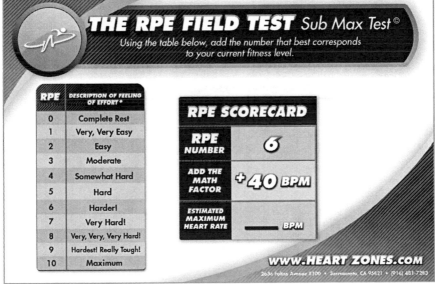

THE RPE FIELD TEST Sub Max Test©

Using the table below, add the number that best corresponds to your current fitness level.

RPE	DESCRIPTION OF FEELING OF EFFORT *
0	Complete Rest
1	Very, Very Easy
2	Easy
3	Moderate
4	Somewhat Hard
5	Hard
6	Harder!
7	Very Hard!
8	Very, Very, Very Hard!
9	Hardest! Really Tough!
10	Maximum

RPE SCORECARD

RPE NUMBER	6
ADD THE MATH FACTOR	+40 BPM
ESTIMATED MAXIMUM HEART RATE	_____ BPM

WWW.HEARTZONES.COM
2636 Fulton Avenue #100 • Sacramento, CA 95621 • (916) 481-7283

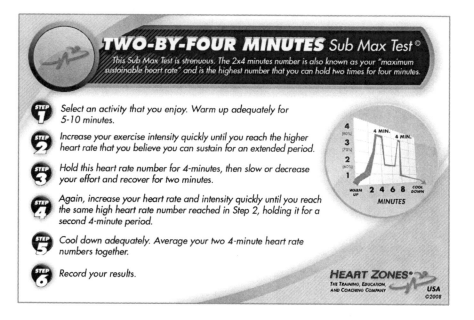

TWO-BY-FOUR MINUTES Sub Max Test ©

This Sub Max Test is strenuous. The 2x4 minutes number is also known as your "maximum sustainable heart rate" and is the highest number that you can hold two times for four minutes.

STEP 1 Select an activity that you enjoy. Warm up adequately for 5-10 minutes.

STEP 2 Increase your exercise intensity quickly until you reach the higher heart rate that you believe you can sustain for an extended period.

STEP 3 Hold this heart rate number for 4-minutes, then slow or decrease your effort and recover for two minutes.

STEP 4 Again, increase your heart rate and intensity quickly until you reach the same high heart rate number reached in Step 2, holding it for a second 4-minute period.

STEP 5 Cool down adequately. Average your two 4-minute heart rate numbers together.

STEP 6 Record your results.

HEART ZONES®
THE TRAINING, EDUCATION, AND COACHING COMPANY
USA
©2008

TWO-BY-FOUR MINUTES Sub Max Test©

Using the table below, add the number that best corresponds to your current fitness level.

CURRENT FITNESS LEVEL	POOR SHAPE	AVERAGE SHAPE	EXCELLENT SHAPE	FIT ATHLETE
FITNESS FACTOR	50 BPM	40 BPM	30 BPM	20 BPM
AVERAGE HEART RATE	+ _____ BPM	+ _____ BPM	+ _____ BPM	+ _____ BPM
ESTIMATED MAXIMUM HEART RATE	_____ BPM	_____ BPM	_____ BPM	_____ BPM

WWW.HEART ZONES.COM

2636 Fulton Avenue #100 • Sacramento, CA 95821 • (916) 481-7283

The Heart Rate Monitor Guidebook

them over the inside surface of your wrist and lightly apply pressure. Wait quietly and move your fingers until you feel the blood flow. The reason that pulse is taken in the wrist is because it is safe and prominent. Other prominent locations are the groin and the neck (carotid pulse). However, taking your pulse rate from your neck's carotid artery can slow your heart rate and sometimes gives you a false reading.

Pulse can best be manually measured when you are stationary, which makes it a difficult method for determining training intensity for those who are exercising. When you stop exercising to count your pulse it almost immediately begins to drop - for some really fit people it plummets like a stone. This leads to calculating a pulse rate that is lower than what you are actually working at. It's common for those who are fit to see their pulse drop a beat per second. That can result in a 10 -15 beat error when counting manually.

The easiest method is to count the number of pulse waves during six seconds and add a zero to that number to obtain the number of beats per minute. For example, in six seconds, if you count 8 beats then you add a zero and have the number 80 or eighty beats per minute. Others prefer to count pulse for ten seconds and multiply that number by six or for fifteen seconds and multiply times four. Accuracy of measurement is what's important here and sometimes it's difficult to multiply when you are tired, and your heart beating slows while you are counting, which is an additional reason why using a heart rate monitor is preferred.

MAXIMUM HEART RATE TESTS

There are a lot of ways to determine your maximum heart rate and, of course, the least-risky method is to have your physician supervise your test. If a physician does this, also ask for a threshold test so you can have an accurate value for your threshold heart rate as well (more on this later). You can also take a supervised graded stress test (GSX) at a sports laboratory. Call your local sports club for a referral. Many fitness testing facilities offer sub-maximal exercise tests designed to bring you to

75-85% of your age-determined maximum heart rate. The usefulness of these sub-max tests is questionable.

Besides comparing your results to tables that suggest how "fit" you are based on your chronological, not biological age, their basic value is in recording your current exercise training load and corresponding heart rate in hopes that you will re-test and see changes. (This might be helpful, but you'll very probably know you are getting fitter without it). Some testing facilities will say they are taking you to your maximum heart rate, but really they will only take you to your age-predicted maximum heart rate (calculated as 220- age). This test is not what you want because it doesn't give you your "true" maximum heart rate, just the mathematical one. Make sure you know what they are going to do in advance or request (maybe demand) a true maximum heart rate test.

If you want an adequate test and exercise screening, invest in a maximum heart rate test performed by a Heart Zones certified Personal Trainer (CPT), Indoor Cycling Instructor (CICI), or one of our Heart Zones CC, Certified Coach (CC). There is a broad range of fees and types of tests but the normal range for just a maximum heart rate test is $75-$150 USA. Add another $100-$300 USA for a blood workup and VO_2 max test. Sometimes, your health insurance covers some or all of these costs. By taking these tests, you are also able to keep a record of your fitness levels and changes as you age. It's advisable to take these tests every five years and compare the results over that time. This practice is good, sound preventive medicine because you take responsibility for measuring and monitoring your aging process.

An alternative is to take one of the self-administered maximum heart rate tests described in this chapter - if you are apparently healthy and have no risks for cardiovascular or other diseases and meet the *ACSM Guidelines* previously mentioned- the fun begins.

2–4 MINUTE TEST

This is a protocol that we have developed and tested that requires (without warm-up and warm-down time) between 2 and 4 minutes to complete. The test is best taken on a track or bike, and it requires a partner who can run/bike with you throughout the test, to give heart rate readings aloud and set the pace. The runner being tested wears the chest transmitter belt and the partner wears the wrist monitor.

Start the test with an easy warm-up of at least 5 minutes or 2 laps. Your goal during the warm-up is to get your heart beating to 100-120 bpm (or to an estimated 60% of your maximum heart rate). Without stopping, begin the test by gradually accelerating your speed so that your heart rate climbs about 5 bpm every 15 seconds. At each 15-second Interval, your partner should tell you the exercise time and your heart rate and offer encouragement as he or she gradually, very gradually pushes you faster.

Within a 2- to 4-minute period, if your partner has set the pace correctly, your heart rate will cease to climb even with increased effort and pace. You'll know you are there when you can no longer accelerate and you hear your partner repeating the same number. At this point you've reached your maximum heart rate and either you or your partner can call an end to the test. For detail description of the 2-4 minute test, go to Workout #4 in this chapter.

5K RACE TEST

This can be taken by anyone skiing, running, biking, or snowshoeing. Enter a 5K race, and during the last 1–2 minutes go to a full sprint. Keep checking your heart rate monitor and add 5 beats to the highest number recorded there during this period. The result should be your maximum heart rate (because of muscle fatigue, you can't drive yourself all the way to true maximum heart rate at this point).

BIGGEST NUMBER TEST

This is one of those that is simply obvious. Given that you've worn your heart rate monitor a while, especially during hard workouts, your maximum heart rate is the biggest number you have ever seen on your heart rate monitor (the biggest *reasonable* number, not 300 bpm, say - you don't want to take one that's influenced by interference).

HEART RATE FITNESS TESTS

Your heart rate monitor is a measurement tool. With a little experience, you are going to learn how to use it to measure your current level of fitness. These assessments are different than measuring your maximum heart rate, the Sub-Max tests. Heart Rate Fitness Tests answer that all important question: How Fit (cardio-fit) Are You? Curious to know the answer? Then let's use our coach and biofeedback device, our heart rate monitor, as a measurement instrument to answer that question.

AMBIENT HEART RATE

It's not as critical to Heart Zones Training as the maximum heart rate, but it is still of value to know your average daily heart rate – your "ambient" heart rate, also known as "sitting heart rate." This number, usually found when in a sitting position like behind a computer or in front of a television, normally varies little from day to day. When it does vary, especially if it goes up, it is a good indicator of your body being under some sort of stress. For example, you could be fatigued, over trained, under mental or emotional stress (which is reflected in your body by physical stress), your immune system lowered by an oncoming cold, etc. The lower your ambient heart rate the better. This is a *trainable* and *moveable* number that decreases with fitness and increases with inactivity.

Raising your heart rate does not make you fit. You can raise your heart rate by thinking.

To determine your ambient heart rate, take your pulse or wear your heart monitor and jot down in your calendar or day planner sitting heart rate numbers that you see or count throughout the day, perhaps for several days over a week. The average number will be your ambient heart rate.

RECOVERY HEART RATE

One of the best indicators of fitness is to take a recovery heart rate assessment. There are a variety of recovery heart rate tests, but one of the most popular is the "120 second" test. The purpose of the test is to measure how quickly you recover back toward your ambient heart rate. The faster the better; the fitter you are. If you recover quickly, it means that your ability to restore oxygen and nutrients to the muscles is more efficient.

There are other recovery heart rate assessments. Recovery heart rate is a measurement commonly used during interval training. Select a recovery heart rate number such as the floor of Zone 2 as your take-off point and the floor of Z5, Zone 5 as your highest intensity allowable interval number. Recovery heart rate is a tool in your training arsenal to provide you with information you wouldn't otherwise have. Most interval workouts use recovery *time* or *distance* not recovery heart rate as the method for determining when to begin the next interval cycle. Time may or may not allow you adequate recovery because it can't rely on your physiological response to your current status. If you are in an over trained or fatigued condition, you'll need more time to recover adequately which heart rate recovery can measure - your stopwatch simply can't know this.

DELTA HEART RATE

By definition, your Delta heart rate is the difference between your standing and prone or lying down heart rate numbers. Some exercise scientists call this the orthostatic test. Whenever you stand, you are changing the training load on the cardiac system requiring the heart to pump blood against the forces of gravity. A low Delta heart rate number demonstrates that your heart can adjust to change efficiently. A higher Delta heart rate number means you are not as fit cardiovascularly and may well be an indicator of increased stress from either internal or external conditions.

RESTING HEART RATE

Two heart rate numbers are frequently confused: resting and ambient. Resting heart rate is that count taken in bed before you rise. It is your pre-rolling over and hugging, getting up to use the bathroom heart rate. Your resting heart rate is found when you *first* open your eyes in the morning.

Your heart rate changes with the time of day, increasing during the daylight hours and decreasing during the night time.

Resting heart rate is one of the key signals or markers for athletes of

150 bpm	–	90 bpm	=	60 bpm
Exercise heart rate		rate at end of 120 seconds		Recovery heart rate (difference)

overtraining or other conditions that might be arising. The five-beat rule applies here: if your resting heart rate is five bpm above normal, you should train only in the low-intensity zones or take the day off.

It's clear that these two heart rate numbers - ambient and resting - drop with training. This is called the "Training Effect." Because of this training effect you save an incredible number of heartbeats in your life-time. Critics can scoff at fitness freaks who love to push their hearts into their upper zones, but over a lifetime, it's a bargain.

Fitness has a cumulative effect. It pays off in the short term and in the long run. In this case, the person who has been working out for their adult life can save over 400 million contractions of their heart muscle. It's your choice. Fitness pays for itself.

Workout #4:

Testing Your Maximum Heart Rate

Because the accurate assessment of your maximum heart rate is crucial to the development of any effective training or fitness program, most coaches and trainers advocate verifying estimates with actual performance tests. These tests can be conducted by exercise technologists and other health professionals in a laboratory setting or self-administered.

A word of caution to all of our readers. Do not take self-administered tests if you are over 35 years of age, have been sedentary, or for any reason are in poor physical condition and have not had a thorough physical exam (including an exercise stress test) and a physician's release.

The American College of Sports Medicine also offers the following warning: At or above 35 years of age, it is necessary for individuals to have a medical examination and a maximal exercise test before beginning a vigorous exercise program. At any age, the information gathered from an exercise test may be useful to establish an effective and safe exercise prescription. Maximal testing done for men at age 40 or above or women age 50 and older, even when no symptoms or risk factors are present should be performed with physician supervision.

You should also know that the American College of Cardiology and the American Heart Association question the value of diagnostic exercise testing in apparently healthy individuals.

Talk to your own personal physician to determine what maximum heart rate calculation or test is appropriate for you.

A maximal stress test and health appraisal by a physician or sports physiologist is the safest and most recommended way to determine your precise maximum heart rate. The test is usually administered on a treadmill or exercise bicycle and it simulates increased training load by increasing the pace, resistance or the surface incline.

During the test you will be forced to exercise extremely hard. The test will continue until an increased intensity of exercise does not cause an increase in heart rate. At that point, you've reached your max.

It is only natural that the test will create some muscular pain and you will feel very uncomfortable. But, if breathing difficulties or any pains occur, especially in the chest, the test should be terminated immediately.

To insure a more accurate maximum heart rate reading, I have developed a refined protocol which requires only two to four minutes of hard effort. Please keep in mind, the maximal stress test cautions mentioned previously also apply to self-administered tests.

Before and after taking any maximum heart rate test, or just exercising for that matter, you should warm up and cool down. How long and how hard is an individual choice. Remember, the purpose is to ease your body from a resting state to an active once and back again.

Just like any other muscle, the heart needs to warm up before going all out and to slow down before coming to an abrupt stop.

The Two-to-Four-Minute maximum heart rate test can be best performed on a track and it requires a partner who can run with you throughout the test, give heart rate readings and set a hard pace. The runner being tested wears the chest transmitter belt while the partner wears the wrist monitor.

Start the test with an easy warm-up of at least five minutes or two laps. Your goal during the warm-up is to get your heart working at about 110-130 beats per minute or about 60 percent of your age estimated

HOW DO YOU SAVE 473,040,000 HEARTBEATS?

Ambient Heartbeat	Unfit Person	Fit Person
Beats Per Minute	70*	50
Beats in a Day	100,800	72,000
Beats in a Year	36,792,000	26,280,000
Total Beats in 45 Years	1,655,640,000	1,182,600,000

Difference: 473,040,000 heartbeats

* Average daily rate including ambient heart rate and resting heart rates.

maximum heart rate.

After warming up, and without stopping, gradually accelerate your speed so that your heart rate climbs about five beats every 15 seconds. At 15-second intervals, your partner should tell you the time and your heart rate and offer on-going encouragement to gradually push harder. Within a two to four-minute window, if your partner sets the pace correctly, your heart rate will cease to climb even with increased effort and pace. At that point, you've reached your max and your partner should call an end to the test or you simply won't be able to run another step! A diagram of your test might look like on the next page.

During that last 15-30 seconds of the test as you continue to gradually accelerate, your partner should keep repeating your heart rate over and over. Eventually, the same number will be repeated because your heart won't go higher - it's a finite number.

for your information:

Your resting heart rate drops 5-8 bpm when you are partially immersed in water because of the reduction in stress on the cardiovascular system. Placing your face in water further lowers your resting heart rate. This is called the "facial reflex" and is common to all mammals.

TRAINING ZONES

After completing a medically appropriate performance test and determining your maximum heart rate, you are ready to develop a training or fitness program around a training zone which meets your current level of fitness and goals. Get out your calculator or pencil and compute your five training zones.

THE POWER OF TESTS AND ASSESSMENTS

Hey, I know, a lot of you may not like to take a test or measure thing - especially exercise. I urge you to give it a chance. Things that get measured get done. And, getting your workouts done gets you a lot of benefit, especially if you use the information from your heart rate monitor. The big bang for your investment in testing is to find out two key numbers and only two:

1. Your maximum heart rate in order to anchor and set your training zones.
2. Your current level of fitness so that you can enjoy the rewards of getting in better shape.

Now that you know how do measure your maximum heart rate and how to measure your cardiovascular, your CV-fitness level, are you ready to learn what to do with that? It's time to get into the zones and become a zoner

8 Reasons Why "220 Minus Age" Is Just Plain Wrong

The age-adjusted maximum heart rate formula (also known as the "age regression formula") was developed a half century ago, at a time when the science of exercise physiology was in its infancy and the technological means to create a more accurate exercise prescription or testing protocol was scarce. The result was that the "220 Mi-nus Age" formula was neither created nor validated based on supported research or clinical testing . Today, the health and fitness industry continued support of an archaic, unproven formula is (a) potentially hazardous to the public, (b) a severe blow to our effectiveness and credibility, and (c) a tragic undermining of the proven advances and discoveries in exercise physiology over the last half century. Here ten reasons why "220 Minus Age" gets a failing grade:

1. The formula's inventor acknowledges its unscientific development. The equation was created in the early 1970's by scientists Fox, Naughton, and Haskell who intended it to be a rough formulation and not meant to be representative of the entire population. All subject in the studies referenced were under 55 years of age and male. Although the equation has become accepted and the standard in the literature and is used widely in clinical and fitness settings, its validity is uncertain.
2. There is no scientific research to support it. There is no scientific validation of this formula. There is simply no research to sup-port it.
3. It is physiologically nonsensical. There is no physiological reason why everyone of the same age should have the same maximum number of heartbeats in a minute's time. In fact, we KNOW this isn't true. For example, as fit individuals age, their maximum heart rate drops very little. Research has shown that the maximum heart rate of individuals of the same age can vary by 11 bpm based on many variables especially sport activity. Yet this formula claims to scientifically prescribe intensity-

based training levels for individuals, even as it ignores their scientifically established individuality.

4. It is useless. There is a common assumption that any of the equations that predict your individual maximum heart rate will be both reasonably accurate and reasonably useful. Such is not the case with "220 Minus Age." Intended to guide users to exercise in the right cardiovascular training zones (CVT), in fact, the formula doesn't accomplish this. "The 220-age formula designed to predict maximum heart rate is useless" according to Carl Foster, Ph.D. and past president of the American College of Sports Medicine, "because it simply is not accurate."

5. It is elitist. Don't believe Dr. Foster? Well, how about trying to convince pro athletes that they should go back to using "220 minus Age," equation if they ever did. Why do we think that pro athletes somehow deserve more accurate training regimens than fitness exercisers? There is value to increased precision, especially for those seeking weight loss or true aerobic benefits from their physical activity.

6. It may be dangerous. The formula is built into and displayed on the consoles of most pieces of cardio-equipment. But, if followed, it can be dangerous overestimating maximum heart rate in young adults and underestimating it in older people. Using 220-age forces fitness enthusiasts, with the air of scientific authority, to exercise at too high or too low a cardiovascular intensity. Similarly, the formula also leads some individuals to exercise at intensities too low to achieve needed health benefits. As fitness professionals, we need to ask ourselves if we could be at legal (not to mention ethical) risk for using an equation to prescribe exercise intensity which we have ample reason to suspect is inaccurate.

7. It is an embarrassment. Savvy consumers can prove for themselves that their Max HR isn't what the formula says it is, so how much credibility do you think they give training professionals who say otherwise? Yet working this formula is a requirement to pass most personal trainer certification tests. And, worse still, the formula is posted in most health clubs. Using dogma, instead of evidence-based science, makes health and fitness professionals appear to be naïve at best and, at worst, incompetent in their chosen field.

8. It allows us to be lazy. In the early 1990s, I created the original five heart rate training zones, each built on 10% of your maximum heart rate. Those zones were first published in my work, The Heart Rate Monitor Book, and have subsequently been adopted as the standard CVT zones programmed into millions of cardio machines. I acknowledge that at that time, almost twenty years ago, I, too, was unwilling to change and to recommend alternative methods for prescribing CVT zones. Accepted by the ACSM, this mythical formula was just too easy, and it was even then a dogma. I have subsequently confessed my error in recommending the formula and apologized for supporting such a simplistic means of deter-mining such an important value.

9. There are scientifically validated alternatives that are safe and effective. To the best of my knowledge, at this time there is no equation that has been proven accurate enough in predicting maximum heart rate. None whatsoever. This does not mean that we don't have any proven means of achieving the same end, because we do. Sub-maximum testing pro-tocols, or "sub-max tests," are a straightforward method of estimating maximum heart rate, based on a physiological response to a safe level of exercise stress. One such test, "The Can-You-Speak-Comfortably Foster Test" is scientifically validated by Carl Foster, Ph.D. There are others. And, yes, I have a business that promotes these alternative tests and protocols, yet I'm sure there are many other means of setting CVT levels that I haven't even heard of and from which we would all benefit. Let's open the doors to actual innovation, and let the best exercise intensity prescription win!

10. We have a responsibility to do our best. Because the estimation of maximum heart rate comes from a professionally sup-ported math-ematical formula, it carries an air of scientific authority. If we health and fitness professionals want to continue to be seen as authorities, we need to do our best for our clients, whether it's easy for us or not. Supporting the use of this out-dated formula is simply not the best we can do.

Chapter 6
The Five Training Zones

Are you on the bus yet? I hope you're in the midst of throwing off the paradigms that were weighing you down and are planning to take a test or two to calculate your maximum heart rate. Now you've come to the good stuff, the "heart" of the matter, so to speak! In this chapter, we're going to introduce you to the basic details you'll need to individualize and maximize your training.

Heart Zones Training is designed around a framework of progressively more challenging heart rate "zones." These zones are based on percentages of each person's maximum heart rate, so Heart Zones Training is actually a doubly individualized system. (That's why it works so reliably and efficiently!). You set your training zones based on your maximum heart rate, and then you choose the zones you want to train in based on your goals at any given time.

Each heart rate training zone covers a ten-percent range of your maximum heart rate. As the zones change, so do the metabolic and physiological events; fuel utilization changes (your body burns fats most efficiently in one zone over another, for example), lactates and oxygen utilization changes (you can train aerobically or non-aerobically), metabolic activity changes (you can train toward your goal of faster competitive performance or having a healthier heart), and most importantly of all, *you* change. Meeting and exceeding your fitness goals is the true pleasure of Heart Zones Training.

It's easy to follow the Heart Zones Training system because it's *your* individualized prescription; it's your plan; it's your body; it's under your control. Not only are you on the bus, you're the driver.

Whichever way you choose to do it, once you start to monitor your heart rate you can watch yourself reach your goals – whether you want to lose weight or fat, gain muscle, body sculpt, get fitter, get healthier, improve your heart, or expand your mind drug-free. It's powerful. Competitive athletes say it's a weapon. For any of us, whatever our goals, it's definitely an advantage. Welcome to a system that's so well-suited to *you* it can't help but work!

ALL ABOUT ZONES

There are some special characteristics of Heart Zones Training zones that make them what they are. Keep 'em in mind as we make our way through the following chapters.

1. Zones have size. The size of each zone is a 10% range of your true maximum heart rate. The size of the zone in number of beats depends on how high your true maximum heart rate is. Given a 200 bpm maximum heart rate (which is very convenient for multiplying), each of the five zones would be 10% of 200, or 20 beats wide. Most zones for most people range from 15 to 20 beats in size; this is big enough to allow for some "wiggle room" when you are working out, but small enough to be on target for your particular training goals.

2. Zones have structure. A zone may be viewed as being made up of two different parts: its top and bottom halves. In other words, inside every zone is an upper and a lower zone. So, while the whole Aerobic zone may be from 70% to 80% of your maximum heart rate, the lower half of the zone is 70%-75% (or 140-150 bpm in our 200 bpm maximum heart rate example), and the upper Aerobic zone is 75%-80% (or 150-160 bpm in this case). It's just a way to subdivide a medium-sized heart window into two smaller, even more focused parts.

3. Zones have dividing lines. The upper and lower limits of each zone coincide with the floor and ceiling of its bordering zones. The floor of the

Z3 Aerobic zone, for example, is 70% of your maximum heart rate. This floor, or threshold, is that heart rate where you first break into this zone. Seventy percent of your maximum heart rate also happens to be where the Temperate zone ends. The Aerobic zone ceiling, 80% maximum heart rate, is the line at the very top of the zone. At this point you are passing through the Aerobic zone ceiling into the floor of the next higher and more intense zone, the Threshold zone.

4. Zone have names. Each heart rate zone has a specific benefit that comes from the physiological activities that happen when you exercise within that zone. For example, the Z1 Healthy Heart zone is exactly that, the range of heart rates where most individuals realize the most cardio-vascular benefits, leading to improved heart and lung function.

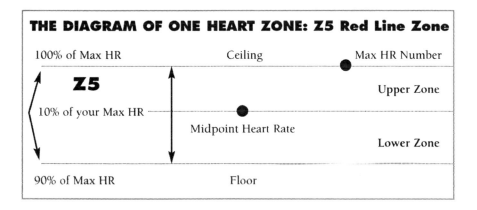

THE DIAGRAM OF ONE HEART ZONE: Z5 Red Line Zone

100% of Max HR — Ceiling — Max HR Number

Z5 — Upper Zone

10% of your Max HR — Midpoint Heart Rate — Lower Zone

90% of Max HR — Floor

5. Zones have numbers. There are certain specific and measurable events that are so exact that they're represented by a single heartbeat value called a heart rate number. We've talked about a few of them: the maximum heart rate number and resting heart rate number are specific heart rate numbers that are located in relationship to (inside or on the dividing lines of) the zones. For example, the diagram below is the location of your maximum heart rate on the ceiling of Zone 5.

6. Zones are a subset of the wellness continuum. The wellness continuum consists of three areas of physical well-being - health, fitness, and performance - and we need to keep in mind that we're not all going to have our goals in the same areas. This is why your friend, who's a veteran marathoner, might complain about what kind of "shape" he or she is in, while you would kill to look the way they do and be so fit and healthy. The health area covers those training zones that promote health but don't primarily improve physical fitness and certainly not performance. To measure improvements in health, we seek positive changes in blood pressure, body fat, cholesterol, etc. To measure improvements in fitness, however, its positive changes in oxygen utilization, lactate concentrations and heart rate numbers we're looking for. And, to measure improvements in performance, positive changes in completion times, accuracy of movement skill, mental attitude, lactate threshold, and other indices are used.

7. Zones use time, not distance, as their measurement tool. That is, the amount of time you spend in each zone is the way you measure your workout, not in miles run or the number of strokes per minute cycled or rowed. This measurement is called "time in zone" and is measured in the number of minutes that you spend in each zone. For example, one day you decide to run for 30 minutes in the Aerobic zone; the following day you might choose to walk for 50 minutes in your Temperate zone. Varying your workouts, both in activity and zone, allows you to get multiple benefits from your training.

8. Zones have specific numerical values. When we talk about "exercise by the numbers," that means doing workouts based on the specific numbers that make up your exact zones. For example, if your true, tested maximum heart rate is 200 beats per minute and you wanted a high fat-burning day as a percent of your fuels burned, you would calibrate that workout to be in Z1-Z3. If you really wanted to fine-tune your training, you might choose to narrow the heart window to Z3. Use the chart on page 66 to determine the specific numerical values for your five zones.

9. Higher zones require less time in zone than lower zones. You can train at the lower zones, or "cruise" zones, as they are sometimes called, for longer periods of time than in the higher zones. As you move up to higher intensity zones, you need to decrease the amount of time that you spend in that zone, particularly in the top two, the Threshold and Red Line zones. This simply makes sense; you can walk farther than you can sprint, and overdoing it is nearly a guarantee of injuries or burnout.

10. Zones are relative. Your five heart rate zones are specific to *your* maximum heart rate, not anybody else's. With two runners, each maintaining a heart rate of 160 bpm, one might well be in their Z4 Threshold Zone and the other may be in their Z2 Temperate Zone. It's all relative.

11. Zones quantify training load. For the first time, using heart rate information can provide us the data to be able to quantify exercise amount, training load. Never before has this been possible outside the laboratory because it requires three different pieces of data assembled together: intensity, frequency, and time. It comes together neatly spelling the word LIFT. Each letter in the word is the first letter of the training load formula: Load (L) = intensity (I) times frequency (F) times the amount of time (T). By adding a little math, you can now measure how much exercise you are getting - easily. This is called exercise dosage. The letter "I" stands for intensity which you now know means which of the five heart zones you spent time in. The letter "F" means frequency or how many or how often you train in a period of time (example: 5 workouts a week). The letter "T" is for time and it is measured in minutes, how many minutes did you exercise in that workout. Similar to caloric
expenditure, the LIFT formula gives you a way to measure the amount of

training that you accomplished.

12. Zones can be used for your emotions. The sum of emotional and physical stress is reflected directly in your heart rate numbers. This is known as "cumulative stress" because it is the sum of all stressors which you are experiencing in real time, at the moment, and throughout your day. There are five different emotional heart zones and you'll read about them in Chapter 17. Emotional Fitness Training.

Several years ago I organized a meeting between our company and one of Japan's largest athletic shoe companies. During that meeting, I first learned about the Japanese expression, translated into English, called "watch - do - be". To them these three words represented three different stages of personal development, the watch-do-be progression. Each of the business men started by explaining that their lives were out of balance, that they worked too much, and that they didn't prioritize what was truly important to them. They said they had come to realize that their health and their families were more important than their business status and the yen in their bank accounts.

All four of them agreed that they were former "watchers" that had developed into "doers," and that this was part of both a cultural and personal transformation for them. But you could tell they wanted to know how to take that final step towards the pinnacle of the pagoda of mental-physical-emotional balance, of personal integrated fitness - they

Zone		Frequency	Intensity	Time	Activity
Red Line	Z5	0-2 times/week	90-100%	2-4 min.	Racing, intervals, speed work
Threshold	Z4	1-3 times/week	80-90%	15-55 min.	Run, spinning, cc skiing
Aerobic	Z3	4-6 times/week	70-80%	20 min-2 hrs.	Jog, swim, cycle, step
Temperate	Z2	3-4 times/week	60-70%	15-30 min.	Jog/walk, swim, cycle
Healthy Heart	Z1	2-3 times/week	50-60%	10-60 min.	Walk, low-impact aerobics

run • bike • swim • hike • cycle • step • ski • jog • walk • race • spin

wanted to *be*.

I told them their goal of "being" healthy, of "being" fit was an attitude, a state of mind. It was all in their head. It was all in their muscles. It was all in their soul. But it could be experienced by connecting the body and the *heart,* with the head through the process of Heart Zones Training.

AN OVERVIEW OF THE FIVE ZONES: THE GRADED STRESS TEST

While you wouldn't normally pass through each of the five zones in a single workout, there is one situation where this happens - what physicians call a graded stress test. The graded stress test is great for accurately setting each of your heart rate zones, but in this case it is also very useful for giving us an overview of what each of the zones is about.

Throughout the test, measurements of the amount of oxygen you consume and the amount of carbon dioxide you expire are tracked. At the same time, the physician might also be taking small amounts of blood to measure your blood concentration of lactate, a by-product of energy metabolism. In addition, your heart rate is continuously measured by a cardiovascular monitoring system.

You start by stretching and warming up, and then you slowly begin to exercise either on a bike or, in our example, on a treadmill. Progressively, the speed of the treadmill periodically increases, and as the intensity changes, your heart rate increases.

The first thing that you'll notice is a time lag between the start of exercise and the heart, respiratory and blood responses. This is because it takes a minute or two for your heart to gear up to the body's demand.

Very soon the appropriate responses occur; the body catches up and gets the message that exercise has begun. This is called "the second-wind phenomenon." To you, it'll feel like the exercise has become easier, when in fact you've just caught up with the jump in metabolic demand from the beginning of the workout. This slow coming up to speed occurs most often in Z2.

As the intensity increases, you pass into the Temperate zone. Here you're in a fairly balanced metabolic state, but the pace is still quickening. During this period, there's a steady increase in oxygen uptake, blood circulation, and your body's fuel requirements. The fuel mixture is now beginning to change more to carbohydrates.

As the pace or effort continues to increase, you begin to stress the cardio and pulmonary systems.. Carbon dioxide continues to be excreted through the lungs and doesn't yet start to accumulate in the muscle tissues. Almost all of the lactic acid produced is metabolized or converted back to glucose by other tissues, so it's also not accumulating. As you pass into the upper Aerobic zone, your fuel mix changes from predominantly fat burning to a state where more carbohydrates are required for fuel.

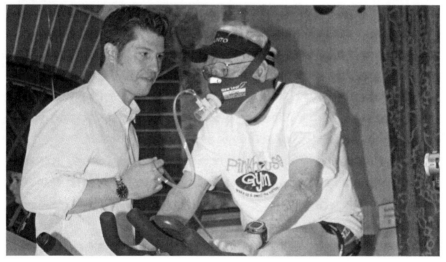

Eventually, as you pass through the Z3 Aerobic Zone ceiling, you enter the Threshold. Aerobic ("with oxygen") metabolism can no longer provide the additional energy required to handle this training load or speed, and the proportion of fats burned is lower in the total energy mix. At these intensities, you are non-aerobic and your muscles start to produce lactates faster than your body can dispose or "resynthesize" them. At this same heart rate number there's a change in respiratory function as well. Breathing becomes noticeably harder. This change in breathing pattern is often referred to as the first ventilatory threshold. But you haven't yet reached your max: as the treadmill goes faster, you can still run faster. You've passed through your low threshold (T_1) or your first ventilatory (VT_1) or lactate threshold (LT_1).

As you pass into the Z5 Red Line zone, you reach the VO_2 max point where you can continue to run faster, but you can no longer increase the amount of oxygen that you are consuming. Right now, you will need encouragement to continue, because you will want to quit. But you can still run faster, and your heart rate continues to increase. After this point, the longest you can run on the treadmill, if you are *super* fit, is a matter of a few minutes - be prepared for the end to come soon. From here on the test requires that you have the internal and external motivation to continue to run so you can reach your maximum heart rate. You're burning almost pure glucose for fuel, and your time is running short - less than a minute. Your lactates are rising exponentially, and within moments you must stop, absolutely exhausted. All you can hear is your breathing, which is at a maximum, your legs are wobbling from fatigue, your heart is pounding in your chest, you might be experiencing confusion and you feel this sense of happiness (or nausea) - because the stress test is over. The treadmill speed drops quickly, and you slow your pace to an easy jog-walk for a cool-down. As you are recovering, you drop back through each of the zones as your heart rate drops and oxygen and metabolic demands once again can be easily met. Now you have the data that you need to determine your heart rate numbers, to set your zones. Oh yes, and it was a little painful as well - exercising to your max anything is always that way.

A final caveat, this standard graded stress test tends to predict a maximum heart rate 3-10 beats below your true max. This is because of the length of time that the test requires - sometimes as long as 20 minutes for performance athletes. During such a long testing time, the fatigue is so great in your leg muscles that your heart doesn't reach its maximum heart rate. Take the 2-4 minute maximum heart rate test described in Chapter 4 to assess more accurately for true maximum heart rate.

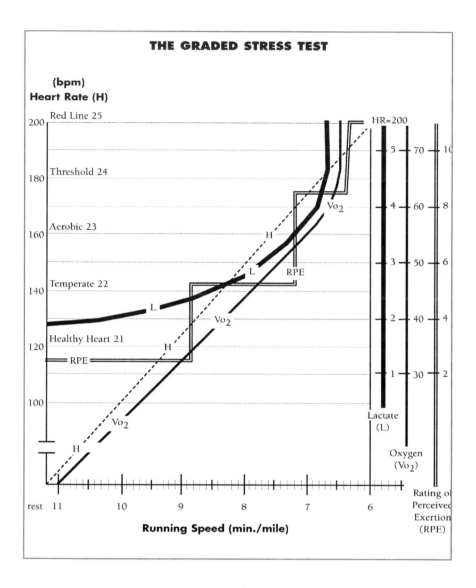

THE GRADED STRESS TEST

(bpm)
Heart Rate (H)

Red Line 25

Threshold 24

Aerobic 23

Temperate 22

Healthy Heart 21

HR=200

Vo_2

H

L

RPE

L

Vo_2

H

RPE

Vo_2

H

Lactate
(L)

Oxygen
(Vo_2)

Running Speed (min./mile)

rest   11   10   9   8   7   6

Rating of
Perceived
Exertion
(RPE)

Workout #5:

X-C SKIING INTERVAL WORKOUT

Introduction. We all owe a debt of thanks to the cross country skiers. They were first to rapidly endorse heart training and help launch the revolution of higher performance conditioning using heart rate monitors. As the colds of winter transition us to cross country skiing and sport snowshoeing season, here's one of my favorite "in-season" workouts. Being a total body sport, cross country skiing puts as much demand and burn on the chest and breathing muscles as on the legs, arms, and mind-body.

Purpose. Intervals are key to Nordic skiing because they simulate racing at high heart rates on the uphills and active recovery on the down hills. A cross country ski race is a series of intervals, so this workout is race specific training.

Workout Preparation. Find a loop course that will take about five minutes to complete. It should be reasonably flat, well-groomed, and secluded from heavy recreational ski traffic. Your maximum heart rate is sport specific. As a result, remember to test it for each different sport.

Workout Plan. This workout is a set of 5-10 loops with a three minute active rest between loops.

Workout. Warm up with one or two loops at 60-70 percent of maximum heart rate. For the first two loops, ski at the top of Zone 3 (80 percent maximum heart rate), then ski the last three loops at the top of the midpoint of Zone 4 (85 percent). Include three minutes of active rest between each loop. (that's a 2:1 work to rest ratio). Warm down by skiing one loop at no more than 60 percent maximum heart rate. Time yourself during this workout and write it in your log along with your heart rate averages.

Frequency. Do this training session once each week. Increase the number of loops per session to 10 by the time you are peaking for your most important race.

Helpful Hints

• *Don't be concerned about your heart rate during the first 60 seconds of your loops. Because of the way the heart rate monitor calculates by averaging the data every 3-5 seconds, the first readings need to be "softened" until there is sufficient data to provide accurate results. This takes about a minute for the displayed data to match your actual heart rate.*

• *Don't sacrifice technique or your biomechanics for top heart rates. If your technique begins to suffer, step back in your interval training and work on longer intervals with more emphasis on technique than speed.*

• *Share your interval sessions with a friend. Match yourself with someone whose times and heart rate percentages (relative heart rate not absolute heart rate) are close to yours so you can encourage and "hammer" each other together as you train. It will make you both better athletes.*

Reference Websites

www.TheSallyEdwardsCompany.com - Learn more about Sally's speaking and presentations and join her by attending them in a city nearby.

www.HeartZones.com - The official website of all those who work with the Heart Zones Training system: School teachers, medical specialists, health club trainers (group X and personal trainers), athletes, coaches, kids, and fitness enthusiasts.

www.HeartZonesCoaching.com - Heart Zones Coaching is the official training company for the Trek and the Danskin women's Triathlon Series. The company trains and certifies coaches, provides coaching support services, and is the licensee of Heart zones USA. If you choose you may contract with a private HZT coach or join a team program coached by a Heart Zones CTC, Certified Triathlon Coach.

www.GlobalRide.net - The company, owned by Heart Zones MICI, Master Indoor Cycling Instructor, Gene Nacey is a video production business that focuses on quality virtual cycling. You may purchase their DVDs and ride indoors feeling the joy of riding outdoors.

Chapter 7

Zone 1, The Healthy Heart Zone

The search has been on for the fountain of youth since before poor Ponce de Leon ever set foot on Florida soil, but it's beginning to look like our goal is in sight. Ponce, a Spanish explorer who arrived in the new world in the 1500's, may have died from the blood-thirsty mosquitoes, but many now are dying from the effects of obesity and sedentarism. The truth is that those deaths today are as needless as Ponce's was.

There's still no miracle cure, unless common sense and sound physiology have become miraculous, but there is a clear route to well-being and life extension: the Healthy Heart zone. Your body doesn't *have* to decline with age; we *choose* to send ourselves into a physical free-fall simply by becoming less active as we get older, triggering an ever-accelerating downward spiral. If you're in one of those spirals, turn your nose upward, look up at the sky and start to soar back up. Entering the Healthy Heart zone is your first step. Here you'll begin a workout program that guides you to the fountain of youth by breaking through the cardiovascular floor - 50% of your maximum heart rate.

QUALITY OVER QUANTITY

As fitness expert Covert Bailey says, it's muscles that make the tiger sleek and let the eagle soar. Well, you'll find your wings in the Healthy Heart zone - it's the launching pad of the wellness continuum. It is probably the most important zone of all because it's the first point where the health benefits of exercise are realized.

Being at the easiest, most comfortable intensity range - 50%-60% maximum heart rate - the Healthy Heart zone has taken some hard knocks from many fitness professionals. For years, many have said that there's simply no benefit to exercising in this zone, because there is no improvement in the body's oxygen utilization. However, there *is* noticeable improvement in several other wellness categories: blood pressure lowers, cholesterol levels improve, body fat decreases or stabilizes, and muscle mass increases.

> *"If you walk 2 miles a day in 30 minutes, 3 times a week, death from all causes is reduced by 55%."*
> *-Ken Cooper, M.D.*

These are the reasons to work out in the Healthy Heart zone – because you want to get healthier. If your goal is to be a competitive athlete, you will probably only spend time warming up and warming down in this zone. If your interests are to improve your health, especially if you are just starting a fitness program, the Healthy Heart zone is the place to be.

The zone floor for the Healthy Heart zone is 50% of your maximum heart rate. When you cross this heart rate line, you will realize health benefits. The amount of energy burned during this time will not be as great as in higher zones, but you will be burning a relatively large percentage of the *type* of calories that are most preferred as your source of fuel - fat. There's a critical, but not well discussed difference between total calories burned and the type of calories burned. Quality, or type of calories burned, is generally more important than quantity, the total number of calories expended in a workout. In the Healthy Heart zone, while the total calories burned per workout may be low, a very large percentage of the calories are fat calories. Carbohydrates are high-grade fuels, perfect for burning in the higher training load training zones. But burning them up doesn't slim you down, it might just make you hungrier!

The Healthy Heart zone is a very comfortable level of exercise - you get the feeling that you could go on forever. The average number of calories burned per minute (about 4-6) is lower than in any other zone, though. So, if your number one goal is not basic cardiovascular fitness, but weight loss, you'll need to move up to the Temperate zone, Zone 2.

Even if you have more advanced goals, the Z1 Healthy Heart zone is a good place to start, as well as to come back to from time to time, when you need a break from more strenuous workouts. Here you'll find the quiet kind of success that sticks with you; you'll feel good about yourself, you won't sweat profusely, and you'll be going at a moderate enough pace to have time to actually enjoy both the scenery and the workout.

Zone	Zone Name	% Max HR	Fuels Burned	Calories
Z1	Healthy Heart	50%–60%	10% Carbohydrates 60%-85% Fat 5% Protein	±4 calories per minute

IS P.E. P.C.?
OR IS PHYSICAL EDUCATION POLITICALLY CORRECT?

Maybe you grew up with the experience of physical education that many of us did. PE teachers only had 30 minutes a day for you to actually experience the joy of exercise, so the teacher worked you hard. At the beginning of the school year, you had to take a fitness test, and if you were like many kids, you did poorly. That teacher with the whistle was trying to whip you into shape. What it probably did was whip you right out of physical fitness until now.

Mandatory physical education has been eliminated from many schools today, and you might be surprised to hear that I think this is a big mistake. Getting sufficient cardiovascular exercise every day is crucial to children's fitness, growth, IQ, and weight maintenance. With the number of obese children growing yearly, this is not a light matter. Many adults have lost their former, youthful fitness and are now struggling to regain it, but just imagine the immensity of your task if you were *never* fit, not even as a child!

I taught time physical education, and when I did, I found the most crucial step was getting the kids to enjoy exercise. Heck, many of the teachers struggled teaching PE because the class was about discipline, not about

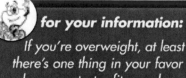

starting youngsters on the path of lifetime fitness. As far as any mention of heart rate zones went, the most physical education teachers were taught was to try to get kids into some target heart rate zone of 70%-85% maximum heart rate, which is far above the Healthy Heart zone and many sedentary kids' abilities.

As adults, we have the luxury of choosing our own preferred forms of physical education, and we can also take advantage of the fact that we now know that working out in the Healthy Heart zone (50%–60% of your maximum heart rate) is sufficient for great health benefits to occur. For those who have been inactive for more than five years, this is a perfect training load level with which to begin a program. If your maximum heart rate were 200, it would mean that you would be spending your time in the 100-120 bpm zone.

The table below illustrates the Healthy Heart Zone ranges based upon 50% to 60% of specified maximum heart rate.

Z1 Healthy Heart Zone 50% - 60% Maximum Heart Rate Chart

Max HR	150	155	160	165	170	175	180	185	190	195	200	205	210 bpm
50%		75	78	80	83	85	88	90	93	95	98	100	102	105
60%		90	93	95	99	102	105	108	111	114	117	120	123	125

GIVE A LITTLE, GET A LOT

The ACSM now acknowledges, after it re-reviewed the scientific literature, that working out in the Healthy Heart zone reduces your risk for certain degenerative diseases. The Healthy Heart zone doesn't fit this prescription because it is below the recommended 60%-90%. And that's the reason for the wellness continuum. Sure enough, if you want to *improve* fitness you will want to be in a higher zone, but if you want to get *healthier*, start out with the Healthy Heart zone.

When I give talks about Heart Zones Training, I often get two types of questions: What is the optimum exercise intensity and duration for a training workout? And, what is the minimum exercise intensity and duration for a training workout? With the Healthy Heart zone, you can get away with doing a little and still get a huge benefit. It's the fitness version of having your cake and eating it, too!

The fact is, a little exercise makes a bigger health difference to you than a lot of exercise. That is, physical activity follows the law of diminishing returns - with more exercise you don't get a commensurate increase in benefits.

The figure below illustrates this phenomenon:

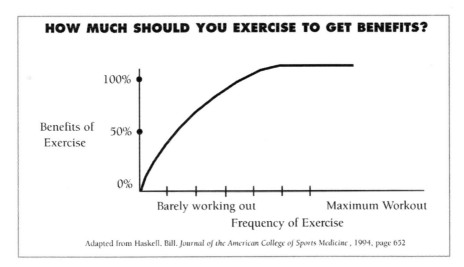

HOW MUCH SHOULD YOU EXERCISE TO GET BENEFITS?

Benefits of Exercise — 100%, 50%, 0%

Barely working out — Maximum Workout

Frequency of Exercise

Adapted from Haskell, Bill. *Journal of the American College of Sports Medicine* , 1994, page 652

A little *can* be better than a lot. A lot of exercise may give you the maximum benefits, but not the optimum benefits. For example, Dr. Ken Cooper in this book, *Antioxidant Revolution,* argues that excessive exercise constitutes a risk because of the release of "free radicals."

If you are working out for your health - to lower your risk of heart attacks, improve your immune system, lower your percentage of body fat - then exercising in the Healthy Heart Zone will maximize your return on your fitness effort invested. Sure, there are additional benefits when you train in the four higher zones, but many of the benefits can already be achieved right here.

The greatest benefits happen to those who need them the most, the least active individuals who begin a low-intensity rate exercise program. They are going to see much greater health benefits than the marathon runner who adds another ten miles a week of running. Sure, the ten miles may produce some incremental speed or endurance benefit, but not the massive health improvements that you will see when a secretary or computer nerd moves out from behind their computer screen and gets into a low-intensity exercise program. The figure below illustrates the point: a little exercise goes a long way towards gaining benefits.

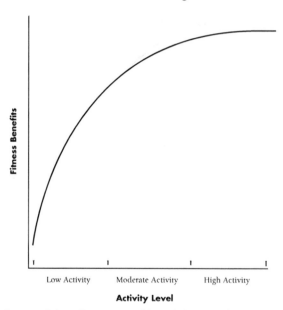

The Exercise Law of Diminishing Returns or

Activity Level

How much benefit you get with each increase in activity

If you've been relatively inactive and want to begin a fitness program, it's not only more efficient to work out in the Healthy Heart Zone, it's also safer. This is the zone that has the least orthopedic or cardiac risk.

Please don't be one of those stereotypical, gung-ho exercise fanatics who wants all of their results in the first week, because for better *and* worse, exercise is a double-edged sword. Training can either make you healthier and increase your resistance to disease or, if you overdo it, can injure you and decrease your immune potential. And, your risk is more related to the intensity of the exercise than its amount or frequency. It's better to exercise a little longer in the low-intensity zones than shorter periods at high-intensity levels. It's *not* true that the more pain, the more gain. For example, there is more of a risk of catching a cold, breaking bones, and heart attacks in the high heart rate zones than in the low ones. In other words, I don't recommend pushing yourself because it's possible that you could fall.

It *is* true that with less pain there's more gain. In fact, *for some health benefits such as lowering blood pressure, reducing platelet aggregation and enhancing immune function, exercise in the three lower zones (the Healthy Heart, Temperate, and Aerobic zones) is more beneficial than exercise in the higher zones.*

TRAINING VOLUMES AND THE PRINCIPLE OF EQUIVALENCY

Everybody wants an exercise program that gets them the most benefits in the least amount of time. You can have it with just two caveats: you've got to measure your heart rate (preferably, but not necessarily, with a heart rate monitor) and you must stay in the Healthy Heart zone the equivalent of 10 minutes a day. Quite simply, it doesn't matter whether you do 10 minutes a day or 20 minutes every other day. What matters is that you do it. After nearly a century of exercise testing, the answer to how much, how long, and how hard has been answered.

The body doesn't care when you indulge in low intensity exercise – it only responds to exercise volume. Low intensity exercise can be accumulated in bits and pieces: twelve 5-minute periods or something equivalent is not better or worse than one 60- or two 30-minute periods. Why this occurs is what exercise scientists call the "last bout" effect.

Your body responds in two ways to any type of exercise: you get both the extended "training response" and the immediate "biological response," both of which produce health benefits. A training response is a change in your body's structure or function from the exercise experience, which may be permanent or extended (for example, your muscles get bigger, your cardio-respiratory system uses oxygen more efficiently, etc.). The biological or "last bout" response doesn't make any sort of permanent change in your body's structure or function, but it does have an immediate reaction to your exercise (for example, a drop in your blood pressure or release of endorphins into your bloodstream).

It's the last bout effect that people who regularly work out get "addicted" to all those warm, energized, positive feelings. Your mind and body are physically uplifted from getting your heart rate up, and good feelings spontaneously arise when endorphins are released. Still, we're not just getting the benefits of the classic "runner's high" here. Most of the time when you are regularly engaged in a health or fitness program, you are going to earn yourself effects that are a combination of both training *and* biological responses.

Here's a good example. If you are an older person with hypertension, and you work out on a stationary bike in the Healthy Heart zone for 15 minutes, you will probably see a significant drop in your systolic blood pressure for up to two hours after the exercise. That's a last bout effect. It's the result of the exercise experience, not of your accumulated training. What's great is that this biological response from the last exercise bout can be augmented by repeated regular bouts of exercise and can become permanent - a training response.

The bottom line? At relatively low exercise frequency and intensity, the body doesn't care about the kind of exercise or the duration or frequency of your workouts. What it does care about is your total exercise volume. Your body just really wants you to move around and spend a reasonable amount of energy in the health area of the wellness continuum. Your body doesn't care if you are raking leaves or shovelling snow or are on a cardiovascular machine at an athletic club. Your body doesn't discriminate against you if you are walking your dog or if you are a mail carrier. Your body only begs for one thing: that you move regularly and spend some energy. If you want to sip from the waters that Ponce de Leon did not taste, then dip your cup into the Healthy Heart zone.

A Z1 HEALTHY HEART WORKOUT

Starting a fitness program is a meaningful, literally *vital,* step; and you want to do so gently to allow your body to adjust to exercise stress. It's your choice whether you start out with ten minutes six days a week or twenty minutes three days a week for this workout. Your body responds to each of them equivalently.

Begin by putting on a pair of comfortable walking shoes and a casual outfit and choose a time of day that is going to be reliably convenient, when there is no competition for your attention.

Determine your specific numerical values for the Healthy Heart zone. If your maximum heart rate is 200 bpm then they will be from 100 to 120 bpm. (If you are using a heart rate monitor, you'll input these numbers as your zone's floor and ceiling.) Stretch for a couple of minutes and then start out walking slowly, smoothly picking up the pace to a brisk speed. It should take you about 60 seconds to break through the 100 bpm lower limit. About every minute or two you'll need to take your pulse rate or make a quick glance at your monitor (if it doesn't automatically beep, vibrate, or flash at you when you go out of your zone) to ensure that you are within the zone. For at least the last two minutes of the workout make sure you are in the *upper* Healthy Heart zone, which would be 110-120 beats per minute if your maximum heart rate were 200 bpm. At the end of the final two minutes, slow down for about sixty seconds to let your heart rate drop below the floor of your Healthy Heart zone. Sixty minutes a week. That's all. Hang out here for several weeks, and you'll get healthier.

Sally Edwards racing on her Kestrel racing bicycle and heart rate monitor at the 1998 Ironman World Championships in Kona, Hawaii. She finished a disappointing 4th in the Grand Master's division.

Chapter 8

Zone 2, The Temperate Zone

As a life-long athlete, I've never had the sort of intimate relationship with the fat battle that some people have, but a woman named Lisa brought reality home to me with her experience. "I was 135 pounds before the birth of my first daughter, but 210 pounds after the birth of my second. One day, my husband came home with a heart rate monitor. I'd heard about Sally Edwards and her Heart Zones Training system and decided to give it a try. I bounded into the Z2 zone and hung out there for one and one-half years, ate everything I wanted but limited my dietary fat intake to 30 grams a day and the fat slowly melted. I have maintained 135 pounds ever since." Lisa sustained a healthy weight loss amounting to about one pound per week.

WHAT IT DOES

The Z2 Temperate zone is so-called for a simple reason: It's a moderate and comfortable zone. In zone 2, approximately 70%-85% of all of the calories that are burned come from fat and the rest from carbohydrates (CHO). However, unlike the 4-6 calories or so per minute you can expect to burn in the Healthy Heart zone, in the Temperate zone an average person will burn about 6-10 calories per minute! So, in ten minutes of exercise, depending on your weight and other factors, you'll burn about 100 calories. Approximately 85 calories will be from fat in

The following summarizes events and conditions within Z2:				
Zone	**Zone Name**	**% Max HR**	**Fuels Burned**	**Calories**
Z2	Temperate	60–70%	10% Carbohydrates 50-80% Fat 5% Protein	± 7 calories per minute

your diet or your own body releasing it's stored fat. This blend of fat and CHO, carbohydrates, changes based on your diet, current fitness level, genetics, amount of exercise, etc.)

As you continue to train into the higher zones, you burn more calories, but you also burn proportionately less fat as a percentage of your total calories.

The chart below shows the percentage of fuels burned by zone:

Is it better to burn more "total" calories during higher heart zone

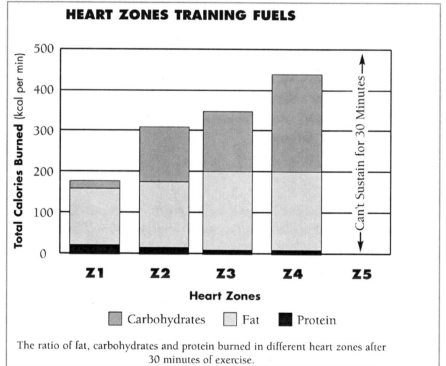

The ratio of fat, carbohydrates and protein burned in different heart zones after 30 minutes of exercise.

Adapted from Butterfield , Gail, et. al. Hershey Foods Corporation: Topics in Nutrition and Food Safety: Fuelling Activity, fall 1994, page 6

workouts, or to burn a higher "percentage" of your calories as fat calories? The answer is - it depends. It is individual, depending totally on your fitness level and your goals. If you're already in shape, it's best to burn total calories; if you are on your way to getting fit, it's better to burn fat calories. If you're in great shape, you don't need to hang out in the low zones, because you are fit not fat. If you are fat and not fit, this is the place for you.

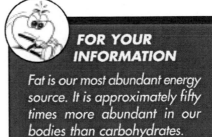

FOR YOUR INFORMATION

Fat is our most abundant energy source. It is approximately fifty times more abundant in our bodies than carbohydrates.

By exercising in the temperate zone, you double your health rewards because you burn more fat and, at the same time, gain muscle mass. Consequently you have more muscle available to burn even more fat as your resting metabolic rate (RMR) increases. In other words, the more muscle mass you have, the more calories you burn just sitting still.

And, when you get into relatively good shape, you can hang out in zone 2 for a longer period of time - it can be a recovery zone or a long, slow endurance zone. If you use the Temperate zone for either purpose, then the blend of fuels your body burns becomes even more in your favor. With longer training sessions, more than 60 minutes in duration, your body begins to run out of the readily available carbohydrates in

> *When muscles demand energy to move, it takes time for your stored fat to break into smaller pieces so it can pass through the **fat** cell wall and into the bloodstream to be transported to your muscle cells.*

your system and relies even more on your body's stored fat. In the first few minutes of exercise, there is a tendency for the muscles to grab carbohydrates for fuel because they are readily available and don't have to be mobilized.

This makes sense because when you first start up, you're body's looking for whatever it can get its hands on to stuff into the furnace. The longer the exercise duration, the more body fat can be broken down and shuttled out to the muscles via the bloodstream. That's what's so great about long, slow training - it increases your fat mobilization. Look at the chart below and you'll see how important fat is as a source of fuel during long work-outs.

Look at the chart below and you'll see how important fat is as a source of fuel during long work-outs.

Glycogen, or stored carbohydrates in the muscles, is depleted with long exercise sessions while fat can remain in abundance.

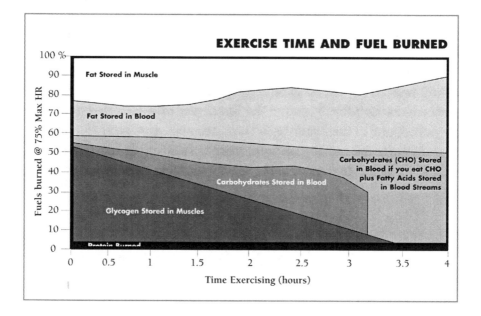

HOW IT DOES IT

The floor for the Temperate zone is 60% maximum heart rate, just above the Healthy Heart zone. The ceiling of the Z2 Temperate zone is 70% maximum heart rate, just below the Aerobic zone. As you exercise in the Temperate zone you realize even more of the health benefits that accumulate from progressively moving from the Healthy Heart to the Temperate zone. Get beyond this zone, and you're achieving fitness more than health.

For someone whose maximum heart rate is 200 beats per minute (bpm), their Temperate zone is 120-140 bpm. This is a moderate level of activity, strenuous, but challenging. It's that zone where you feel that you are working - you break a sweat early on but you can carry on a conversation the entire time and there isn't a feeling of discomfort.

Exercising in the Temperate zone allows your body to accomplish three things. Fat mobilization is the first - getting the fat out of your cells. Fat is stored in fat cells as triglycerides, large molecules that can't pass through the cell wall into the bloodstream. When the muscles demand energy, as in exercise, the fat cells are stimulated by enzymes to divide the fat molecules into smaller pieces (fatty acids), which are then freely released into the bloodstream where they travel to the muscles. However, if your heart rate goes *above* the Temperate zone, more lactic acid is produced which begins to block the enzymes that allow the fat to be liberated from the cell. And, of course, trapped fat can't be burned.

The second accomplishment of the Temperate zone is getting the now-freed fatty acids not only out of the cells but into the bloodstream. This is where the lower training zones become even more important, because blood is still circulating in the fatty tissues at these lower heart rates. When you train in more intense heart rate zones, blood flow is restricted in fatty tissue. Therefore, even if the fat is released from the cells, it can't effectively enter the bloodstream.

Once in the bloodstream in sufficient concentrations, the free-floating fatty acids are drawn into the muscle fibers. Inside these fibers, the fatty acids are activated by more enzymes which prepare them to be broken down within the muscles' energy factories, the mitochondria.

It makes sense that the higher the concentration of free fatty acids, the more accessible they are for the muscles to utilize. However, mitochondria also depend on the presence of another player in the fat-burning process: oxygen. This is key: for fat to burn, oxygen must be present. If your heart rate goes too far above the Temperate zone, you end up training anaerobically, that is, "without oxygen." At these intensities, carbohydrates are burned, not fat.

These three steps in the process of fat loss - the release of fat from cells, the transportation of fat to the muscles, and the higher concentration of fatty acids, combined with the availability of oxygen with which to burn the fat, happen far and away the most efficiently in the moderate intensities of the Temperate zone. In other words, hanging out in the Temperate zone allows you to open up your fat cells and let the fat come out.

GETTING BETTER ALL THE TIME

The benefits of exercising in the Temperate Z2 zone go on and on. Studies show that those who work out at low heart rates burn more fat, even when they are not in the midst of a training session, than do those who don't exercise. Training teaches the metabolic processes how to preferentially pick fat over sugar.

How does this happen? Remember when we talked about the training response in the last chapter? Working out in the Temperate zone causes these kinds of extended changes in your body's structure or function.

Specifically, the amount of stored fat you can burn is related to the rate at which you can supply fat to your muscles. When you increase the rate, you increase the percentage of fat burned. That's what training in the Temperate zone does - the more you train in the Temperate zone, the more efficient your body becomes at using fat for energy since, with exercise, there is an overall increase in the activity of the fat burning enzymes. This makes more fatty acids available leading to an increase in the availability of fat as the primary energy source. There is another factor that determines the rate at which you can supply free fatty acids to be burned: the amount of blood flow to the muscle. When you engage in regular training, you increase the blood transport system's ability to deliver blood by increasing the number of capillaries surrounding the

muscle fibers, so more blood flows to your muscles. Training in the

Temperate zone allows you to increase the amount of free fatty acids released out of your cells and into your bloodstream as well as to increase the amount of blood flow to your muscles.

Also, by training in the Temperate zone, you substantially increase the number of mitochondria in each muscle fibre. Since fat combustion takes place in the mitochondria, the more you have of these small energy factories, the more fat calories you can burn. Next, the size of the mitochondria increase with exercise. With bigger energy factories – mitochondria – you can combust even more fat calories. Research has shown that mitochondria get about 35% bigger with training, while there can be as much as a 15% increase in the quantity of mitochondria.

The mitochondrial enzymes' activity increases, too. Increasing this activity increases the mitochondria's efficiency and, thus, the muscles' aerobic capacity (your ability to utilize oxygen). With an increase in the number, the size, *and* the activity of the mitochondria, the Fat Burner is well-equipped to release, transport, and burn more and more fat as a source of energy.

As you hang out in the different zones, another one of your body's training responses is to increase the amount of your muscle tissue or lean body mass. You want this. The more muscle mass you have, the more calories you burn at rest and your resting metabolic rate, the amount of calories you burn by just being alive, increases.

None of these changes happen overnight, so don't expect to start a Heart Zones Training program and see improvements on your second day. When you add a weight loss component to your training there usually isn't immediate weight loss. This is normal. We often think we can "beat the system." We can't. Heart Zones Training works within the system, optimizing the way the body works.

At some point as you increase the intensity of your exercise, your muscles shift to using a higher percentage of carbohydrates than fats. This intensity level is called the "cross-over point." That is, as your heart rate increases, your metabolic response crosses over from using mostly fat as the energy source to predominantly CHO. One of the definitions of fitness is to change this crossover point to a higher heart rate. As you get fitter you burn more fat calories at lower heart rate numbers than when you are less fit.

In the old school, coaches preached the philosophy of "LSD" workouts. Now, before you start thinking that all those runners out there in the '70s were so stoned out of their minds that it was a miracle they weren't tripping over their own feet, let me clarify. To us, "LSD" stood for "Long, Slow Distances." We did twenty a day'ers - twenty *miles* a day of running - as frequent workouts. We were convinced that the longer we ran, the more fat we would burn (which is generally true) and that this was one of the tracks of the road to true runners' high. We ran and ran and ran for years and years and years. But, as students of both our experience and of ongoing scientific research, we began to cut back, run fewer miles, *and* set more personal bests. We learned the Heart Zones Training lesson, that the quality could be more important than the quantity of our exercise.

Today we've entered the era of SSDs - short, slow distances. That's really what the Temperate zone is, at least in the beginning. The results are huge on the health continuum as well as in the mind.

So, how do you put the Z2 into practice? Do what a friend of mine named Juanita does four times a week - twenty-aday'ers but minutes not miles. She loves a variety of cross-training, so in the summer she swims one day, circuit trains in gym for one, bikes another, and walk-runs a fourth — each for twenty minutes, and each in the Temperate zone. In the winter, one day a week she circuit trains for 20 minutes, the next she sport snowshoes for 20 minutes, the third she cross-country skis, and on the fourth she uses a stair-stepper or treadmill machine. Twenty minutes, four times a week is enough to melt the fat away, so long as it's twenty minutes in the Temperate zone.

Each time, fitness enthusiast Juanita burns fat calories as her primary fuel source, even though she doesn't burn as many total calories as if she were in the Aerobic zone. And she enjoys the workout because it's fun and not painful. Because of the variety, she keeps her motivation and interest high. Each time she knows that she is investing in her health – the most important thing she has in her life.

Remember, though, training in the Temperate zone is only half of the fat-loss game plan. If you eat a high fat diet, then your fat cells are competing with what you just ate as the source of fat for energy. Muscle fibers prefer dietary fat over stored body fat, after all.

Z2 Temperate Zone 60% - 70% Maximum Heart Rate Chart

Max HR	150	155	160	165	170	175	180	185	190	195	200	205	210 bpm
60%	90	93	96	99	102	105	108	111	114	117	120	123	125
70%		105	109	112	116	119	123	126	130	133	137	140	143	146

CHAPTER 9
Zone 3, The Aerobic Zone

The Aerobic zone gives you the most "bang for your buck." Here you'll get the most benefits in the least amount of time. If you said, "I want everything from exercise," this is your zone. The Z3 Aerobic zone gets you fitter, gets you faster, gets you thinner. That's why it's been touted for decades as the guts of the one mythical "target zone." The Aerobic zone might be called the heart of the heart of it.

The word "aerobic" itself has been the hallmark of the fitness revolution which began in the late 1960s with the launch of Ken Cooper's legendary book *Aerobics*. Following right behind him were the other icons that drove the principle of aerobic fitness to the forefront. Women should take most of the credit for turning the theory of aerobics into practice - what we all now know as the "aerobic class." Starting with Jackie Sorenson, aerobic dance guru, dance exercise leaders have taught classes in their homes, schools, company cafeterias, and of course, health clubs. Credit should go, too, to Judi Shepherd Misset, who created Jazzercise.

Simultaneously, the running craze struck, and America started jogging. Jim Fixx's *Complete Book of Running* emerged as an unlikely hit and landed, feet-first, on the best-sellers' list. Jump forward into the digital age of the 90s. It's the era of machine exercising and digital readouts - stair climbers, spin bikes, cross conditioning machines, and recumbent bikes. It's the heyday of cross-training and adventures in the outdoors: quadrathlons, hiking, canoeing, ultra-distance events, and power-walking. But there are plenty of fans of the new wave of indoor sports: step aerobics, heart aerobics, lateral slide training, boxerobics, and personal training.

You have now arrived at the web-apps age of the 2010's. The 21st century, and the faster-lifestyles that got even faster as we spin like a dervish from emotional, physical, environmental, and financial crisis to the planet and all of it's inhabitants. Wars on obesity, terrorism, and sedentary lifestyles make heroes out of ordinary villains. The interests of fitness enthusiasts grows with new technologies like the Wii system, digital TVs connected to every cardio-machine at the health club, and fitness competitions from reality TV weight loss shows to web-racing. Smart fabrics make sensing physiological responses even easier and more non-intrusive with blood pressure, heart rate, sweat rate, body position and temperature more readily available. And, all of the entertainment and data in the world is being connected with social networking and web 2.0 technologies and devices.

Wondering which marvelous activity to turn to? Choose any of them, and do as many of the indoor and outdoor sports as your fun-loving inner child desires; just remember it's the zones (and the amount of time you spend in them) that matter.

THE TRANSITION ZONE

The Aerobic zone has very specific parameters. The aerobic zone floor is 70% of your maximum heart rate and it is at this point that you begin to realize substantial cardiovascular benefits. If your true maximum heart rate were tested at 200 bpm, then the aerobic floor heart rate for your purposes would be 140 bpm.

Its neighboring zone to the lower side is the Temperate zone. Once you cross over from the Temperate to the Aerobic zone, it doesn't mean that you stop burning fat as a source of calories. It just means that the percentage of types of fuels burned changes. No longer are you burning the vast majority of your calories from fats; instead you're shifting into the zones that use more carbohydrates as their fuel source.

The ceiling for the Aerobic zone is 80% of your maximum heart rate. This is actually quite strenuous for the novice exerciser. For someone who has been training for a few weeks or months, this might be considered "somewhat hard" or "hard" if you were to give the feeling a verbal description. Above the ceiling of the Aerobic zone is the Threshold zone. When you cross this line you've entered the world of performance training. If your true maximum heart rate were tested at 200 bpm, then your aerobic ceiling heart rate would be 160 bpm. This Aerobic heart rate zone is also known as the "talk test zone" because it is within this zone that you can speak without a shortness of breath or loss of words; if you start to exercise above it, however, a friendly chat soon becomes the last thing on your mind.

The Aerobic zone is the fitness area at the heart of the wellness continuum. It is the transition zone between the two health zones and the two performance zones. It's also the first of the zones where performance training effects begin. In the Aerobic zone you begin to realize the changes that lead to athletic conditioning versus basic health and fitness. That is, this is the zone where tremendous (but somewhat technical) physiological changes occur. As indicated below, the cardio-pulmonary changes from rest to the aerobic level are enormous.

	Active Rest (sitting quietly)	Aerobic Zone (70-80% Max HR)
Heart Rate:	30-80 bpm	120-180 bpm
Oxygen Utilization	3.5 ml/kg/min	50 ml/kg/min
Respiratory Rate:	12 breaths/min	35-45 breaths/min
Expired Airflow	5 L/min	180 L/min
Cardiac Output	5 L/min	40 L/min
Working Muscles Blood Flow	1.2 L/min	12 L/min
Blood Flow to Kidneys	1.1 L/min	6 L/min
Heat Production	100 kcal/hr	1,000 kcal/hr

The changes are incredible - it's a comfort zone. (Don't forget - it's also comfortable.) The Aerobic zone is where you break sweat, raising your core temperature to just above the sweat point, but not much beyond.

You feel like you have had a workout when you train here, but you don't feel any of the burn or the pain. If you do, you have pushed yourself through the Aerobic ceiling and into the Threshold zone, which isn't the place to be if your goal is to achieve fitness. It feels great to take a shower after an Aerobic zone workout because you can feel that you have released both emotionally and physically some of your stored-up toxins. The Aerobic zone is a place where you get a lot of rewards and feel good about both your mental and your physical muscles. Quite simply, when you are an active exerciser, the Aerobic zone is the place to spend some of your most memorable workouts. It's a training zone that enhances the features of most of the other zones, and it's a wonderful place to be.

The following summarizes events and conditions within Z3:

Zone	Zone Name	% Max HR	Fuels Burned	Calories
Z3	Aerobic	70–80%	60% Carbohydrates	± 10
			35% Fat	calories
			5% Protein	per minute

AEROBIC PERFORMANCE TRAINING

Now, even though we just said that the Aerobic zone is in the fitness, not performance area of the wellness continuum, ironically enough, for the performance-oriented individual, the Aerobic zone is where you want to spend the bulk of your workout time. Time spent training in the Aerobic zone is called "base work time" or just "base." The Aerobic zone is really the comfortable center to your performance training program. Training in the zones below the Aerobic zone provides little measurable effect on performance, but may add to your training stresses. Training above the Aerobic zone causes excessive dependence on glycogen and not fatty acid metabolization. For athletes, the Aerobic zone provides enough of a stimulus to improve joint and tendon strength, but without excessive stress impact. It is a zone that teaches the metabolic pathways to spare carbohydrates and metabolize fatty acids. Exercising in Zone 3 leads to other cardiac and pulmonary changes but typically does not result in over-training.

> *If you are new to training, your resting heart rate may drop as much as 1–2 beats per minute for every 1–2 weeks that you train in the Aerobic zone, until you reach a new and lower resting heart rate number.*

For those returning to performance training after a lay-off or injury, the Aerobic zone is ideal because it provides an adequate training load to drive the training effect from adaptation mechanisms, yet it is gentle and fun. Quite simply, it is an endurance-building zone. Training a certain amount of time in Z3 builds resistance to fatigue and increases cardio-vascular efficiency.

The Aerobic zone is the place where enhancements to the functional capacity of the heart, lungs, vascular and skeletal systems really occur. Maybe that is why the Aerobic zone is also the one loved by so many exercise purists. Maybe it's because of the mood-altering endorphins that become so profuse when training in the Z3 and Z4 zones. Discovered in the 1970s, the blood level concentrations of these opiate-like stress reducers can increase up to five-fold from the resting state as a result of exercise. Labeled the "exercise high," this state of euphoria, which arises particularly in these two zones, can result in mood improvement and is implicated in increased pain tolerance, reduction in anxiety, tension, stress, and improved appetite control. The beauty is these benefits continue for hours after you've worked out.

Endorphins are still highly controversial because of limited and varying research data. It seems that the higher the exercise heart rate levels, the greater the production or sensitivity to endorphins. That's one of the reasons the Aerobic and Threshold zones can become addictive.

Compounding this increase in quantity of endorphins from brief bouts of higher intensity training is the slower rate of disposal of endorphins in trained individuals compared to the untrained. This slower rate of disposal allows for the effects to linger and might increase one's tolerance for high-intensity extended training. Clearly, all of the results are not in yet.

Remember, though, that the benefits of zones are not cumulative. You have to train in a specific zone to get its specific benefit. If you are a Z3 junkie, but you really need to maximize your fat loss, you're going to have to slow down sometimes to do fat burning zone (Z1-Z2) workouts. Or, if you really need to improve your 10K run time, you're going to have to occasionally ease yourself out of the smooth comfort of the Aerobic zone, and into something a little more challenging, say Z4. But on the other hand, if you haven't spent much time here because you love one of the other four zones, it's time to try Z3. Once you've gotten sufficiently fit, the Aerobic zone is a great place to spend gobs of time and live it up.

CARDIO IMPROVEMENTS

If you were shocked at the amount of unfamiliar exercise terminology before, you'd better steel yourself, because it gets worse before it gets better. Once you enter the fitness and performance zones, you start hearing people toss around long and impressive words, like "cardiovascular" or "cardiopulmonary," or short and weird ones, like "VO$_2$ max" (but more on that later).

Taking the roots of the first word, "cardio" for heart and "vascular," referring to your blood vessels, this is the zone that works the heart and its blood-transport system. The Aerobic zone gives us cardiopulmonary - referring to both the heart and the lungs - benefits, too. In reality, all three parts - heart and lung and vessels - are simultaneously worked by the wonderful Aerobic zone.

How many actually know what "aerobic" means? Well, literally, "aerobic" means "with air." In fitness terms it means that you are exercising at an intensity level such that the lungs can infuse sufficient oxygen into the blood, while the heart can pump sufficient quantities of the oxygen-laden blood to all of the muscles - including the heart muscle.

Some of the cardiovascular improvements that your body undergoes as a result of Aerobic zone exercise are:

• *increase in the number of blood vessels,*

• *increase in the size of blood vessels,*

• *increase in blood delivery to your muscles,*

• *increase in oxygen delivery to the muscles for fuel,*

• *increase in the oxygen delivery to the fat cells to free them into the blood,*

• *increase in the blood to carry the fat from fat cells to the muscles,*

• *increase number of mitochondria within muscle cells that convert fuels for muscle combustion,*

• *increase in size of each individual mitochondria,*

• *increase in number of capillaries in the working muscles,*

• *increase in size of existing capillaries,*

• *increase in size of coronary arteries,*

• *reduction in blood pressure.*

An increase in both the size and strength of the heart, resulting in increased stroke volume (the amount of blood pumped with each heart-beat),

• *increase in cardiac output (stroke volume times heart rate),*

• *decreased heart rate for the same intensity level training load.*

• *increase in red blood cell volume, plasma volume, and total blood volume.*

Some of the cardiopulmonary or respiratory changes that result from training in the Aerobic zone are:

• *Increased vital capacity (the amount of air that can be breathed out after a maximal intake of breath).*

• *Decreased respiratory rate (the number of breaths you take in response to a given level of training load).*

• *Increased maximal pulmonary ventilation (the volume of oxygen per minute you can breathe).*

• *Increased pulmonary diffusion (the amount of oxygen exchanged by the lungs).*

• *Increased difference in arterial-venous oxygen (more oxygen is extracted at the tissue level).*

VO₂ MAX

Another value of the Aerobic zone is that if you train in Z3 your VO₂ max improves. This rather cryptic benefit may not mean much to you if you are unfamiliar with fitness jargon, so let me explain. The more oxygen that you absorb and feed to your muscles, the better you will be able to exercise. With increased oxygen utilization at a given intensity level, your heart rate at that training load will be lower. Why? Your heart rate increases to provide more oxygenated blood to your muscles, but if you've trained your body to the point where it's already circulating more oxygen, your heart isn't going to need to work harder. *That* is a key definition of aerobic fitness improvement, and it is one of the primary benefits of the Aerobic zone.

Exercise scientists have devised a way of measuring the quantity of oxygen that your muscles burn and the quantity of carbon dioxide that they release as one of the by-products of exercise metabolism. This is called VO_2 or volume of oxygen. It is quoted as a percentage of your maximum amount or your VO_2 max. The average middle-aged unfit, sedentary woman's VO_2 max is about 30-40 milliliters of oxygen per kilogram of body weight, and a sedentary man's is about 45-55 milliliters. The reason that men's numbers are higher than women's is because typically men have more muscle mass as a percentage of their total body weight. The larger muscle mass uses more oxygen because muscle is active oxygen-demanding tissue. The larger the fat mass the less oxygen used because fat is inactive tissue. For a woman with equal muscle and fat tissue percentages as a same-size male, the differences would not be great.

FUELING UP

As you travel up through the heart rate zones, there is a continual shift in the percentages of different fuels burned. As you transition into the Aerobic zone, you are for the first time utilizing a higher percentage of carbohydrates than fats as a source of muscle fuel. This has several effects on your performance.

First, we don't have as many carbohydrate calories in storage as we have of fat, because while our bodies may have plenty of fat cells, there are no such things as handy, quick-access, calorie-storing carbohydrate cells. We can only store a limited supply of carbohydrates in our muscles, blood, and liver in the form of glycogen. So, there is a limited supply of quick-energy carbohydrates stored within the body and a limitation on how much we can get out of our gut from foods that we

Z3 Temperate Zone 70% - 80% Maximum Heart Rate Chart												
Max HR	150	155	160	165	170	175	180	185	190	195	200	205	210 bpm
70%		105	109	112	116	119	123	126	130	133	137	140	143	146
80%		120	124	128	132	136	140	144	148	152	156	160	164	168

consume while we exercise.

The average person's body contains between 375 and 475 grams of carbohydrates at any given time. Since one gram of carbohydrates equals four calories, if you multiply 375 grams times four and 475 grams times four, you know that the average person carries on board a supply of about 1,500 to 1,900 calories of glycogen. For example, if you burn 13 calories per minute in the Aerobic zone, then you would have about 2 hours of workout time available. That , of course, is if you burned only pure muscle glucose, which we don't. Our bodies always burn some sort of blend of fat and carbohydrates together, which is why we can exercise longer than 2 hours, without having to refuel. But, the body's increasing need for carbohydrates over fats at ever higher exercise intensity levels is why it is important to consume carbohydrates during Z4 and Z5 or very long Z3 workouts.

The quantity of carbohydrates stored in your body is dependent to a great deal on your diet. If, for example, you ate a low-carbohydrate diet or even worse, you fasted, when you started to work out there would be a huge drop in the amount of stored glycogen in your blood, muscles, and liver. This would limit your ability to train in the Aerobic zone and your overall energy level. The opposite is also true. If you eat a high carbohydrate diet you can store more glycogen on board and hence have more available to fuel you through the Aerobic zone.

One of the best, most reliable Aerobic zone workouts we've found is Step Aerobics. With this kind of workout, you use your heart rate to determine the height of the step, selecting a height that allows you to complete a steady-state 20-minute step training session all within the Aerobic zone.

It will take you several training sessions to achieve the best combination of step height and music cadence to get your steady-state Aerobic workout. This is because of the effects of heart rate drift, which means that at the same training load, over the duration of a workout, your heart rate gradually drifts upwards. The same happens with your respiration rate, which drifts to a progressively increasing number of breaths per minute with any steady-state exercise.

Start with your favorite workout tape or your favorite instructor's class and only put one riser on your step (which should make the step approximately 4" tall). For the next twenty minutes, exercise at this intensity level (one riser and at a fixed number of beats per minute for the music) and watch your heart rate change. Throughout the entire time you should be above your Aerobic zone floor yet never break through the Aerobic ceiling.

At the second session, keep the music intensity the same but add one more riser, making your step 8". Now, determine the heart rate cost of adding that 4 inches of step height. For most, this equates to a 5–10 beat increase in average heart rate (if you have a heart rate monitor, measure the difference in the average as well as the high and low heart rate values). If it results in an increase of more than an average of 15-25 beats per minute, this is a clear indication that your current fitness level could use some improving. It also means that you should take the second riser off and go back to a lower step level in order to stay in your Aerobic zone.

On the third exercise session if you haven't already gone through the Aerobic ceiling, add the final riser, which should make your step 12", while keeping the choreography and the music identical. The only change will be in your step height. Again, measure your change in heart rate and adjust your step height accordingly for next time. After three sessions, you should have a pretty good idea of which step height gave you the best Aerobic zone workout, but keep in mind that as your fitness increases, you'll need to start adding steps again, and retesting yourself.

Variations of this workout include mixing the choreography as well as the music cadence. Play with these variables and teach yourself how to change your zones (perhaps working through both your Z2 *and* Z3 zones in one workout) by varying the elements of your training load - music beat, resistance as step height, and choreography - to enjoy multiple training effects.

Triathlon and running legend Sally Edwards is the Founder and CEO of Heart Zones USA and The Sally Edwards Company; both are based in Sacramento, CA. She encourages everyone to read her blog and follow her on Twitter and Facebook and her two company's websites.

Chapter 10
Zone 4, The Threshold Zone

Welcome to the Threshold zone! Even if you don't choose to train in the Z4 Threshold zone, it's a place you're no doubt familiar with, though maybe you are unfamiliar with its name. Here's a hint: this is also known as the "shortness of breath" zone. Sound familiar? It's the zone where you feel the burn in your legs as you quickly climb a set of stairs; where, when you reach the top, lean over, put your hands on your thighs and try to catch your breath, your mind slowly reminds you, "You're really out of shape."

The Threshold zone is so-called because, for most *fit* people, within this zone of 80-90% maximum heart rate is your threshold - your second lactate threshold and your high ventilatory threshold. Because these thresholds are so similar and so close together, for our purposes now, we are going to wrap them up and call this exercise intensity, heart rate number "threshold" (see Chapter 18 about the Threshold Training System). Above the threshold, oxygen debt starts to rapidly accumulate and lactates are spewing out. It can be a very uncomfortable place. But here's the startling part about the threshold. In the *unfit* individual, it is common to see thresholds at around *60%* of their maximum heart rate. And, in the extremely fit, it is common to see thresholds above 90% of their maximum heart rate. The chart on the next page gives you a view of the parts of Z4.

This is very important: if you are unfit and your threshold heart rate point is within your low zones, Z1-3, you *can't* train in the Threshold zone. It's simply too high a heart rate intensity. You need to stay below your threshold for *all* of your exercise. This is one of the primary reasons why exercise fails the healthy unfit: we're asking them to train far above their thresholds.

The following summarizes events and conditions within Z4:

Zone	Zone Name	% Max HR	Fuels Burned	Calories
Z4	Threshold	80–90%	80% Carbohydrates 15% Fat 5% Protein	±15 calories per minute

Let's say you are beginning an exercise program; you're healthy, and you're motivated to be successful. You are told to follow the arithmetic formula to calculate your exercise heart zones, so you use the 220 minus your age formula, which is on the wall charts at your athletic club.

You start your program, jump into the 70%-85% heart rate range and can't maintain that for more than 5-10 minutes, but you're told that you are to stay there for at least 20 minutes, 4 days a week. At that intensity level, your chest is pounding, your breathing is faster than you could have imagined, and the pain is enormous. What do you do? If you are like most, you quit and then try and restart at some future time. The reason you failed is that you were told to train at a level that is above your threshold and cannot be sustained. It's not your fault that you couldn't do it. You were given the wrong information. Don't be too hard on your trainers and coaches, though. In all likelihood, they didn't know the correct information either. They were blinded by the accepted paradigms.

So, be warned that we are now leaving the comfort of the health and fitness areas of the wellness continuum. If you aren't already fit or aren't interested in training for performance's sake, this might be where you choose to get off the bus. In other words, it's okay to skip this chapter and the following one, which covers the Red Line zone, but do pick up the book again after these chapters, because there's more to come for everyone. More on weight loss. More on performance. More.

HIGH INTENSITY, HIGH PERFORMANCE

Some fit folks hate this zone. There are others, though, who are threshold Z4 addicts, spending all of their training time hanging out here, producing endorphins and eating up lactic acid as if it were chocolate. We are concerned about the latter group (threshold junkies is their nickname) and encourage the former to try a few more sessions here because, if your goal is performance, you can get a lot of bang for your buck in the Threshold zone.

As we've just discussed, your threshold heart rate number changes with your conditioning. As you become more fit, your heart rate at this point is higher; as you become less fit, your heart rate at this point lowers. This is a moveable and trainable heart rate number – not a fixed one like maximum heart rate - threshold heart rate is dynamic.

If you are interested in high performance, one of your goals must be to raise your threshold as close as you possibly can to your maximum heart rate. In other words, your goal is to improve your *maximum sustainable heart rate.* It is the highest heart rate that you can sustain for a given distance without having your performance suffer. Racing at your maximum sustainable heart rate improves your performance in any athletic event. Researchers have discovered that maximum sustainable heart rate is one of the best predictor of your success. This high heart rate number is expressed as a percentage of your maximum number. For example, if I can run a 10K at my maximum sustainable heart rate of 175 bpm, for me that translates to 85% of my maximum heart rate.

The most obvious question is what kind of training is necessary to improve the threshold heart rate and maximum sustainable heart rate? For the answer, you would need to jump forward to Chapter 12 ("High Performance with Heart Zones Training"). For here, the brief answer is called the "At/About/ Around" Principle. That is, a large percentage of your "time in zone" needs to be at/about/around your threshold heart rate - up to 25%-50% of your training time if you are training to race competitively in the final training period.

Keep in mind, too, that your threshold heart rate number is specific to the activity in which you are engaged. If your threshold heart rate is 185 bpm running, it might well be 178 bpm cycling. It is postulated that these differences are related to the muscle mass used during the specific activities, as well as whether the activity is weight-bearing or not. Threshold heart rate is not only sport-specific, it is conditioned sport-specific. If you are currently fit running and unfit swimming, you can have a high threshold heart rate for running and a low threshold heart rate for swimming.

Triathletes are great examples of Threshold zone aficionados. We love to hammer as much as possible and to constantly test ourselves in all three sports: swimming, cycling, and running. When I first began doing triathlons in the early '80s, there was little to nothing written on cross-training or multi-sport programs. So, using the laboratory of the self and what little available research I could find, I decided to devise a self-test to determine my threshold. Each week I took this self test in one of the three disciplines, and, as the weeks went by, I watched my scores improve.

TWO NEW THRESHOLDS - LOW AND HIGH

The history of the term "threshold" dates back to 1923, when two exercise scientists, Doctors Hill and Lupton, first noticed that when skeletal muscles are subjected to increasing training loads their metabolic demands exceeded what the body could provide to them. It wasn't until 1964, when the testing equipment became available to measure oxygen and carbon dioxide consumption and blood lactate changes, that the threshold first became measurable with lab tests.

Physician scientist Karl Wasserman used the term "threshold" to define a particular training load where blood lactates first begin to rise above their resting levels. Since then, the meaning has evolved to refer to that effort when blood lactates concentration increases dramatically over their resting levels.

Of course the controversy over the true definition of threshold continues today among coaches but no longer among exercise researchers. The scientists have settled their arguments among themselves. The majority now agree that there are many different ways to measure threshold using gas exchange, taking blood samples, using rating of perceived exertion, measuring shifts in breathing or ventilation to name a few. And, there is general agreement among scientists that there is not one, but two thresholds and that there are two major corresponding physiological shifts: the low or first threshold and the high or second threshold. At each of these two thresholds there is a change, a shift in metabolic (think fuels) processes, a change In concentrations of lactate in the blood (lactate thresholds), an altering of total respiratory air inhaled compared with oxygen absorbed or carbon dioxide exhaled (ventilatory thresholds).

Generally speaking, the low threshold, also known as the first threshold or T_1, is approximately but not precisely around 80% of one's maximum heart rate. This is the point where blood lactate first begins to accumulate from the steady state[1], this is the effort when fat utilization begins to decrease, this is the intensity when there is a substantial increase in the absorption of oxygen compared to total inspired air[2]. This is the low threshold heart rate number. This is the first threshold.

Move now to the high threshold, the second threshold. This is the exercise intensity at-about-or near 90% of maximum heart rate. This is the cross over point between aerobic and non-aerobic exercise. This is the intensity which is only sustainable for 20 to about 40 minutes for fit individuals. This is the point where blood lactate makes an exponential increase in concentration, this is the effort when fat utilization nearly turns off and pure glycogen is demanded, this is the intensity when there is a substantial increase in the expiration of carbon dioxide compared to total inspired air[3]. This is T_2, the high threshold heart rate number. This is the second threshold.

---

[1] Also called OBLA or onset of blood lactate accumulation and sometimes measured as 2.0 mm/L.
[2] Referred to as VT1, the first ventilatory threshold.
[3] Sometimes referred to as VT2, the second ventilatory threshold or "the respiratory compensation for metabolic acidosis threshold".

Both the low and the high thresholds are important exercise bio-markers. Both T_1 and T_2 have a role in training because they mark changes in the body's response to exercise stress or higher intensity levels. For those just beginning exercise, avoid going above either threshold - it could be hazardous. For those training for performance, the second threshold is critical for raising your aerobic capacity, your max VO_2. The more oxygen you can efficiently process, the longer and the faster you can train and race.

There are two ways to measure the first and second thresholds:

• *Take a lab-quality test at a testing center, like the Heart Zones Testing Centers located throughout the USA.*

• *Take a field-test on your own or with a certified Heart Zones personal trainer or coach. Heart Zones has a packet of workout cards that include four different field tests for low threshold.*

The first test provides more accurate results as well as more robust information. You learn more about threshold training in Chapter 18 so hand on, help is on the way. You can learn a ton from taking the lab test because it is the gold standard of endurance fitness testing. You find out your total caloric expenditure in each of the five zones, you find out the ratio of fat-to-carbohydrates that you burn; that is, if you are a better carbo or a better fat burner. You find out how fit you are comparatively - are you in the bottom 50% of your peer or age group or the top and if so where? The test costs about $160-$200 and can be done on a bike, treadmill, rower, or whatever your sport speciality.

Field tests for T_1 and T_2 are accurate but not precise. They are done with you and a heart rate monitor coupling heart rate data with respiratory response, rating of perceived exertion, and changes in your ability to speak comfortably. Field tests can be done on your own and are explained in detail by reading the free articles at www.heartzones.com/resources or by working with a coach or personal trainer who has been certified to conduct them, a Heart Zones CMS, Certified Metabolic

Specialist. If you want to get the most out of your test results and the quality of the test, make sure that the lab or test center has experience with all levels of fitness enthusiasts and not just the competitive types.

Workout #6:

Threshold Workout: At-About-Around

Introduction. It is difficult to sustain your threshold heart rate for longer than about 20-60 minutes depending on your fitness level in any single activity. And, since threshold heart rate is sports specific, you may need to do this workout in each discipline. The closer you can race at or above your threshold heart rate the higher your maximum sustainable heart rate. And, the higher your maximum sustainable heart rate is, the faster you can race.

Workout Plan. This workout can apply to almost any activity but it is not for the beginner. It is based on the principle that the threshold heart rate number is an individual heart rate buried in the center of a very, very narrow heart rate range. For this workout, the range is five beats per minute, with a top number or ceiling of your threshold heart rate and the bottom or floor of the workout range five beats lower. The workout is two by 20 minutes. After warming up take yourself up to your threshold heart rate and hold "at-about-around" that number for two minutes, then drop five beats to your floor and hold for two minutes. Cross back and forth every two minutes between this narrow bpm window for 20 continuous minutes. Do an active recovery for five minutes between sets then repeat the main set before a warm-down.

Workout Example. This is what the workout would look like for someone who has an threshold heart rate of 185 beats per minute (bpm). If you don't know your threshold heart rate do a field test or use your average heart rate during the middle of a 5K race or subtract 5-10 bpm from your average heart rate for 10 minute all-out effort.

Warm-up: 5 minutes up to 140 bpm.

Main Set:

2 minutes at 185 bpm

2 minutes at 180 bpm

2 minutes at 185 bpm

2 minutes at 180 bpm

2 minutes at 185 bpm

2 minutes at 180 bpm

2 minutes at 185 bpm

2 minutes at 180 bpm

2 minutes at 185 bpm

2 minutes at 180 bpm

Active Rest: 5 minutes at 145 bpm

Repeat Main Set

Warm-down: 5 minutes at 145 bpm

Comment. What you are trying to accomplish with this workout is to push your threshold heart rate up toward your maximum heart rate and then step back on the throttle just enough to breathe more comfortably before you push up to your threshold again. This is two minutes hard followed by two minutes slightly easier This isn't an easy workout.

I recommend that you modify it to fit your current fitness level. Your first time you might just try one main set. By the end of your training program you might want to try three sets.

Another way to modify this workout is to drop the recovery heart rate by 15 bpm for two minutes and then take it up quickly to threshold. Or, Change the interval time from 2 minutes during the hard effort to one minute.

It is definitely a challenging workout and you will feel the results of high intensity training the following day. A quick tip, the following morning you take your resting heart rate before you get out of bed to make sure you have not pushed yourself too hard the day before. The next day's workout needs to be a recovery or a Temperate Zone day.

Sally Edwards greeting triathlon participants at the finish line.

Chapter 11
Zone 5, The Red Line Zone

If you've made it to the Red Line zone, with heart rates from 90% to 100% of your maximum heart rate, you have arrived at the top of the heap. Maybe we should say, if you've made it to the Z5 Red Line zone *on purpose,* you have arrived. Like the Threshold zone, this is another one of those places that most people end up visiting only unwittingly: chasing their escaped dog or cat down the street, or running to catch their train, plane, or boat. You already know Zone 5. This is the place where your heart feels like it's going to burst and your legs soon feel like lead. While no one would ever want to live there, the vast majority of us wouldn't even call the Red Line zone a nice place to visit.

If you've arrived at the Red Line zone on purpose, you're one of a proud, perhaps crazy, minority. It's a place I love. I love to eat lactates. I love to go hard. I love to see how long, how fast, how high I can go. It's that place where we suffer excruciatingly from metabolic processes. It's the place for masochistic athletes. Quite frankly, it's wonderful - for me.

You simply can't hang out for long periods of time in the Red Line zone without dropping out of it for a breather. Your heart rate cannot hang out at or near maximum, because of its exceedingly high demand for fuels. Every second you are in the Red Line zone, your body's oxygen and glycogen needs exceed your ability to deliver them. The heart muscle is a "work now, pay now" muscle, and it will not go into oxygen debt. Because skeletal muscles operate under the principle of "work now and pay later," they have the ability to keep on going, past the balance point, and drive themselves into oxygen and glycogen debt. You might wonder what the price is for skeletal muscle deferment of metabolic payment. The ability of those muscles to continue to contract without fuel is the extremely high production of lactates!

Lactic acid junkies like me, love hanging out in the Red Line zone because we get faster while training at the same heart rate or intensity. Since the Z5 zone is the outermost zone in the heart zone chart, sitting just above Z4, all of your time spent in the Red Line zone is at a heart rate that is higher than your anaerobic threshold heart rate (if your anaerobic threshold heart rate is less than 90% of your maximum heart rate). After all, the best way to improve your anaerobic threshold is to train at-about-around your anaerobic threshold heart rate. This zone is also affectionately known as the "lactate tolerance zone" because this is the zone that conditions the body to buffer or withstand the high acidosis as well as to shuttle away the lactic acid to be resynthesized.

It is in the Red Line zone that you squarely, up front and with no way around it, meet your maximum heart rate. When you see your maximum heart rate, know that exhaustion – complete and total exhaustion - is no more than a minute away. Very soon, you will quite simply peter out. Z5 is a dangerous place, because if you don't come visit often enough you can't reach your peak, but if you overstay your visit your body won't invite you to return.

The Red Line zone is feared by many and misunderstood by more. One

Why do we use our maximum heart rate numbers as the anchor point for zones rather than thresholds?

Answer: We do this because maximum heart rate is a fixed number so we can fix the five zones. Anaerobic threshold heart rate changes with conditioning, so as you get fitter, it goes higher. Because anaerobic threshold heart rate number moves with conditioning, all of your zones also change with conditioning. With each beat of change in anaerobic heart rate, there is a change in all of the floors and ceilings of all of the zones. The use of maximum heart rate is, therefore more practical, less confusing, and easier to use because they are static and not dynamic.

of the most frequently asked questions about Heart Zones Training applies here: are the benefits cumulative?

In other words, if you hang out in Z5, are you going to get all of the benefits from the Healthy Heart, Temperate, Aerobic and Threshold zones. The answer is no. In each zone, a different process occurs that is specific to that process; if you want to receive that benefit, then you have to pay your dues in that zone.

The following summarizes events and conditions within Z5:				
Zone	Zone Name	% Max HR	Fuels Burned	Calories
Z5	Red Line	90–100%	90% Carbohydrates 5% Fat 5% Protein	±20 calories per minute

RED LINE FUELS

For those wanting to burn off a high percentage of fat calories, the Red Line is one of those zones that won't help you in the slightest. In the Red Line zone, since there isn't any extra oxygen available, and since fat needs oxygen to metabolize, additional fat burning is all but turned off. The 5% of the total calories burned or so of the total energy burned in the Red Line zone that is from fats isn't as helpful as in your lower zones.

For the calorie counters in the crowd, the Red Line is a great zone, because you are burning the highest number of calories per minute of any of the five zones - up to 20 calories per minute depending on your weight and muscle mass. But, unfortunately, there aren't very many minutes involved in Red Line training, because you are in and out of the Red Line zone because you can't sustain the intensity for long.

The Red Line zone is so hot that it demands the purest of fuels - the highest octane available to get the maximum combustion and thrust out of each muscle contraction. Our body's preferred high-octane fuel is glycogen, or broken down carbohydrates. Even if your body could use the low grade fuels, fats or fatty acids, in the Red Line zone, it would be like putting diesel in your Ferrari - not recommended.

Our skeletal muscles love glucose or, as we like to think of it, "muscle sugar." Glucose, when it is burned at high-intensity heart rates, is chemically transformed into lactates which, as we know, are acids. It's the build-up of these acids which leads to acidosis, that tell-tale feeling of overall fatigue, heavily wooden limbs, hard breathing, and burning muscle pain.

RED LINING AND OVERTRAINING

If you want to get fast, you have to train fast. It's a standard rule that SSD (short slow distance) and LSD (long slow distance) workouts aren't valuable as anything but recovery workouts for the individual training for high performance. However, the Red Line zone is so hot that an overdose or miscalculation in training here can result in long-term damage and the need for long-term recovery.

There are some serious consequences of hanging out too long in this zone. First, with the high levels of acidosis from the presence of lactic acid, muscle cell enzymes are affected. That is, the enzymes that are responsible for aerobic metabolism are sabotaged, and one's aerobic endurance capacity is hurt. Repeated days of high intensity red lining results in damage to these enzymes, and you simply can't train aerobically without problems.

What really happens is that the lactic acid damages the muscle cell

for your information:

The purest of the forms of glycogen is ATP, or adenosine triphosphate. When you are in the Red Line Zone and sprinting a 100-yard dash, you are burning principally ATP. Here's the catch - we only have enough ATP available in storage for about 10 seconds, before it's exhausted, Clearly ATP is not a fuel to be dependent on - it burns off as fast as it takes a match to burn out.

wall. Like any wall, the damaged muscle cell wall breaks down, and the cell material leaks out into the blood. That's when you see increases in certain blood panel concentrations like urea and CPK. It means that the walls are leaking.

If you don't heed the warning signs and do some training in the lower zones - or simply rest - your ability to train will continue to diminish substantially. A cell wall takes a long time to recover.

Among the common negative outcomes of too much time in the Red Line zone:

• **Interference with coordination capacity.** In sports like soccer, skiing, martial arts, basketball, and ice skating, where both endurance and coordination are requirements, there is little to no improvement in technical skills when the individual is exposed to the upper Red Line zone and near exhaustion. High lactic acid contents in the blood interfere with coordination, lessening the benefits of training, not increasing them.

• **Increased red blood cell destruction rate.** Red blood cells are responsible for carrying oxygen, and their health and numerical stability in the bloodstream is obviously of vital importance to anyone, let alone the endurance athlete. Yet, when training in the Red Line zone, acidosis causes the membranes of red blood cells to become unstable, which makes them more fragile. This fragility is augmented by the number of red blood cells that are destroyed because of mechanical trauma and the increased speed of the blood flow into small capillary vessels.

• **Increased risk of injuries.** High acidosis within the muscle tissues result in weakening of the muscles to such an extent that severe muscle injuries occur more readily.

• **Diminished ATP energy renewal.** Again because of the high concentration of lactic acid, ATP, the energy source for short bursts, does not reformulate as quickly. This delay in reformation severely limits one's ability to perform short sprints of exercise during training sessions.

• **Damage to aerobic capacity.** The lactic acidosis also causes damage to endurance capacity because it interferes with the various enzyme mechanisms which enhance oxygen utilization.

All that being said, we shouldn't place *all* the blame for the Red Line zone's possible ill effects on lactates. The current thinking is that there are a number of different occurrences that cumulatively prevent you from continuing to contract those muscles and move forward. One of the current suspects, generated through exercise along with lactic acids, are hydrogen ions (also known as free radical – which are cell-damaging agents, by the way). In brief, it seems that when your blood is loaded up with hydrogen ions, from high intensity exercise, the muscle pH drops (producing acidosis), and it is this drop in the pH which additionally hurts or impairs the metabolic processes that produce energy and muscle contractions. For more details on this, read Ken Cooper's book, *Antioxidant Revolution*

Z5 TRAINING HAS ITS RISKS.

Individuals who spend a lot of time training in high zones are not only taking a risk of potential overtraining from too much high intensity work-loads, they are also at increased risk of impairing their immune system. As well, those who accumulate high Heart Zones Training weekly points, are also at higher risk, regardless of their time in each zone. High training volume has been shown to result in a higher number of individuals who become ill from respiration and other infections.

> *Heart Zones Training Points are a way of measuring training dosage. More details on this in Chapter 12.*

It's not just the high zone or the high heart rate numbers which determine frequency of illness - it can also be one single exhausting work-out. For example, in a recent study, after running a 26.2 mile marathon, 13% of the runners who completed the marathon became sick shortly after the race while only 2% of runners who trained for the same marathon but who didn't actually run it became sick. It seems that a high dose in a single day of exercise weakens the immune system as well.

High zone training can downgrade the immune system because it results in a physiological response of the body which produces an increase in stress hormones (such as cortisol and catecholamines). Stress hormones decrease the activity of certain immune cells (T cells and NK cells) which are responsible for directly killing infected cells and invading microorganisms. Your defense or your resistance against infectious agents is compromised by high zone training.

Just as you may know about the "stress-makes-you-sick" problem, psychological stress can make you stupid, too. Exercise coupled with psychological stress further impairs immune function. Stress from competition, your coach, family expectations, sponsors, and spectators added to the stress of lack of sleep, travel to events, and absence from home can increase the risk of infection and may lead to sub-par performances.

> *To calculate HZT Points, Heart Zones Training Points, multiply the zone number by the number of minutes you train in that zone.*

Overtraining caused by high-volume and/or high intensity training with inadequate recovery results in the loss of performance. It's not reserved for competitive athletes. First timers and recreational exercisers who crank up their Heart Zones Training points too high and too fast are subject to the overtraining syndrome. It's usually too late when the symptoms appear, and they can literally appear "out of the blue" with little or no advance warning signs.

There is a way to reduce the risk if you have sophisticated and effective ways to monitor immune cell concentrations and blood sampling, but this is expensive and not available to most. Even with an optimal fortified nutritional program, with regular recovery and rest periods, it's difficult to avoid the immune-suppressing stress hormones associated with high zone training.

RED LINE INTERVALS

Ultimately, the Red Line zone is the place where you can exercise yourself into exhaustion and optimum athletic training. This high level of fatigue has always fascinated exercise scientists. In my graduate years at UC Berkeley, I began my research by attempting to answer the fatigue question. In my athletic years, I have trained and raced in some of the longest and hardest races in the world in a continuing attempt to understand what makes us exhausted and what we can do about it.

The personal reason I want to find the source of fatigue is to combat it - to override it so we can go further and faster. It's altruism that love-hate relationships are the most dangerous. You thirst for the love and suffer from the hate, and together the ambivalence can drive you crazy. For me and others, the Red Line zone is exactly that same relationship. You thirst for the benefits (enhanced performance) and suffer from the experience (pain), and together they can drive you to stardom or failure.

Still, because it is difficult, if not downright dangerous, to hang out for any length of time in the Red Line zone, it is time that needs to be carefully planned. We stay there for a short time, then recover and hop back into it. Then it's out to rest again. This is called interval training, and there are actually two types of intervals: the exercise interval and the rest interval. The exercise or training interval is the amount of time that we spend at a certain heart rate or workload. The rest interval is the time that we spend recovering from the exercise interval.

For example, let's say you want to do lower Red Line zone intervals (90–95% maximum heart rate). You could do short, or "sprint" intervals (rather than middle or long intervals) of one minute at that heart rate, with a one-minute active recovery interval. That's called a 1:1 ratio of effort to rest, because you are spending equal amounts of time (a minute each, in this case) exercising and resting.

Z5 Red Line Zone 90% - 100% Maximum Heart Rate Chart

Max HR	150	155	160	165	170	175	180	185	190	195	200	205	210 bpm
90%		135	140	144	149	153	158	162	167	171	176	180	184	189
100%		150	155	160	165	170	175	180	185	190	195	200	205	210

If your maximum heart rate were 200 bpm, then to do this lower Red Line workout you would exercise in a narrow zone of 180-190 bpm for one minute. Then you'd slow considerably and rest, still moving (this is an *active* rest), letting your heart rate drop for one minute. Each group of one minute in Z5 and one minute out of Red Line is the "interval set." You may choose to do 6-10 of these sets for your workout.

This Red Line workout can be done on a track, on a bike, Nordic skiing, running, or swimming.

In your monitor, set the upper zone to 95% of your true maximum heart rate. In the case of someone whose maximum heart rate is 200, they would set the monitor to 190 beats per minute. Next set the monitor's alarm to sound at every one minute. Use an active recovery of 30-60 seconds by walking, gliding or slow pedalling before you begin the next interval. Break the workout into two sets of five different 1:1 interval repeats, with a 3-5 minute rest between each set.

The reason you want active recovery between the exercise interval is to sustain high levels of lactates in your blood.

That's one of the main purposes of the workout - lactate tolerance training. You are trying to build up your lactate concentrations during the session. When there is too much recovery, your lactates drop. If you can't finish 5 repeats the first couple of tries, that's fine. Start with 2-4 and build your way up.

There is a slight delay between your real heart rate and the monitor reading. That's because your heart rate is higher than the monitor because it is updating the data each 5 seconds, so it is always delayed - on both the active and the recovery times.

This lagging of your monitor behind your true heart rate is one of the drawbacks to the technology as it exists today. In the near future there will be real-time heart rate monitors. But for now be satisfied that the data is so close (far better than you could derive from taking your pulse) and remember that we are only listening for the alarm as we accelerate our heart rate into the Red Line zone.

For runners who like track workouts, two of my favorites are called "ladders" and "dropping 1 second per quarter."

Both add new dimensions to an already overtaxing experience. With ladders, change the heart rate ceiling by 2 beats (or 1%) per lap. In our example, the first lap is 190 bpm, second is 192, third is 194 until the fifth lap and then go back down the ladder. The second variation is to use time as the stimulus.

Drop one second in time for each quarter for the last five quarters. This is truly a delayed gratification workout. Tomorrow you will be tired and sore and wonder why - you're thinking just a few laps around the track in the Red Line zone shouldn't fatigue you to this extent. But it does! All Red Line training sessions will cheerily work you to the max. Only if you allow yourself recovery time can you arise as a stronger and faster athlete.

HEART RATE IN THE ANIMAL KINGDOM		
(From W.S. Spector, *Handbook of Biology*, 1956.)		
Animal	**Average Heart Rate (bpm)**	**Heart Rate Range (bpm)**
Camel	30	25-32
Elephant	35	22-53
Lion	40	N/A
Horse	44	23-70
Ass	50	40-56
Human	**70**	**58-104**
Giraffe	66	N/A
Sheep	75	60-120
Cat	120	110-140
Dog	N/A	100-130
Rabbit	205	123-304
Squirrel	249	96-378
Rat	328	261-600
Hamster	450	300-600
Mouse	534	324-858

Workout #7:

Red Line Workout: Ten Max Quarters

Introduction. This is one of those track workouts which can be used for different sports - cycling, Nordic skiing or running. Even swimmers can do 200s and the workout is the same. When you are performing it, you have one of those contradictory experiences. You wonder is it the leg burn that hurts or is it my lungs from breathing so hard? Metal to the floor! That's what the Red Line training is all about. If you have that masochistic sense of feeling it in every cell, here's where you will be in your own element. It's best to do this workout with some fellow lactic hedonists as you can push yourself even harder.

Purpose. The purpose of the workout is lactate tolerance training. You are trying to build up your lactate concentrations during the session by exercising in the Red Line zone or 90- 100 percent of maximum heart rate.

Workout Plan. This track workout is a series of 10 quarter-mile repeats performed at 90-95 percent of your true maximum heart rate. For someone with a maximum heart rate of 200, this number would be 180-190 bpm. The workout is broken into two sets of five quarters with a short recovery between quarters and a longer rest between sets.

Workout. Set the ceiling or upper limit of your monitor to signal at 95 percent of maximum heart rate. A lower limit will not be necessary. After a warm up, cycle, ski or run hard for your first quarter mile (or 200 yards, if swimming). The goal is to set off your alarm before you reach the end of the quarter. Use an active recovery by jogging, skiing or pedalling slowly until your heart rate breaks through the 70% of max rate then start with the next quarter. Take a 3-5 minute rest after the first set of five quarters and then do a second set.

If 10 quarters are too difficult in the beginning, start with five and build your way up. Be sure to keep your recovery active to sustain the level of lactates in your blood. You are trying to increase your lactate concentration and too much recovery will allow your lactates to drop.

Recognize that your heart rate is actually higher than displayed because the monitor is updating the data every few seconds and running the information through a series of mathematical equations called algorithms. This lag behind true-time heart rate is one of the drawbacks of monitor technology as it exists today. The data will be close enough so just listen for the alarm as you accelerate into the Red Line zone.

Comment. This is truly a workout which offers delayed gratification. Tomorrow you may be tired and sore. You'll also wonder why just a few laps around the track in the Red Line zone are so fatiguing. All lactate tolerance training sessions stress you to the max as they also build you up.

Chapter 12
Heart Zones Training Points

Thanks to Ken Cooper, MD, writing the paradigm-shifting book *Aerobics* almost fifty years ago, the world has taken a giant step forward by following his exercise prescription of counting "aerobic points". He carefully designed a new generation of exercise and sparked a revolution in fitness that was based on important principles, including self-testing, measurement tools to manage your workouts, and a quantification method to reward exercise outcomes - the Aerobic Point System.

I was an undergraduate student at UC Berkeley's Physical Education department in 1968 when Cooper, then a young Air Force officer and physician, came to campus and lectured on the principles of aerobic training. Those same principles have stayed with me and allowed me to better appreciate what's needed for high performance training and racing.

The Heart Zones Training Point system is truly one of the first high performance athlete, coach and trainer systems that has allowed to quantify workload. This is a pivotal step which can take you to an entirely new level of training and performing.

Training load is the quantity of exercise stress as measured by the LIFT formula of frequency, intensity and time (or duration) equals load. If you were to multiply these three parameters of an exercise bout, you would have a measurement of total workload called dosage. Now, with the Heart Zones Training Point system, there is a way to calculate these three variables.

The formula is as follows:

LOAD = Intensity x Frequency x Time

The missing piece in this formula which has prevented the measurement of exercise workload and eluded and frustrated us for all of these years is the "I" for intensity. A heart rate monitor measures exercise intensity. Only now, with the use of this piece of fitness hardware, can we measure workload.

The Heart Zones Training Point system uses the quantification of frequency as number of workouts per week, intensity as measured by numerical heart zones, and time as the amount of time in each zone to determine daily, weekly, and monthly points.

The first step to determine your Heart Zones Training points is to use heart zones. If you spend twenty minutes a day in zone three that workout is valued at 60 points which is 20 x 3. If you did that workout for five days, which meets the ACSM Guidelines for minimum exercise, you'd discover that you'd earn 450 points, the minimum number of points

---

ACSM Guidelines

5 days x Z4 x 20 minutes = 450 Points   4 days x Z3 x 30 minutes = 360 Points

It appears that to meet the requirements set by the American College of Sports Medicine, you would need to get about 400 points a week to meet the minimum standards.

---

needed to obtain the minimum exercise requirement.

What's the maximum number of points? What's a healthy number of points? What's the ideal number of points? What's the best number of points you need to set a PR (personal record) in a race?

Here's the incredible news. We can now, using the Heart Zones Training Point System and the Variability Index or, V.I., predict when you will be at your peak performance level. You can now know when you are training towards the point of injury or over-training or when you are at high probability for a breakdown - mental or physical. That's because each person has an individual **training load threshold** or a quantifiable amount of exercise that they can sustain which allows them to achieve peak performance.

If you are wondering how, the answer is that your training load threshold is a certain range or number of Heart Zone Training points. You may have a threshold of 4,000 points per week and someone else may have a workload threshold of 1,000 points. It doesn't mean you're a better athlete, faster, or fitter but that your tolerance of exercise quantity is higher than mine. I may have a more sensitive immune system than yours or you may have an injury that, after a certain amount of stress, just says it's enough or you will re-injure yourself. The workload threshold for exercise varies widely among individual athletes. It's your responsibility to train at different weekly point levels to determine just how much, how hard, how long you can exercise to reach high performance and your goals.

HOW MANY HEART ZONES TRAINING POINTS ARE OPTIMUM?

How much training load is optimum varies between individuals based on a number of factors. It depends on your current level of fitness, the rate at which you can adapt to training stresses, the type or mode of activity, and much more. There are ranges based on the sport and the speciality within that discipline for optimum training. Use these ranges as a guideline for determining how many LIFT points you might use in your training plan and what is realistic given the amount of training time you have available:

Cycling:

50-75 Endurance Ride = 1,000-1,200 points
100 Mile Century Ride = 1,200-1,500 points

Running:

5 Kilometer = 750-1,00
10 Kilometer = 1,000-1,200 points
13.1 Miles/Half-Marathon = 1,200-2,000

VARIABILITY INDEX (VI)

Read on if you are interested in the most advanced concepts of applied sports training systems. This information is directed towards coaches, high performance athletes, researchers and such. It's technical. Just skip this section and don't get bogged down in this level of information if you don't want to.

Variability in training has been shown to be one of the most significant parameters to successful high performance improvement. Variability means changes in the workload within a training cycle. A training cycle is a certain number of days of training which usually is a period between 7 and 21 days. In coaching lingo, it's called a mesocycle.

Changing the frequency, intensity and time- the LIFT formula is one of the most important exercise stressors. It results in training adaptation and, hence, improvement. This improved fitness occurs because changing your LIFT creates a stress-recovery adaptation leading to a higher fitness level and higher work capacity or exercise capability. In other words, if you want to swim, bike, skate, run faster and stronger, progressive variability must occur in your training regimen.

Progressive variability can be measured and monitored.
Progressive variability is periodization.

Training Variability is changing the number of Heart Zones Training points day to day. Progressive training means changing the total Heart Zones Training points from week to week.

Variability indexing is how we measure the amount of training variability within the same week. VI means that each week you change your Heart Zones Training points, in a progressive and variable way during the week. Within each week vary your Heart Zones Training points systematically increasing them until, at some point, you reach your workload threshold.

The graph below demonstrates a typical Variability Indexing within a single week: This graph shows high Variability Indexing for weekly training, which is what you are trying to achieve.

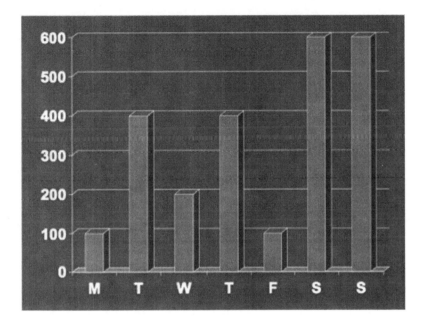

Why do you want high variability within the weekly schedule?
Answer: It allows for the stress-adaptation response to occur.

Thanks to Karl Foster, Ph.D., author of *Physiological Assessment* and Professor of Exercise and Sport Science, University of Wisconsin-La Cross and his work with high performance athletes in particular speed skaters (many of whom live in Milwaukee which is the headquarters for their sport), "I can almost accurately predict when an athlete, almost any athlete will breakdown. Here's how. I take their logbook, calculate their Heart Zones Training points and then I know their workload. Next, I plot that value along with their racing performances, injuries, illness over a year period of time and can then determine quantitatively their individual workload threshold value. When they surpass their workload threshold for a relative period of time - Kaboom, they are hurt, drained, destroyed, fried, trashed."

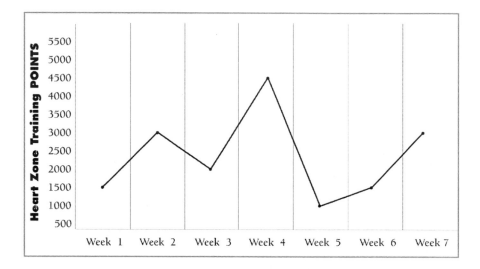

According to Foster, for recreational runners and skaters, that individual workload value is about 2,000 Heart Zones Training points per week. Working with some of the US Olympic speed skaters he has seen them reach thresholds of 6,000 Heart Zones Training points and sustain it without injury. For many elite level performers, the 3,000 point threshold seems to be about the norm.

This is an area of high performance training that begs for longitudinal research. Why can some athletes get overtrained at 2,000 points and others at 6,000? Do different sports tolerate different threshold values? You are invited to be an experiment of one – use your log over the last year and plot the points. You'll probably have to guess at the I, or intensity level, but you should have the time and the frequency. Then, calculate your VI and maintain a high weekly and monthly variability that is planned and scheduled out.

Workout #8:

The 5 By 5 Workout

Introduction. There are a few classic heart training work outs in my standard weekly sessions. I do this one, the "Five by Fiver," every Thursday morning because it fits within the 48-hour Rule: Rest 48 hours before your next Zone 4, Threshold Zone or higher workout.

Purpose. To teach your running-specific metabolic systems to adapt to constantly increasing training load every five minutes, which trains both your cardiovascular ability as well as your lactate clearance systems.

Workout Plan. Simply, this is a five-beat ladder every five minutes. Subtract 20 beats from your maximum heart rate to determine the top rung on your ladder and subtract 50 beats from your maximum heart rate for your heart rate starting point or the first rung on the ladder. The range between these two numbers if your training zone for the "Five by Fiver."

Example: 195 (maximum heart rate) - 20 = 175 (ceiling or top rung). 195 (maximum heart rate) - 50 = 145 (starting point or first rung). Training zone for workout = 145-175 beats per minute (bpm).

Workout. For a warm-up, gradually increase from a walk to a slow jog to the starting point for the first five minutes. Begin the main set ladder by moving into a new five-beat every five minutes as shown in the example on the following page.

Minutes	Heart Rate Zone
0-5	Warm-up
5-10	145-150 bpm
10-15	150-155 bpm
15-20	155-160 bpm
20-25	160-165 bpm
25-30	165-170 bpm
30-35	170-175 bpm

Total Workout = 35 minutes at 145-175 bpm

Recommendation. I recommend that you start by only going up the ladder once. When you are in great shape, try going up only twice in a workout. The up and then downs are really hard.

Quite honestly, this is one of my very favorite training workouts because I work myself through all of the different zones -Temperate, Aerobic and pierce into and then train to the top of my Threshold Zone. Log it as a 10-pointer for difficulty. It's a challenge but guaranteed to get you faster, stronger, and fitter!

Chapter 13
The Training Tree -The 10 Step Program

Climbing trees has always been fun for me. Even as a kid when my three older brothers and I had a tree fort and played games in the fort, it was adventuresome. It's the same today. I love to climb trees and I hope that you fall in love with climbing this tree because it is the route to your best fitness. The tree that I want you to climb is the Training Tree. The Training Tree requires just as strong a trunk as one that would withstand the weight of a tree fort and four kids and all of their friends scrambling up it. The Training Tree is a step-by-step, well a branch-by-branch, way of getting to the top of your training, the top of your game, your highest level of fitness.

The Training Tree is a useful tool, a model, a way of planning your training over discrete periods of time called mesoocycles. There are six limbs on the Training Tree. Each limb is a new specialty period of training, it is a new cycle of training. The Training Tree allows for the distribution and sequencing of training load. It is a way to spread out, distribute, training load and it provides a way to determine when to apply training load, how to sequence it. The Training Tree progressively increases training load in a logical manner, allowing for regular, daily, stress-recovery cycle that leads to positive adaptation.

THE TRAINING TREE

When you're ready to assemble all of these parts - your goals, heart rate zones and points, and your exercise time - into a cohesive and integrated program, remember that like snowflakes, flowers, or redwoods, no two training programs are alike. I like to look at my training program as a tree with many branches, each of them lifting me higher, yet remaining there, solid as ever, when I want to pull back on the intensity of my experience and climb down a little.

The training tree starts at the bottom, with its roots. The roots of the tree are information and education, thirsting for the water of learning and nearly as large below the ground as the branches are above. The branches are at different levels and each must be scaled to reach the tree top, which holds your goal. As you start to create your own personalized training tree, always focus on the top limb. That is what drives all of the parts or branches in the training system.

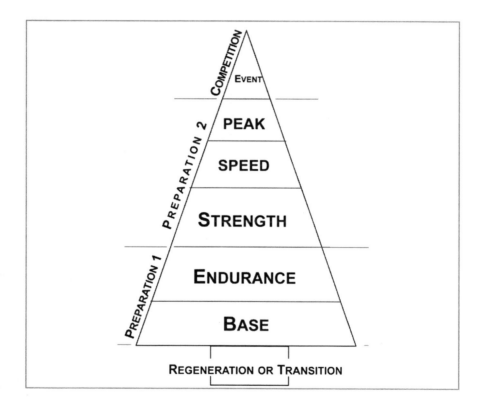

BRANCH 1: ENDURANCE BRANCH

This is the starting point of any training program. Base training is slow, easy, fun. It is the lower three zones; endurance training is the same as basic training. The purpose of spending time in the first branch is to develop your cardiovascular endurance to the point that you can easily sustain a workout without a great deal of fatigue and muscle soreness. The base endurance branch is a great place to hang out because it's so easy and relaxing with no pressure – just simply time in the low zones.

EXERCISE PHYSIOLOGY OF BRANCH 1

Adaptation	Explanation	Information
• Improved VO_2	VO2 is the volume of oxygen that you can consume in one minute	Because your lung, heart, and skeletal muscles are in better condition you can deliver more oxygen to the muscles
• Movement Efficiency	Balance, coordination, proficiency	As you do a specific movement, you develop more motor coordination so you can go farther on less energy.
• Enhanced Fat Burning	You become a better fat burner	Increased amount of movement increases the amount of calories that you burn. And at low intensity you burn a higher percentage and a higher total number of fat calories.
• Joint System Stronger	Ligaments and tendons that connect bones, muscles, and joints become more capable of securing you during weight bearing activity.	Ligaments and tendons thicken in the adaptation process as the strain of weight bearing activity requires them to become stronger. You may become less flexible which is why stretching exercises become important to maintain your range of motion.
• Psychological Patience	With longer workout time some people say they experience boredom from exercise.	By slowly building your exercise time you become accustomed to working gently for longer time without getting mentally stale.
• Improved stamina	Your ability to sustain longer periods of exercise at a sub maximal workload	Aerobic endurance is the starting point for fitness because it allows you to sustain an increased amount of exercise dosage until it begins to feel easy which is when it's time to move up the HZT Training Tree.

Frequency per week: 3-5 workouts *
Time: 15-30 minutes per workout**
Period: 2-4 weeks
Heart Zones: Z1 through Z3
Benefits: Comfortable, sustained, steady-state exercise

There's a reason to hang out on each of the branches. While you are spending time on the branch change occurs. In exercise science this change is referred to as "adaptation". Adaptation is a response process in which change occurs. On each of the five different branches, there is a different response because as the stress increases, the adaptation to that stress occurs. As you progress through each of the branches look for the explanation of the physiological changes which occur. The explanation on the previous page – Exercise Physiology of Branch 1 – should help you to understand this better.

BRANCH 2: STRENGTH BRANCH

It's time to add that all-important exercise stimulus: resistance training. Following many of the same principles that weight lifters use, athletes stimulate muscle power by applying appropriate resistance stimuli to the specific activity that they are training for. That is, it is known that if you "overload" the specific muscle by repeatedly asking it to work at higher levels of workload, usually at a slower rate, the muscle responds by getting stronger. Favorite examples of resistance training are stairs - use office buildings, bleachers, stair machines at the club or hill intervals. Find a few rolling hills - mountains will do - and work the uphills in Z3. The downhills are active resting in the Z2 zone. The benefits are enormous. The ability to climb hills is a specific stimulus that leads to increased speed and strength.

Frequency: 2 workouts per week of strength +3 workouts of endurance
Time: 20-60 minutes

Period: 3-4 weeks
Heart Zones: Z2 through Z3
Benefits: Sport-specific muscle strength

The strength branch is a time for more than just doing strength resistance training with weights and machines. Since a lot of lower body weight training is in the seated position, it isolates different muscles than when you are standing. Further, you aren't required to support your body weight during seated repetitions. As a result, your specific lower body muscles do get generally stronger and they become adept at exerting power while you are sitting down. It's then important to take this improvement in general strength to the specific muscle strength required by that sport activity.

Most weight training routines focus on individual joints and muscles and don't require your muscles to support full body weight. That's why training on hills or in the water with resistance devices builds more sports specific strength. For example, running up hills forces the muscles in all parts of your leg - from your hips, legs, ankles and feet to exert power while fully supporting your body weight. Hill workouts stress the lower leg muscles resulting in dramatic increases in running power. With more power, you get the benefits of longer, faster running strides.

Kenyan runner would be a good example of this. They are some of the best runners in the world, in spite of the fact that they never go to a gym and lift weights. Their "gym" consists of the hills and mountains of their rugged homeland and upon their daily training regimen.

Research supports what runners have known for a long time about hill running. Bengt Saltin, Ph. D. has examined the muscle tissue of hill runners and found they have higher concentrations of "aerobic enzymes" (those are the chemicals which help muscles to consume oxygen at higher heart rates for longer periods of time without fatigue) than the muscles of the runners who only train on flat ground.

To improve your leg-muscle power, to enhance your sport-specific economy, to protect your legs against soreness and, in running, to increase stride length, the strength branch of the tree is the place to hang out. The most common kind of strength training session is called "hill training".

EXERCISE PHYSIOLOGY OF BRANCH 2

Adaptation	Explanation	Information
• Improved VO$_2$	The volume of oxygen burned per pound of body weight per minute increases, which is good.	You are training more time in higher zones which means more intensity. As you train at higher heart rates you burn higher amounts of oxygen per minute.
• Movement Efficiency	More distance per calorie expended. (As in a car getting higher miles per gallon.)	You are now moving faster, which requires more coordination than in lower branches.
• Enhanced Fat Burning	Changes in the blend of fuels burned, which is the ratio of carbohydrate (CHO) to fat.	You are burning more total fat calories and, since you are training in the lower three or Fat Burning Zones, you are burning more total calories. You'll also be burning more fat when you are at rest than before.
• Joint System Stronger	Thickening of the connective tissues that hold joints together.	Tendons connect muscles to muscles. Ligaments connect muscles to bones. Both are part of the support system of every joint. By getting thicker they get tighter so you have a more secure joint.
• Psychological Patience	Exercise intensity is increasing but time in zone is staying the same so your patience now begins to shift to the feeling that results from higher heart rates.	At higher heart rates you are breathing harder and will feel the intensity as an expression of less comfort in the sport specific muscles and harder breathing.
• Improved endurance stamina	Aerobic endurance is extended.	You'll be able to go further, faster, longer, easier because you have become more efficient and your ability to sustain work longer and longer improves.

There are two different basic kinds of hill workouts. To boost your leg-muscle power, one of the best methods is find a very steep slope at least 25 meters from the bottom to the top.

The second way of optimally improving your performance during this stage of strength training is to increase the aerobic capabilities and to improve the fatigue resistance of your muscles is by finding a "set" of hills that are moderate in nature and which you can train over for 20-30 minutes. Find a hilly park or a bunch of sand dunes along the shore or rolling terrain in the country and use them for this workout. You'll do your recovery phase as you saunter down the backside and your high intensity phase as you work your way to the top of Z4 and hopefully, on your recovery back into Z2.

BRANCH 3: SPEED

If you want to race fast, train fast and train strong. This is the phase that builds upon the lower three branches by adding your first Red Line workouts with short or endurance intervals. It's the branch where you start time trials at specific heart rate points to test improvement. It's the period of seeing big heart rate numbers, because you are pushing towards your maximum heart rate. It's time to watch for the highest sustainable heart rate and to work at raising that value. For cyclists, it's time to breathe hard and stare at the monitor as you push yourself and your monitor to new dimensions. This is interval training - specific interval training that matches your racing or performance goals. If you are a sprinter, then long intervals are not going to be of as much value. Use a variety of interval training regimens and workload ratios during this phase.

Frequency: 2-3 workouts plus endurance and strength workouts

Time: 20-60 minutes

Period: 3-4 weeks

Heart Zones: Z3 through Z5

Benefits: Improved speed, lactic acid removal and glucose fuel utilization.

EXERCISE PHYSIOLOGY OF BRANCH 3. SPEED

Adaptation	Explanation	Information
• Improved VO_2	Your ability to transport oxygen into the muscle and carbon dioxide out of the muscle greatly improves.	This is the phase of training when you go beyond an RQ or respiratory quotient of 1.0, which is the anaerobic threshold, when more carbon dioxide is produced than oxygen can be delivered, so you shift into oxygen debt stage or anaerobic metabolism.
• Lactate Tolerance	Lactic acid is a byproduct of energy metabolism.	When lactic acid is produced because of insufficient oxygen present, it needs to be shuttled out of the muscle to be resynthesized. The amount of lactic acid as measured in pH or acidosis levels is called your lactic tolerance buffering ability.
• Improved Biomechanics	Like efficiency, this is enhancement of your structural alignment and enhanced coordination	When your biomechanics improve so does your ability to move the same distance in the same time at a lower heart rate reading. That's truly the outcome of improved efficiency and biomechanics.
• Enhanced Glucose and Fat Burning	You become a better fat burner and a better carbohydrate (CHO) burner.	You are burning higher amounts of both fat and CHO because you need more of the easy to burn CHO for higher intensity training.
• Joint System Stronger	Ligaments and tendons that connect bones, muscles, and joints become more capable of securing you during weight bearing activity.	Ligaments and tendons thicken in the adaptation process as the strain of weight bearing activity requires them to become stronger. You may become less flexible which is why stretching exercises become important to maintain your range of motion.

continued next page

Adaptation	Explanation	Information
• Psychological Patience	With longer workout time some may experience boredom from exercise.	By slowly building your exercise time, you become accustomed to working gently for a longer time without getting mentally stale. Diversify training partners and mode of exercise.
• Change in Muscle Fibre Recruitment	There are two types of muscle fibers: fast twitch and slow twitch.	During this phase more fast twitch Type II muscle fibers are required such that they are converted to look and behave more like slow twitch fibers which are the ones needed.
• Economy	Improvement in stride length, capillary bed build-up, all around efficiency of movement.	Like in a car, it's you getting the most miles per gallon because you are so efficient in your biomechanics, oxygen uptake, muscle recruitment, and it's demonstrated by your ability to hold pace over the entire distance of a race.

BRANCH 4: PEAK

This period of training is a favorite for many athletes. The peaking phase is the time when you put all of the other branches together into one: endurance, strength, and intervals.

It is the variety branch. It is the time when you are incredibly fit and loving it. It's the time when you get to experience all of the heart zones. It's a precision training period. It's high intensity, it's resistance training, it's growing endurance, it's recovery workouts, it's incredibly challenging. And through all of it, it is a period of listening to your body, because it's during these weeks that overtraining most frequently occurs.

Frequency: 6-7 workouts (e.g: 2 endurance, 2 interval, 2 strength, 1 recovery)

Time: 30-120+ minutes
Period: 2 weeks through entire season
Heart Zones: All
Benefits: Putting it all together to optimize high-performance fitness

Adaptation	Explanation	Information
• Improved VO_2	As you train at higher intensities for longer periods of time you can increase your Max VO_2 levels. This is how you train your stamina.	Your Max VO_2 continues to improve until you reach a point that is your sport specific and genetic maximum amount, after which additional training will no longer improve your oxygen carrying capacity.
• Lactate Tolerance	Like VO_2 as you train your ability to tolerate higher concentrations of lactic acid increase. This branch is called "lactic acid land" because you will be spewing the stuff out of your muscles.	Like VO_2, there is a limit to the amount of acidosis or lactic acid that you can buffer at any one point. You will reach your highest value and then no longer improve. If you overtrain, however, this tolerance level is compromised.
• Improved Biomechanics	During this phase you are training all three building blocks:endurance, speed, strength.	The power branch is the most important because you are training at your hardest and driving all four systems: muscle contraction speed (intervals), aerobic and anaerobic endurance (stamina), and muscle strength (ability of muscle to contract under higher loads).
• Enhanced Glucose and Fat Burning	As measured in calories per minute, this is the peak number of calories burned during any of the branches.	Because of higher heart rate levels and workload levels, you are burning the highest amount of fat and highest amount of carbohydrates (CHO) of any of the branches.
• Joint System Stressed	This is a time to beware of connective tissue problems.	With high workloads and intensities come the potential for tendon problems or joint stress or ligament complications. Listen to your body's pain levels and stress.

continued next page

EXERCISE PHYSIOLOGY OF BRANCH 4.

Adaptation	Explanation	Information
• Psychological Intensity	It's a high limb on the tree and high psychological intensity comes with it.	Staleness can come from more than just physiological stress. It can also result from the mental toughness needed to grit your teeth through increasingly harder workouts.
• Economy	You are at the top of your sport specific training period and you might feel the stress of all out training.	Note that you might see a decreased appetite, both in your libido and your dietary appetites. If you don't stretch, you'll notice a certain lack of range of motion in your joints. Maintain flexibility during this period.

PEAK
BRANCH 5: RACING

Racing is a very tenacious branch. It's as much psychological as it is physical. The demands are arduous because it requires constant testing, usually against other athletes as well as against your own goals and that great truth-teller - the clock. It requires constant recuperation and resting, too. I've been asked more times than I can remember which I prefer - training or racing. I always answer that training is like eating cake, but the racing is adding the ice cream; I love the two together. Racing is my favorite branch because it challenges so much more than just my body. It requires toeing up to the line and test-ing yourself against yoursel. That is who the race in life is really with. But, it also requires the ability to cut back after the race, to recover, to regain speed and power and strength and endurance to race again.

Frequency: If racing: 4 workouts. If not racing that week: 6-7 workouts

Time: 30-120+ minutes
Period: up to 12 weeks
Heart Zones: All
Benefits: To successfully race throughout a season without injury or staleness.

EXERCISE PHYSIOLOGY OF BRANCH 5. RACING

Adaptation	Explanation	Information
• Improved VO_2	You are there. It happened in the Power Branch, not now.	Your goal here is to maintain the high level of training that got you here. You are trying to make sure that your fitness does not diminish, and frequent testing is advised to measure this.
• Lactate Tolerance	You are here. Your anaerobic threshold heart rate should be at its highest number.	This is a time you want to go into an exercise lab and have your VO_2 and lactic acids measured so you have some information, because "you can only manage what you can measure and monitor" - one of our five principles.
• Biomechanical Efficiency	Because you are trying to hold a high physiological training level, it's a great time to work on improving your movement efficiency.	Continue to concentrate on moving smoothly, effortlessly, in a way such that you feel like you can get into "the flow"- a physiological state during training where it feels as if time has no dimension or responsibility.
• Enhanced Glucose and Fat Burning	You need to maintain efficient fat and CHO burning ability.	Since muscles are fueled by high octane fuels that are carried in high octane blood, eat a balanced and high carbohydrate diet.
• Joint System Stronger	Propensity towards skeletal injuries.	During any high performance phase of training, there is a higher risk of breakdown from both skeletal as well as immunity compromises.
• Psychological State	Varies tremendously among individuals.	For many, this is the best of all times on the training tree and for others it's the most psychologically stressful.
• Economy	Balance of all parts of life is the key to reaching high economic state.	Look to keep all parts together: social, family, emotional, spiritual, financial, and job responsibilities, as well as physical well being.

RECOVERY: THE TRUNK, NOT A BRANCH.

Recovery period is one of the least understood and appreciated parts of the training tree, yet it is a critical part of your training phases or periods. The recovery period does not consist of "junk workouts" or time just spent in a low zone. Rather, it is a period in your annual training schedule when it is time to take a break while still maintaining fitness. Some athletes choose to develop a training plan with a recovery period in the "off season." In this cycling of workouts, a recovery period is critical to allow the body a long period of rest-up to 4-8 weeks-to recover from the rigors of high-intensity training regimens. All recovery workouts are in the two lower zones with an infrequent lower Aerobic zone workout. The benefit is recuperative in all ways from intramuscular to emotional rest.

Frequency: 4-6
Duration: 15 minutes - 1 hour
Period: 4 weeks - 3 months
Heart Zones: Healthy Heart, Temperate, Lower Aerobic
Benefits: Rest and to regain energy

HEART ZONES TRAINING TREE CHART

Maximum Heart Rate (beats/min)	Base/Recovery	Endurance	Strength	Speed/Interval	Peak
Z5 Red Line 90-100% of Max.	-	-	-	6 mins	6 mins
Z4 Threshold 80-90% of Max.		-	6 mins	6 mins	12 mins
Z3 Aerobic 70-80% of Max.	-	30 mins	42 mins	36 mins	36 mins
Z2 Temperate 60-70% of Max.	42 mins	24 mins	6 mins	12 mins	6 mins
Z1 Healthy Heart 60-70% of Max.	18 mins	6 mins	6 mins	-	-

Example of how to distribute your training time through a progression of training phases for a one hour exercise period.

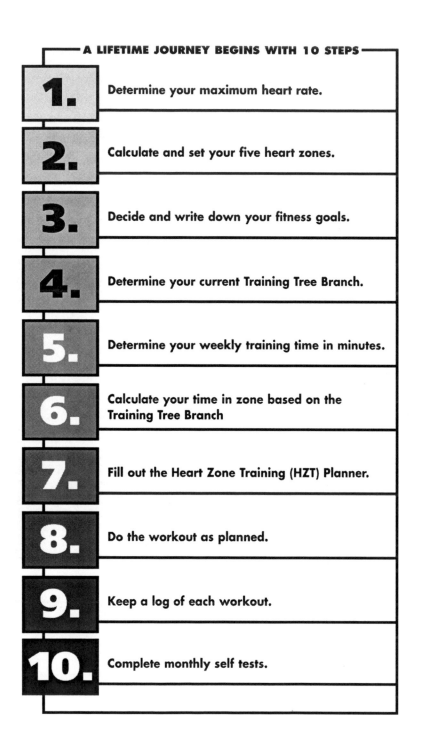

A LIFETIME JOURNEY BEGINS WITH 10 STEPS

1. Determine your maximum heart rate.

2. Calculate and set your five heart zones.

3. Decide and write down your fitness goals.

4. Determine your current Training Tree Branch.

5. Determine your weekly training time in minutes.

6. Calculate your time in zone based on the Training Tree Branch

7. Fill out the Heart Zone Training (HZT) Planner.

8. Do the workout as planned.

9. Keep a log of each workout.

10. Complete monthly self tests.

STEP 1.

Determine your maximum heart rate.

Maximum Heart Rate: Tested:_____ bpm Estimated _____ bpm

STEP 2.

Calculate and set your five heart zones.

Heart Zone	Number of Beats per Minute
100% Maximum Heart Rate	_____ bpm
90% Maximum Heart Rate	_____ bpm
80% Maximum Heart Rate	_____ bpm
70% Maximum Heart Rate	_____ bpm
60% Maximum Heart Rate	_____ bpm
50% Maximum Heart Rate	_____ bpm

STEP 3.

Decide and write down your fitness goals.

Training Goal 1: _____

_____

_____

_____

Date to be Accomplished:_____

Training Goal 2: _____

_____

_____

_____

Date to be Accomplished:_____

STEP 4.

Determine your current branch on The Training Tree. _____.

STEP 5.

Determine your weekly training time in minutes.

How many days per week? _____days per week

How many minutes per day? _____minutes per day

How many minutes per week? _____minutes per week

TIME IN ZONE

Developing a training program that fits into the training tree depends on you and your schedule and commitments. It must be in written form, and it's best to post it. Old paradigm training programs are usually written using the measurement controls of distance or speed - it's a 50-mile running week or a 10,000-yard swim week. Your new paradigm training program works with the time in zone (TIZ) plan, so the workouts are written in time and in zone, not distance.

Time in zone starts with determining how much time you can commit to your high performance program. Then, develop the plan around that amount of time. Let's use the example of someone who has seven hours a week available for training. Dividing that by seven days to get a daily value, we find that this athlete has one hour per day to train. This means that a typical workout could encompass a range from 45 to 90 minutes. This individual is a single-sport athlete, with five years of training and racing experience, and is training for a half-marathon. Here's an example to be used by you only as a guideline of what a weekly workout looks like.

Determine your weekly training schedule by starting with the amount of time available and multiply it according to the percentages given for each training branch. The percentages depend on the training tree limb that you are currently scaling. To fine tune your program, adjust it based on the specific sport and event that you are training for.

SAMPLE HEART ZONES TRAINING WORKOUT PLAN

Time: 420 minutes (7 hours per week)

Branch: Peaking

Goal: 90-minute finish time for a half marathon with the race in 4 weeks

Daily Average Time: 1 hour

Range: .75 to 1.5 hours   **Max HR:** 200

	Time	Zone	Zone #	Type	HZT Points
M	60 min	Aerobic	Z3	Continuous run at 150 bpm Stretching for 1/2 hour	180
T	45 min	Red Line	Z5	9 x 5 min at 180-190 bpm	225
W	60 min	Temperate or	Z2	Recovery: slow and easy Complete Rest Day	120
Th	60 min	Threshold	Z4	Hill intervals	240
F	60 min	Lower Aerobic	Z3	Cross Train: bike, swim, ski, snow shoe, circuit train, skate	180
S	45 min	Threshold	Z4	Continuous at race heart rate pace or... Highest sustainable heart rate pace 10 K fun run or race	180
S	90 min	Aerobic	Z3	Endurance Day	270

Summary of Week

Total Time: 7 hours	Time in Zones:	1 Temperate workout	60 min. /14%
Total HZT Points: 1,375		3 Aerobic workouts	210 min./50%
		2 Threshold workouts	105 min./25%
		1 Red Line workout	45 min./11%
			420 min./100%

After determining the number of minutes you have available for the week, divide these minutes into their respective zones. Then, plug the minutes into a weekly schedule. For example, let's continue with the 420 minutes per week - an hour a day - high-performance trainer. Here's what this individual's percentage of training time by zone resembles:

STEP 6.
Calculate your time in zone based on the Training Tree Branch

Zone	Max HR	Zone	Endurance		Strength		Speed		Peak	
Z5	90–100%	Red Line	---		---		10%		10%	
Z4	80–90%	Threshold	---		10%		10%		20%	
Z3	70–80%	Aerobic	10%		70%		60%		60%	
Z2	60–70%	Temperate	80%		10%		10%		10%	
Z1	50–60%	Healthy Heart	10%		10%		10%		---	
			100%	Min.	100%	Min.	100%	Min.	100%	Min.

STEP 7.
Fill out the Heart Zones Training (HZT) Planner.

Day	Date	Sport/Activity	Time in Zones					Daily Points
			Z1	Z2	Z3	Z4	Z5	
Mon								
Tues								
Wed								
Thurs								
Fri								
Sat								
Sun								

Zone Name:	Zone Points	% of Max HR						Weekly HZT Points Total
Red Line Zone	5	100-90%						
Threshold Zone	4	90-80%	Z1	Z2	Z3	Z4	Z5	
Aerobic Zone	3	80-70%						
Temperate Zone	2	70-60%						% TIZ
Healthy Heart Zone	1	60-50%						

*Total Weekly HZT Points: Multiply the time in each zone by the number of that zone.

STEP 8.

Do the workout as planned. Do the workouts as you wrote them in your HZT Planner.

STEP 9.

Keep a log of each workout.

STEP 10.

Complete monthly self tests.

• *Test 1: Sport specific maximum heart rate test*

• *Test 2: "Improvement effect heart rate" test - hold distance and heart rate constant and measure elapsed time.*

• *Test 3: Resting heart rate test*

• *Test 4: Ambient heart rate test*

• *Test 5: Delta heart rate test*

It's time for you to put all of this together into a system with the proper tool for the job - your heart rate monitor. A heart rate monitor is your coach, your personal trainer. It's at your side whenever you wish, giving you the hard data on what your body is experiencing. Your Heart Zones Training success really all depends on you linking it all together - the plan, the workout, the information, the motivation, the results. That's what a heart rate monitor can do for you. It's the link between your mind and your body. It is this dynamic interaction that gives you the power to make it all work and to see the results. It's your personal power tool.

In order to give you the information you need, the heart rate monitor needs to get a little info from you first. So the first thing to do is to set your training zone, the high and low numbers of beats per minute, into the watch portion of your monitor. There are many different models of heart rate monitors, with many different features, so it's difficult to make suggestions as to how you'll set the numbers in any given monitor. Remember, though, that keeping track of your zone numbers is the most basic, essential thing that most heart rate monitors do, so it's always quite simple. And, if in doubt, refer to your owner's manual, even if your manual is hard to read. The low-end heart rate monitors only give you a constant heart rate read-out, so if you use this model you're going to have to memorize your zones and keep the floor and ceiling numbers in your mind.

Workout # 9:

Climbing The Interval Ladder

Introduction. This is one of those really hard workouts, so watch out if you aren't ready to tackle those upper zones. If you're ready to feel the flavor of high performance Heart Zones Training, this workout is a good way to begin your interval training. Heart zone intervals are similar to the intervals that you may have been doing in the past because they consist of hard and easy timed sessions. The tough part of this workout is that the rest is at the beginning and as you climb up the ladder there is no relief until you hit the top rung.

Workout Plan. This workout is sometimes called a "progression ascent" because you work progressively harder and harder as you ascend to the top of the session. With each step on the ladder, you move up one zone and drop one minute off the interval time. Start out in the warm-up phase by spending five minutes in your Healthy Heart zone (Z1) or 50-60 percent of Max heart rate. After five minutes, move up one zone to the Temperate Zone (Z2) for four minutes. Continue this progression through each zone and end with one minute in your Red Line zone (Z5).

If you find this workout is too strenuous, modify it slightly by dropping the Red Line zone and shortening each of the other zones by one minute. For those of you who are accustomed to high intensity training, do two or three repeats or repetitions of this workout.

Comment. I personally love the high zones but I'm a lactic acid junkie, so that feeling of complete exhaustion when I finish my Red Line time is for me the best. Also, I know what the benefits are and that keeps me motivated. By training in the upper zones, I get the performance benefits of improved cardiovascular function and faster speed. I need both of these for competitive performances. However, it really is good for most of us to get a little faster and a little fitter.

Former Ironman marathon course record holder, Sally Edwards running in her sixteenth Hawaii Ironman race at the age of 51 enjoying every step of the 26.2 mile distance.

Chapter 14
Heart Zones Weight Loss Program

You don't have to be thin to be healthy. You don't have to be thin to be fit. You don't have to be thin. If your genetic heritage, body type, and metabolism make you susceptible to gaining weight very easily, don't feel bad. You could be one of evolution's triumphs, successes. In prehistoric times, the people who fared the best through times of sporadic food supply were the ones whose bodies made the most efficient use of energy and stored away as much as possible for tough times. Scientist now know we evolved to succeed in an environment when food supply was unreliable and the physical activity demands of life were high.

Imagine yourself in prehistoric times, pitted for survival against that skinny fashion model with no apparent body fat. Who would live longer? To paraphrase Darwin, it all comes down to "survival of the fattest and yes, the fittest." But, you might be saying "I don't want to be the fattest guy in the cave. I need to go on a diet and get some of the excess weight off before I survive a stroll through the jungle." That's where you are wrong - dead wrong. Fitness and thinness are not the same thing. They are not connected. Sure, you probably know a lot of fat and unfit people. They got fat in large part because they are unfit, because of their emotional disconnections, maybe because of their low energy. But it is possible for a person to be fit AND fat and perfectly healthy. Fitness correlates to how well your engine is running, not to streamlined fenders or narrow tires.

The Heart Zones program - HAL - is built on just several foundation principles:

- *It's not about fatness - it is all about your fitness.*
- *It's not about thinness - it's all about your healthiness.*
- *It's not about weight - it's all about your energy.*

The program's very foundation is to focus on fitness not weight. Weight takes care of itself easier as you get fitter and fitter. The majority of weight loss programs focus on food intake, food composition, food consumption, food types, and weird plans like dieting based on the color of your eyes. Rather than focusing all of the time on food, the focal point of the Heart Zones Weight Loss Program is about being healthy and active in the zones. And, this is not just one zone methodology - but putting together all three: emotional, physical, and metabolic (energy) zones into a HAL lifestyle. HAL stands for Healthy Active Living and you'll learn a lot more about putting that altogether in the final chapters.

FAT IS NOT THE PROBLEM

Fat is a symptom of overweight or obesity, not the cause. That's so important I'll repeat it - fat is a symptom, not a cause. It's like looking at a case of measles and calling it "skin lesions," when we really know it is a respiratory infection caused by the measles virus. The spots are just a symptom.

Defining overweight or obesity by one of the physical symptoms ignores what goes on inside the body. In truth, obesity is the condition by which the complex mechanisms of appetite and satiety (how your feel and how the body converts the food you eat into energy, that's called metabolism, have, quite simply, become messed up. Our body's weight-regulatory system has gone haywire, usually because of disruptions and disturbances in the metabolic, physical, and emotional abuse of the body. And your genes, your DNA are involved too.

ABUSE

An all too common example of metabolic abuse is serial dieting, weight cycling. The body fights periodic starvation by making key metabolic changes that make sure you gain the weight back when you eat even a normal, healthy diet. The metabolism can become so dysfunctional that the body can function only by grabbing and storing all the energy that comes its way - and it stores it very efficiently.

We commit a form of physical abuse when we don't perform the basic physical activity we need to stay healthy. Amazingly, we readily accept that our dog, our Labrador Retriever needs exercise to stay trim and healthy, but we don't insist on the same for ourselves.

Finally, and long overlooked by weight and fat loss specialists, we subject ourselves to emotional overload, such as stress, anxiety, anger, and depression that can throw the body out of synch and disrupt its weight regulating system. Because of the emotional connection with the brain and your genes, this emotional overload results in changes to the brain structure that results in neurotransmitter sensitivity - and hence changes in the release of hormones.

ARE YOU A GREYHOUNDS OR A ST. BERNARD?

If you have always been a little fat, yet you've cared for the three basic aspects of your health - physical, emotional/mental, and metabolic - then consider your specific biological makeup, your inherited genetics, and your individual physiology. Our genetic heritage extends not only to whether we possess our mother's eyes or our father's chin, but to the nature of our metabolism and how our weight and body responds to physical fitness training. Our individual biological make up even means that each one of our internal biochemical processes work, including everything from adrenaline and cortisol production, digestive processes, our personal chemistry of fat metabolism, insulin, and regulation and fluctuations of sex hormones.

Once you understand your bio make-up, you can stop fretting over the fact that you didn't inherit the physique of a teenage fashion model. Perhaps you should stop trying to be something you can't be. After all, you'd never buy a St. Bernard dog and think, "Ah well, if I starve Bernie enough, maybe I can make her look like a Greyhound. Greyhounds are so fashionable this year, and I want a fashionable dog." No, you treasure all your big, lovable St. Bernard's qualities. You like big dogs. Why not like your big self? We humans come in all shapes and sizes, so why should we all want to look like those skinny people, an Angelina Jolie?

Sometimes we talk ourselves into a corner, saying, "Well, even though I was born with this body type, it can't be natural for me to be like this, because this is an unhealthy state. How can it be okay that I was born unhealthy? Such thinking reflects one of the problems the fat-free movement has created for us: we have forgotten why we have fat and what it does for us. We've forgotten that it is natural for some of us to be fatter than others, even if it places us outside of the recommended weight for our height and weight. Fat is a natural thing, an essential ingredient in a healthy body. It's not just a nasty lump of inanimate matter. Most fat works for us in life-sustaining ways, protecting our vital organs, insulating us, and storing energy so we can function without constant eating. Some special types of fat cells perform absolutely crucial tasks, such as dealing with toxins in the body and maintaining a healthy hormonal balance. We need fat, and we need to store extra fat. It's also natural for us to gain more fat as we age. It's natural for some of us to carry more fat than others. But it's not natural for us to be unfit. Our bodies require physical activity as much as they require air, water and fuel. Without it, we die. And this brings us to the crux of the matter: we have become stuck in the mind set that fat makes us sick, when, in truth, being unfit makes us sick. When we grasp that fact, we begin to realize that fat loss as a solution to health problems is just a big fat lie.

FITNESS VERSUS FATNESS

Let's explore what we mean by fitness and fatness. Fitness measures how healthy you are, how functionally able you are to carry out your daily life. Fatness measures the amount of padding you carry, how big your fenders are, not the strength of the inner engine that gives you the power to do things in life.

Fitness may mean one thing to a professional triathlete or marathoner and another to a young woman with a family and career, but, basically, it all boils down to being healthy and in good condition, with the energy and optimism to tackle your dreams and goals. To attain fitness you must consider the three components we mentioned before:

Metabolic Fitness: Your blood pressure, glucose sensitivity, and blood chemistry.

Physical Fitness: Your cardiovascular fitness (heart and circulatory system), muscular strength, and flexibility.

Emotional Fitness: Your ability to manage your feelings and mental capacity.

Keeping this list in mind, try answering these three questions:
• *Can people display healthy blood chemistry and a healthy metabolism even if they are fat?*
• *Can people possess a strong, healthy heart and be physically strong and flexible even if they are fat?*
• *Can people maintain emotional balance even if they are fat?*

The answer to all three questions? A resounding Yes. It's that simple. Fatness does not prevent fitness. The amount of fat you carry around represents but one aspect of your health and fitness, and not necessarily a terribly relevant one at that. In contrast, physical, emotional and metabolic fitness provide the keys to a healthy and long life. Being thin will never guarantee you a long life. Being fit in terms of cardiovascular, metabolic and blood chemistry health will. The proof depends on scientific research, not on myths and fads.

Our obsession with weight and weight loss has misled us to blame fat and fatness as the root of all illness. In fact, according to Dr. David Richards, author, Being Alive, nothing can improve your health risks more than fitness.

> **"USA Scientist: Fat can be Healthy"**
> Did you see that headline on the CNN news service on July 18, 2001? American researcher and currently a professor at the University of South Carolina, Steven Blair had sparked controversy at a meeting of the Association for the Study of Obesity in London by saying that body fat can be healthy. Results from the studies at Blair's institute, the Cooper Aerobic Institute, on obesity and risk of death showed that previous research had missed the crucial link between fitness and health. "The focus is all wrong," claimed Blair, P.E.D., who continued to say, "it is fitness that is the key." In fact, he even went on to report quite simply that "fat people who exercise are at no greater risk from disease than their thinner counterparts." Optimum health is more about fitness than fatness.

Not surprisingly, claims by Richards and others ignite criticism. In the October 2003 the head of the Center for Disease Control, Dr. Julie Gerberding, told a meeting of the National Health Council, which groups companies and non-profit health advocacy organizations, that Americans are much more likely to die from cancer, heart disease, and diabetes caused by smoking, eating too much and exercising too little. She claimed that obesity is the Number 1 health threat in the USA.

In recent years, however, the evidence supporting Blair's claim that fitness confers a lower risk of disease and mortality, independent of fatness, has been pouring in:

• *A study published in the October 1999 issue of the Journal of the American Medical Association found that overweight men who exercised had death rates, to any cause, only slightly higher than fit men of normal weight and twice as low as normal weight men who were unfit.*

• An observational study carried out by three researchers, Chong Do Lee, Steven Blair, and Andrew Jackson at the Cooper Institute for Aerobics Research in Dallas, Texas, demonstrated that it's fitness not fatness that really counts when it comes to longevity. In their observational study of 22,000 men, they found that death rates doubled for unfit men. Interestingly, obese men had no greater risk of dying than unfit men, as long as they were fit. The researchers concluded that being fit reduces the health risk of being obese.

• A study of 17,000 men in the Harvard Alumni Health Study found that mortality was lower for each of three degrees of fatness when the men were fit.

• Researchers Steven Blair and Suzanne Brodney at the Cooper Institute, Dallas, conducted a review of all studies that had been done up to 1999, examining over 700 scientific articles. They concluded that regular physical activity clearly mitigates many of the health risks associated with being overweight or obese, and that fat people who are fit have lower death rates than normal weight individuals who are not fit.

The American College of Sports Medicine (ACSM) and the US National Institute of Health and National Heart, Lung, and Blood Institute (NIH) commissioned reviews of all this new evidence, hoping they could prepare consensus statements concerning the benefits of physical activity for overweight people. The review concluded that the recent scientific research had shown the following:

1) Overweight and obese individuals who are active and fit have lower rates of disease and death than overweight and obese individuals whoa re inactive and unfit.

2) Overweight or obese individuals who are active and fit are less likely to develop obesity-related chronic diseases and suffer early death than normal-weight persons who lead sedentary lives.

3) Inactivity and low cardio-respiratory fitness are as important as overweight or obesity as predictors of mortality, at least in men.

GET FITTER, LIVE LONGER

Great news continues to pour in about fitness and the benefits it bestows. Not only does fitness help free you from life-shortening disease, it can extend your life expectancy. But, don't just take my word for it.

A new study published in the New England Journal of Medicine provides new evidence regarding the relationship between fitness and survival. In it researchers examined over 6,000 male patients referred to a clinical exercise-testing laboratory and then followed the group for 6 years. They found that the peak exercise capacity (i.e. a measure of their fitness) achieved by a person during the exercise test was the best predictor of the risk of death, whether the individual suffered with cardiovascular disease or not. For both groups, the fittest, regardless of their fatness, had four times less risk of dying compared to the unfit groups. As with earlier studies, fatness, when accompanied by fitness, did not figure significantly in risk of death. Fitness extends life. I shouldn't need to repeat it at this point: the fitter you are, the longer you can live.

MOVE ABOVE THE LINE

So, there we have it. Don't expect great health benefits from fat loss and dieting. Yes, you may have a problem losing weight, but the problem is not your fatness. Fatness is merely a symptom, not a cause. And fat loss cures nothing and can actually do some harm. Forget "fit OR fat." It's a myth. Remember "fit AND fat." It's the truth. Fitness protects against the many diseases, and it prolongs life. When you are fit you can be just as healthy as your thin cousins. Now, armed with what you've learned so far, where would you place yourself in "The Fit AND Fat matrix"?

This matrix includes four different quadrants representing various combinations of fitness and fatness.

THE FIT AND FAT MATRIX

Fit and Fat	**Fit** and Not Fat
Not Fit and Fat	**Not Fit** and Not Fat

This one diagram helps you figure out where you are today and where you might want to go tomorrow. We know from all we have learned so far that the quadrants with the least risk of death, lowest disease rates and best quality of life are the top two above the line (fit and fat or fit and NOT fat). If you want to enjoy a long and healthy life, you need live above the line, you need to be fit. Now what surprises most people is that the two top quadrants provide the <u>same</u> benefits in terms of health and longevity. It doesn't matter for your health whether you sit in the Fit AND Fat (top left) quadrant or the Fit and NOT Fat quadrant (top right). If at the moment you reside below the line in either of the lower two quadrants, you obviously want to move above the line. How do you do that? Well, there's only one escape route: you need to get fit and that means emotional, physical, and metabolic. Becoming less fat will only allow you to move sideways on the quadrant, not to a higher level of health and well-being.

WHO WANTS TO BE FAT AND FIT?

Most of us want to be thin. Society tell us to be thin. Markets and the media want us to be thin. But, deep down, do you want what others demand, or would you prefer the good health that will give you a better and longer life? We've been led into thinking that thinness will win both fashionable good looks and a good life. However, the scientific evidence says, "Hogwash!" Long life comes from health, not thinness. And health comes from fitness, not lack of fatness. So, what do you really want? I honestly believe most of us place a long healthy life first and foremost, fashion way down the list. That's why you should make getting fit your number one priority. Once you gain the health benefits of fitness, natural weight loss becomes easier, almost automatic. When it comes to losing weight, living "above the unfit line" gives you a huge advantage over those who languish "below the unfit line."

If you still need convincing, consider this one last reason why you should focus on getting yourself fit, even if you are fat. If you've tried to get thin, you've undoubtedly waged a long, hard battle. To date, only 5%-10% of people who successfully lose weight by dieting keep it off for the first year, not a very encouraging statistic.

If you focus on long-term physical, emotional and metabolic fitness, your health will improve. It's all a matter of basic human physiology, the way the body works, and how your bio make-up responds. I promise you that if you follow the HAL, Healthy Active Living program you will get the health benefits you seek. You can achieve really big fitness gains in just 8 weeks and hugely significant changes over 8 months. You'll find the benefits and changes you make in your life far greater than those obtained by decreased fatness. No matter what your current body weight, you'll enjoy a better self-image, improved self-confidence and increased mobility. And you will know deep down you are doing something for your own health, for you, and not other people. Under the hood, your engine will start firing on all 8 cylinders.

You can be fit and fat. You can be fit and not fat. You may have extra body weight or you may not, but if you participate in a physically, emotionally, and metabolically sound program, you can attain a healthy body free from the risks of the diseases once so commonly linked to obesity, from coronary heart disease to adult-onset diabetes. People who are fit, even if they are fat, can expect to live longer than similarly fat people who are not fit, and even longer than lean people who are not fit. And you can much more easily achieve fitness than leanness.

LIVE LIKE HAL - LIVE A HEALTHY (H) ACTIVE (A) LIFESTYLE (L)

I've designed the Heart Zones Weight Loss program that not only works, it changes more than "just" your lifestyle. I guarantee that if you follow it, your life quality will improve in metabolic, physical, and emotional ways. It's not a game of counting calories, starvation and guilt, but an empowering way to learn how to give your body what it needs in terms of physical and emotional activity, energy, and care. It focuses on fitness not fatness, and it will enable you, regardless of the amount of extra fat you carry on your body, to reach optimum health and energy.

I want you to know that you may not lose all of the fat that you dream about losing, at least not in the short run. But I also want you to know that a long-term commitment to living like HAL, which means living the three letters - HAL - living a healthy, active, lifestyle, creates the positive changes that ease off plenty of pounds. If you live like HAL you burn lots of stored body fat and you do it in surprisingly simple ways. I'll show you exactly how to do it, how to build that wonderful body into a metabolically efficient and fat burning engine by being active.

FIXATE ON YOUR FITNESS

What, exactly, do we mean by "fitness"? Like "beauty," it can mean different things to different people, and, in fact, the term spans a broad range of levels and types of fitness. It is not a static point, or an on-off button. It is a continuum between zero-level of fitness to your personal, individual best-ever level of fitness. Think of it, then, as a sort of sliding scale from zero to ten. Your ten will differ from mine.

Don't compare yourself to me or to anyone else. Your own fitness is unique to you and your specific bio make-up. Fitness is also activity-specific. Venus Williams is perfectly fit for tennis, but she would not fare well if asked to race against the world's fittest triathletes like Karen Smyers or Beijing Olympic gold medal winner, Australian Emma Snowsill. I doubt whether Venus could finish any one of the three Ironman triathlon sports, either, although it would be fun to watch her try. Fitness is also fuel-specific. You can be fit at metabolizing carbohydrates but not fit at oxidizing fats, or you can be fit at using oxygen but not at re-synthesizing lactate. Finally, fitness is function-specific. You can be fit at lifting heavy weights doing bench presses at your health club, but you can struggle to lift a bag of groceries up to a high shelf.

Are you fit? You would probably answer, "Sort of" or "it depends." It depends on where you are on your own fitness continuum, plus where you are with respect to specific activities, fuels, and functions. As you work out and participate more in physical activities that you love, you move towards a ten on the fitness continuum, while if you slack off and do less, you fall back toward zero, no to low fitness on the continuum.

HEART ZONES TRAINING — THE ZONES CHART

ZONE	MAXIMUM HEART RATE	FUEL BURNED (per min)	CALORIES BURNED (Calories) (Cal/30min)	WORKOUT TYPE	BENEFITS	HZT POINTS	WELLNESS ZONES	LACTATE CONCENTRATION	VO₂	RATING OF PERCEIVED EXERTION	DESCRIPTION OF RPE	TALK
5 REDLINE / RED ZONE	100% ↓ 90%	~20 Cal/min ~600	Max effort, sprinting, high speed intervals / GET FASTEST	Improved lactate tolerance	x5		>8 mmol/L	100 ↓ 83	10 ↓ 7	maximal effort to very, very hard	Can't talk except for very short phrases
4 THRESHOLD / ORANGE ZONE	90% ↓ 80%	~15 Cal/min ~450	Time trials, intervals, tempo, hill work / GET FASTER	Improved anaerobic capacity, lactate clearance	x4	PERFORMANCE ZONES	4-8 mmol/L	83 ↓ 70	7 ↓ 5	very, very hard to hard	Can still talk, but not comfortably
3 AEROBIC / YELLOW ZONE	80% ↓ 70%	~10 Cal/min ~300	Endurance and steady-state / GET FITTER	Improved aerobic capacity, optimal cardiovascular training	x3	FITNESS ZONES	3-4 mmol/L	70 ↓ 58	5 ↓ 4	hard to somewhat hard	Very aware of breathing, still comfortable to talk
2 TEMPERATE / GREEN ZONE	70% ↓ 60%	~7 Cal/min ~210	LSD (long slow distance), recovery and regeneration / STAY FIT	Improved fat mobilization, basic cardio training	x2		2-3 mmol/L	58 ↓ 39	4 ↓ 2.5	somewhat hard to easy	Aware of breathing, very comfortable talking
1 HEALTHY HEART / BLUE ZONE	60% ↓ 50%	~4 Cal/min ~120	Warm-up and cool-down rehabilitation / GET FIT	Improved self-esteem, stress reduction, blood chemistry	x1	HEALTH ZONES	<2 mmol/L	39 ↓ 28	2.5 ↓ 1	easy to very easy	Easy conversation, just like sitting and talking

HEART ZONES TRAINING
A Pruning & Meadors Company
2636 Fulton Avenue, Suite 100, Sacramento, CA 95821
ph: (916) 481-7283   fax (916) 481-2213
email: info@heartzones.com   web: www.HeartZones.com

amount of fat burned
amount of carbohydrates burned

— In all zones, approximately 5% of the calories burned are protein which is negligible.

* A measurement of training load.

* Lactate is the concentration of lactic acid in the blood.

§ VO₂ is the amount or volume of oxygen used.

* Only an estimation, highly variable between individuals. Approximate for 150lb person, walking or running, 20-25% body fat.

Your answer also might take a certain activity into account. You may feel fit for a 5 km (3.1 miles) walk but not at all fit for a 26-mile 385 yards (42.2 km) marathon. Physical fitness is one part of a fitness triad. The HAL program consists of not one, but three different kinds of fitness.

THE FITNESS TRIAD

1) *Metabolic Fitness: Efficiency in burning fuel to make energy.*
2) *Physical Fitness: The ability to enjoy body movement, including cardio respiratory endurance (aerobic capacity), muscular strength, muscular endurance, and flexibility.*
3) *Emotional Fitness: A relatively high level of emotional and mental balance and strength.*

Any fitness program should address all three components: metabolic, physical, and emotional fitness. Otherwise, you're not taking into account all the features that contribute to a long, happy, healthy life. What follows is the definitions and schematic representation of "fitness".

Metabolic Fitness:
- *low LDL cholesterol,*
- *high insulin sensitivity,*
- *high caloric burn rate.*

Physical Fitness
- *high cardio-endurance*
- *high strength and flexibility*
- *high balance and coordination*

Emotional Fitness
- *Feeling balance and flexibility*
- *Positive mental outlook*
- *Ability to manage feelings/thoughts*

Metabolic Fitness - the processes that digest, utilize, and store energy, release energy from storage, and control appetite and satiety signals are all working well. Healthy levels of glucose tolerance, insulin sensitivity, blood fats, and fat metabolism are all examples of good metabolic health.

Physical Fitness - the process of attaining cardio-respiratory endurance, muscular strength and endurance, balance and coordination, and flexibility.

Emotional Fitness - ability to cope with stress, build positive relationships, deal with change, maintain balance in life, maintain mental acuity. To put together your emotional fitness training plan, review the chapter on emotional fitness training and the emotional zones - it provides you with the information and tools to do so.

Do you see the word "fat" in the HAL Triad? No, because fitness does not depend on lack of fatness. Many fitness and medical experts measure body fat as a way of defining fitness. Some even use it as the sole criterion for fitness. In fact, society has placed so much emphasis on the measurement of body fat (skin fold calipers, underwater weighing, etc.) that most people automatically accept them as tests of fitness. It all springs from the same prejudice that body fat is bad and that lean tissue (muscles, bones, etc.) is good. Body fat in and of itself is not bad. It is an essential part of good health. And, as the evidence shows, high percentages of body fat do <u>not</u> cause decreased longevity or poor health. You can be fat and have perfectly good health, provided you include all components of the HAL triad.

No fitness weight loss program should focus on one goal of losing body weight and body fat. Rather, you should concentrate on the goal of gaining metabolic, physical and emotional fitness and the health improvements that occur as a result. Never make the mistake of measuring fitness and health improvements in terms of weight loss or fat reduction. Neither science nor common sense link either body weight or body composition to fitness.

METABOLIC FITNESS

Avoid the numbers on your bathroom scale and pay attention, instead, to the numbers that mean the most: your cholesterol, your blood pressure and your insulin sensitivity. Those numbers reflect metabolic fitness.

Metabolism includes all of your body's energy activities, the chemical reactions and processes that occur every second of your life to provide energy for vital processes and movement. According to Professor Glenn A. Gaesser, Ph.D., author of a book that I love *Big Fat Lies* "Being metabolically fit means having a metabolism that maximizes vitality and minimizes the risk of disease -- particularly those diseases that are influenced by lifestyle, such as heart disease, type 2 diabetes, and cancer." Recent studies indicate you might even add Alzheimer's to that list. Measures of metabolic fitness reveal how well or efficiently your metabolism work. Metabolic fitness is a relatively new part of the fitness puzzle, one you can measure in a lot of ways, including assessments of your insulin resistance and sensitivity (blood sugar levels), resting and exercise metabolic rates, blood pressure, and cholesterol levels.

EATING FOR METABOLIC FITNESS

Your choices for foods are a vast landscape of choices. The number of new food products grows daily. Likewise, your decisions about quantity, quality, packaging, preparation, and so forth for your healthy and fit eating provide you with even more challenges. These challenges for many, lead to confusion about how to eat. One of the most common questions asked of me is this one, "Sally, what should I eat?" The answer to that question on one level is complex and on the other is as simple as looking at a 5.5" x 8" card – I am about to show that to you.

There are lots of reasons why Americans struggle with what to eat – and this isn't the place to list them all. You probably know of this confusion first-hand and welcome a simple solution to it.

To provide you with a metabolically sound nutritional way to dine, an easy to understand and simple diet plan is in order. That's just what I have for you and it's called eating in the Food Zones©. I have designed the Sally Edwards' Food Zones chart to make one picture capture a thousand answers. The primary chart classifies foods based on its inherent metabolic load or stress. That is, what is the weight of that food on your physiology, your vital processes? The metabolically light foods, the low zone foods are the healthiest for your metabolism and you want to select foods from this zone and eat them often.

There are five different Food Zones. Each zone is number with low numbers 1-4 being low and lower metabolic load foods. Eat foods from the low numbers, lower is better.

Each zone is color coded with the lowest zones in shades of blue to green to yellow. The high load zones are in the hot colors from orange to scarlet red. One more time, the reasons that you want to eat in the calmer and gentler shades of colors is that foods from these zones optimize your energy and health. They are the foods that are least likely to lead you down the dreadful pathway of degenerative diseases like Syndrome X or metabolic disease.

In discussions around our household, we talk about what color or number zone we spent most of our nutrient intake in. I'll hear conversations and encourage you to do the same like this one, "I had a tough day and ate mostly in the Orange Zone. It is a Zone 4 day for me but I had a Blue Zone breakfast.

Before you can engage in understanding the language of the Food Zones study the five different colored Food Zones that is the foundation of eating a low metabolic load diet:

THE THRESHOLD LINE

A threshold, like a door threshold, is a cross over point between two spaces. In the Food Zones chart, the Threshold line is the white line. Above the Threshold line are the red zones which are the least healthy; some are even toxic. Below the white line are the healthier foods, enjoy them with care.

In one way, eating well can be summarized in a few words - eat below the threshold line. And yet, we know that it isn't easy to eat well for more reasons than I want to discuss. Rather, make every attempt to eat foods in the low zones.

FOOD ZONES CHART

ZONE NUMBER	ZONE NAME	FAT	CARBOHYDRATE BREAD•GRAIN	PROTEIN	BEVERAGES	CHOCOLATE	FIBER GRAMS	GLYCEMIC INDEX	COOKING	QUALITY
5c	TOXIC ZONE		white crackers, chips		hard alcohol, high fructose corn syrup					Avoid
5b	UNHEALTHY ZONE	Chemically Modified Fats: saturated fat, beef, whole milk, bacon fat	white crackers, chips	chicken, turkey	digestive, diet sodas, light alcohol	white chocolate < 10-20% cocoa	1	>75	seared over very high heat	Very Poor
5a	LESS HEALTHY ZONE	cheese, cream cheese	enriched or bleached breads, grains	chicken legs	fruit juices	Milk chocolate < 20-30% cocoa	1	>75	fried	Poor
THE THRESHOLD LINE										
4	HEALTHY ZONE	Monounsaturated Fats: olives, olive oil, peanuts, peanut butter, almonds, cashews-salted/roasted	couscous, white rice, bread	beef, chicken, turkey fillets	beer, white/red wine	Dark chocolate < 30-40% cocoa	1-2	70	microwave	Good
3	MORE HEALTHY ZONE	Polyunsaturated Fats: safflower oil, sesame seeds, walnuts, salmon, flax seeds- salted/roasted	whole wheat breads/crackers, cereals, mixed grains	all nuts, whole eggs, beans	decaf coffee, soy milk	Sweet dark chocolate < 40-50% cocoa	2-4	60	baked	Very Good
2	HEALTHIER ZONE	Monounsaturated & Polyunsaturated Fats- unsalted/roasted	bulgur, barley, wild rice, bran	extra lean meats, fish	low-fat, fat-free milk, herb tea, raw juices	Semisweet chocolate < 50-60% cocoa	4-5	50	steamed	Excellent
1	HEALTHIEST ZONE	Monounsaturated & Polyunsaturated Fats- raw	whole oats, brown rice, buckwheat spelt, millet	skinless meats, 99% fat free salmon, soy protein	water	Bittersweet chocolate < 60-85% cocoa	more than 5	under 50	raw	Superb

Across the top of the Food Zones chart are the headings for each column. Read them carefully to understand the quality of what you are eating.

Zone Number	The higher the number, the lower the quality of the food. Eat in the low number zones.
Zone Name	Describes what happens if you eat in that zone on a regular basis.
Fat	Lists the different types of fat with the fats in the low zone the highest quality.
Carbohydrate/ Bread	Describes the types of grains that are in bread in order of quality.

Protein	Lists the meats and vegetables with the least fat or the best quality of protein.
Beverages	Qualifies the best liquids with water being the best.
Chocolate	This is a fun column for all of the chocoholics that want to know which chocolates have the best health benefits.
Fiber Grams	Lists the roughage with the highest quality in the blue zones and foods with little to no fiber in the 5c zone.
Glycemic Index	Ranking carbohydrates according to their effect on our blood glucose levels. Choosing low GI carbs.
Cooking	Ranks how food is prepared with the least amount of altering of food the best choice.
Quality	A way of giving each rank a value from superb or avoid at all costs.

SALLYisms

Following a few diet guidelines can make your eating for fitness and health which results in weight loss a simpler challenge. Here are a few Sallyisms or tips that I follow:

Individualized Nutrition: Each person needs to eat in accordance with their lifestyle and not a one-diet fits all plan.

• Food Dynamics: Add a variety of foods including new foods to your food selection.

• Emotional Foods: Comfort foods and food cravings are normal. Try to respond by choosing foods in the lower Food Zones.

• High Energy Foods: High in fruit, vegetables, whole grains, fish, and

lean meats.

• Support: Surround yourself with those who also eat a cardio-metabolic diet. Encourage your entire family to eat from the Food Zones Chart and to eat in the blue-green-yellow zones.

• Eat In or Make to Go: To better control portion sizes, nutrient density, and less processed food, eating in or packing a meal-to-go is your best choice.

• Flexibility: Not essential to eat only in the four low Zones. Exceptions are permitted, that is only human nature.

• Eating habits and behaviors: Eat frequent small amounts of nutrient dense foods.

• Quality: It is better to eat less quantity but more quality.

• Food Group Balance: Each meal should contain the three food groups: carbohydrates, protein, and fat.

• The Rule of 3 Times: Eat three times the fruits and vegetables as you do meat and fat.

• Drink and Be Merry: Drink lots of fluids preferably water and below Threshold fluids.

• Follow the Weight Formula: Practice emotional zones, metabolic, and cardio-zones everyday.

• Not a Diet but How You Eat: Think of Low Zone eating as the way you eat, not as a diet for a certain period of time.

• Eat Low Glycemic Load (GL) Foods: Eat foods that have low glycemic load because not all carbohydrates are equal.

HOW TO BURN THE MOST FAT

Fat is burning in every heart zone. The percentage and total amount of fat burned changes in every zone. The change in the amount and percentage of fat burning depends on principally these three factors:

• How fit you are
• How hard you exercise
• What is the carbohydrate, protein, and fat amounts in your diet.

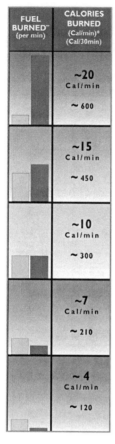

FUEL BURNED¨ (per min)	CALORIES BURNED (Cal/min)* (Cal/30min)
	~20 Cal/min ~ 600
	~15 Cal/min ~ 450
	~10 Cal/min ~ 300
	~7 Cal/min ~ 210
	~ 4 Cal/min ~ 120

Using the Zones chart that follows, find the two column headed "Calories Burning" and "Fuels Burned". You can quickly see that the amount of calories burned increases the higher the intensity, the bigger the zone number. And, the higher the zones the more fat that is metabolized. For example, 30 minutes in Zone 3 is worth about ~10 calories per minute or a total of 300 calories. Also note that in Zone 3 about 50% of the calories metabolized are carbohydrates and about 50% if from fat or about 5 calories of fat and 5 calories of carbohydrates.

Of the many myths in the world of weight loss, one of the worst is the existence of the fat burning zone. There is no fat burning zone. The concept was invented to try and simplify how calories are burned and the concept is invalid. It has led to a great deal of confusion about how fat is utilized in exercise training. What does exist is the "fat burning range", a dynamic range of exercise intensity where you burn the most fat. By definition, the fat burning range is the exercise intensity and exercise time when metabolically, you burn the most total fat. What is important for weight loss is to burn the most total calories. Since oxygen must be present for fat to burn, when you go above your threshold intensity, the cross over point between aerobic and non-aerobic exercise effort, there is no additional fat burned. To burn the most fat, stay aerobic.

The ceiling or top of the fat burning range is your threshold, T_1. The floor of the fat burning range is the point where aerobic benefits are fist measured, about 55% of your maximum heart rate. As you get fitter, your threshold moves upward towards your maximum heart rate and your fat burning range gets bigger. The goals for weight loss then is to enlarge our fat burning range by raising your threshold.

Here is a diagram of those changes using the metabolic Zones Chart:

THE ZONES CHART

The bigger your fat burning range, the more the fat that you can burn per minute of exercise. This is known as the burn rate for fat. Here's a list of more details about the dynamic fat burning range:

- *The amount of fat used increases as exercise intensity increases until you go above threshold.*
- *Fat only burns when oxygen is present.*
- *Fat burning is not a "zone" but a dynamic range of heart beats.*
- *The range of exercise intensity where fat burning changes is affected by your: fitness level, diet, nutritional state, fatigue, stress, genetics, and body composition.*
- *Fit people burn more fat because their fat burning range is larger.*
- *Unfit people are poor fat burners because their fat burning range is small.*
- *The top of the fat burning range is your threshold.*
- *The bottom of the fat burning range is about 55%.*

KEEPING THE WEIGHT OFF

Every year, millions of new diet books are sold. Readers are looking for a solution to the accumulation of fat that leads to obesity. But, are the true experts of getting and keeping fat weight off those who have succeeded for 5 years or more? Are they the ones who have discovered and applied what works for their individual physiology, their genetics, and their emotional nature. They are the applied weight loss experts, applying their personal experiences of what works as they strive for weight management solutions.

One of the worst parts of failing to maintain weight loss, that is, of weight cycling (the losing and gaining of body weight in a repeated cycle), can be the redistribution of body fat to what is known as the "upper compartments," your abdomen. This abdominal or "visceral" fat resides in and around your organs, and it has been strongly associated with chronic high-risk diseases. If that weren't bad enough, weight cycling also leads to a reduction in metabolic rates known as adaptive thermogenesis. Basically, the more often you weight cycle, the lower your resting metabolic rate, your base caloric burn rate, becomes.

Where's the hope in all this bad news? Well, that's where those applied weight-loss experts come in. The National Weight Control Registry (http://www.nwcr.ws) is a non-profit organization that tracks people who have kept more than 30 pounds of weight off for more than one year. Their noteworthy statistics on the over 5,000 Americans that they follow are as follows:

- *80% of persons in the registry are women, and 20% are men.*
- *The "average" woman is 45 years of age and currently weights 145 lb., while the "average" man is 49 years of age and currently weights 190 lb.*
- *Registry members have lost an average of 66 lb. and kept it off for 5.5 years.*

There is a great deal of diversity within their ranks:

- *Weight losses have ranged from 30 to 300 lb.*
- *Duration of successful weight loss has ranged from one to 66 years!*
- *Some have lost weight rapidly, while others have lost weight very slowly—over as many as 14 years.*

The National Weight Control Registry is also now able to report on the how factor of weight loss:

- *Some lost it on their own (45%) and others have lost weight on a dietary program (55%).*
- *98% of Registry participants report that they modified their food intake in some way to lose weight.*
- *94% increased their physical activity, with the most frequently reported form of activity being walking.*

Though there are risks in averaging research results, they still provide meaning as long as you consider the variability among individuals within the report. The three keys to what their members (and they are looking for new members—you can register on their website) report for weight maintenance are (1) low caloric consumption, (2) low fat in their diet, and (3) high level of daily physical activity. For example:

- *78% eat breakfast every day.*
- *75% weigh themselves at least once a week.*
- *62% watch less than 10 hours of TV per week.*
- *90% exercise, on average, about 1 hour per day.*

Each of us must find what works for our individual metabolism and our genetic makeup. We can follow their lead, test to see if their experiences work for us. Each of us must still take ultimate responsibility on our own with support from our friends and family.

LIGHTEN THE LOAD HEART ZONES WEIGHT LOSS PROGRAM

If gaining fitness and losing weight was easy, then two out of three Americans would not be overweight, nor would one out of three be obese. If the formula calories in = calories out really worked, then we wouldn't have a weight epidemic in the USA. In fact, this formula doesn't work. If maintaining fitness gains and weight loss was achievable without much effort, then people would remain thin not fat. But, for most, changing their fitness and their body fat, weight loss or stopping the accumulation of stored fat, is one of the most difficult tasks to accomplish. Most people really do find it to be more difficult to keep weight off than to lose it in the first, or second, or third place. So, what do you do?

What you do is get up, get out, get going by living a HAL life of emotional, physical, and metabolic fitness. That's the secret of the Heart Zones Weight Loss Program. By lightening the "allostatic" load - live in emotional Zones 1-3, by lightening the physical load by working out in the aerobic Zones 1-3, by lightening the metabolic load eating in the blue-green-yellow Food Zones, you get the results that you deserve: better health, more energy, and a longer lighter life.

Allostatic load was first coined by Bruce McEwen in his book titled *The End of Stress as You Know It* (2000). The term refers to the physiological cost of chronic exposure to stress eliciting the stress response. What do I recommend - here's the prescription: lighten the load, stay in the right zones, and live like HAL - and it works every time.

DO YOU WANT THE REAL THING? THE Wii THING?

If you have been thinking about buying a Wii system, don't you want to know if it is good for you first? And, don't you want to know if it as good as The Weal Thing? One of the first studies comes from Carl Foster, Ph. D. from the University of Wisconsin found that the Wii Sports was not as good as the real thing but better than nothing because it increased heart rate, oxygen use, and perceived exertion. Yes, if you play Wii you burn calories, but you burn more calories doing the activity:

Reasons to buy a Wii:
- Gets traditional gamers "off the couch".
- Better than sedentary games like bingo or Monopoly.
- Can be more "fun" than the real thing.
- Can use your heart rate monitor and see your zone.

Reasons not to buy or use Wii:
- No substitute for real sports
- Doesn't burn as many calories as doing the real sport.
- Most Wii sports are Zone 1 which is 50%-60% of your maximum heart rate so little cardio-metabolic results.

Just how many calories are burned doing the activity depends on which activities you do. Here's a run-down from Foster's study:

Sport Caloric Expenditure of Wii Sport (30 minutes)	Percent of Maximum heart rate Heart Zones
Golf - 93 calories	50% - Zone 1
Bowling - 117 calories	52% - Zone 1
Baseball - 135 calories	55% - Zone 1
Tennis - 159 calories	59% - Zone 1
Boxing - 216 calories	74% - Zone 3

Sally's Wii Recommendation? Get up. Get out. Get going. If Wii makes this happen for you then play Wii sports. If Wii is a kick off to your fitness program - do it. Use it. Get it. But, don't trade real tennis for Wii tennis. Don't quite real sports participation for Wii sports. The real thing is better for you and you deserve the best.

Sally's Challenge. Don your heart rate monitor and see for yourself. Play 30 minutes of real tennis and measure your caloric expenditure using your heart rate monitor. Then, play 30-minutes of Wii tennis and see for yourself that real sports trump Wii sports in the real world every time.

THE PERFECT METABOLIC STORM IS HITTING

Gaining force and mass on the horizon, is the perfect metabolic storm. This near perfect calamity is the result of increased work hours, elimination of physical labor, the popularity of sedentary forms of entertainment, eating nutrient-poor meals, dangerous environmental conditions, and what do you have? The answer: staggering statistics from Centers for Disease Control and the US Surgeon General that shows the dramatic increase of sedentary diseases that make up the five parts to a new disease or condition called the "Metabolic Syndrome X". The metabolic syndrome is a cluster of conditions that occur together - increased blood pressure, elevated insulin levels leading to insulin resistance, high triglycerides, obesity and high LDL (bad) cholesterol levels. So, how do we prevent this health and fitness crisis from striking?

One way of averting this metabolic storm is to get people active, using a heart rate monitor to keep in the zones, eating well, lowering chronic stress, and improving CVT, cardiovascular trained fitness. By lightening the load, lowering allostatic load, it is possible to stem the storm.

LISA ALLEN'S STORY

Psychologist say that gaining weight after marriage and motherhood is no accident. There are many complex, tangled emotional issues involved. For me, understanding intellectually what made my weight gain happen did not give me the tools to make it go away or stop continuing.

I had amassed 75 extra pounds over the five years since my marriage and the birth of my two children. I tried the counting calories approach - dieting caused more problems that it ever solved. I'd lost a fast five, hang in there and starve until ten came off. But then the inevitable loss of will power would come and bingo, I'd put on fifteen. If my math is right, that would be a net gain of five, with a bonus of a slowed metabolism that would hang onto everything I ate for fear of being starved again.

I actually did lose something - my self esteem. The scenario is quite familiar to anyone who has ever tried to lose weight. I felt alone, frightened, and downright miserable. How could I have gone from being a fit National Champion in down river marathon canoeing, a marathon runner, and an athlete extraordinaire to being 75 pounds overweight? I would look in the mirror and see a woman I didn't recognize staring back at me.

I knew that I had to exercise and feel better about myself. I tried. The problem was that I had this concept that exercise was something you did as fast as you could for as long as you could, and anything less was not worth doing. I would start running or doing aerobics and go like a maniac until I would aggravate a previous back injury. Forced to lay off exercise for week at a time, I felt my weight was taking control of my body and my life.

One day my husband came home with a heart rate monitor and it's companion book, *The Heart Rate Monitor GUIDEBOOK* by Sally Edwards, and my life changed forever. I read the book and discovered that to lose weight I didn't need to go at a break-neck speed. I'd stay in the lower zones and go for longer time, easy enough not to re-injure my back. I didn't even get up into Zone 3, the Aerobic Zone, for six months.

At about the same time, I began to eat differently - I ate rather than dieted. With the combination of eating in the zones, using heart-rate monitored exercise, and sharing my husband's love for working out, my life and my body shifted. It shifted enormously.

I went slowly, but steadily. It took me 18 months to lose all the weight, but today, I remain 135 pounds with only 16% body fat. I demonstrated that aphorism that sometimes "slow and steady wins the race." I have made peace with food and I rarely give a thought to eating the right foods, I eat below the Threshold line. And, I eat more now than before, when I get hungry, I eat. Emotionally, I don't feel one ounce of guilt and I enjoy eating. Heart rate monitored exercise the Heart Zones Training way has been a true key to my continued success and happiness.

Because I want to share with others what I have learned and experienced, I have no finished my professionals certificate as a personal
trainer. I am living proof that HZT, Heart Zones Training is the best CVT
and weight loss program possibly in the world. Whether the Heart Zones
Weight Loss Program results in a change in your life's work or merely a
change in your clothes size, it will change both you and your lifestyle. I
now know that when we change, all things change

Lisa Allen, *Lawrence, Kansas*

NEATness Counts!

Researchers from the Mayo Clinic have discovered a new trick to fire
up your metabolism—they call it NEAT. NEAT stands for non-exercise
activity thermogensis. NEAT is all the little movements that make up our
day. Not the big movements like exercise, and not the motionlessness
of sitting still or deep sleep. NEAT activities are those such as standing
(rather than sitting), fidgeting, walking around, shopping, cleaning,
gardening, and playing the guitar.

Why does NEAT matter? Well, according to research results published
in Science Magazine, obese persons sit, on average, 150 minutes more
each day than their naturally lean counterparts. This means obese
people burn 350 fewer calories a day than do lean people. And, over
time, that's a huge difference.

To detect even the smallest tap of the toe, the Mayo Clinic researchers
invented a movement monitoring system that incorporates technology
used in fighter-jet control panels. They embedded sensors in customized,
data-logging undergarments that the researchers designed for both
men and women. The researchers' conclusion: Obese people are
NEAT-deficient. It's unclear why that's the case, but, in the meantime,
in between exercise bouts, keep those fingers tapping and those toes
wiggling. To read more: http://www.sciencemag.org

Workout #14

Don't Get a Speeding Ticket

Purpose: Build cardiovascular fitness to raise your fitness level.
Type of Workout: Endurance
Course: Flat or slight rollers
Duration: 45-60 minutes
Zones: 1-4 from Healthy Heart to Threshold

Activity	Description	Zones (Z) Percent of Maximum heart rate	Duration (min.)	Distance (running miles)
Warm-up	Easy	Z 1-Z 2 50-60%	5 -10	.5-1.0
Main Sets 1.	Moderate intensity at an even pace	Z 3 70%	10	~1.0
	Active recovery	Z 2.5 65%	1	NA*
Main Sets 2.	Harder intensity at an even pace	Z 4 80%	10	~1-1.5
	Active recovery	Z 2 65%	1	NA
Main Sets 3.	Hardest intensity doing intervals. Set of 5 intervals 1 minute at 85% and 1 minute drop to 65%	Z 4.5 85%	10	~1-1.5
Cool Down	Active recovery	Slowly recover down to 60% or bottom of Z 2	5 -10	.5-.75
		SUMMARY:	50-60 min.	~5 miles

Description: You get a speeding ticket if you choose too high a heart rate number and you have to decrease your speed and heart rate towards the end of the workout because you held too high a number, too fast a pace or speed. This is a great workout to raise your threshold between aerobic and above-aerobic fitness which means that you can burn more fat as the source of calories.

Heart Zones Training Points: 135 Points

---

*NA means not applicable. The recovery is a slog, focus is to drop heart rate to 65%
*Modification: Modify run to a bike easily by keeping the same time and just adjusting the distances covered. If this is too hard a workout first decrease the intensity by 5%-10% or next by change the duration of the run by 10%-20% in time.

Chapter 15

For Competitive Athletes

If you exercise regularly, you are an athlete. Believe it, don't deny it, take pride in it, because you are.

That being said, we should note that there are different types of athletes: competitive and non-competitive ones. Training for high performance is mainly the domain of competitive athletes, whether they are competing against other athletes, the time clock, or themselves. If you are currently a competitive athlete, by all means, jump into this chapter and go! If you are a non-competitive, health or fitness athlete, you don't *need* to read this chapter, but we do recommend skimming it for the tidbits which will come in handy - if not now, then down the line.

INTERVALS

The first workout type in a high performance program is intervals. Intervals add variety both in your training and in your training benefits, adaptations, so you can most efficiently improve your fitness level. If you are not doing interval training as part of your schedule now, it's time to start.

"Interval" can be a somewhat muddled term. By definition, interval training is a type of workout which consists of a period of high intensity exercise followed by a period of rest - complete or incomplete rest. Several intervals are called a *repetition* (reps). Several repetitions are called a *set*. Following each exercise interval is a *recovery time* (rest) which allows for recuperations.

Intervals are written in a standard way, a coaches shorthand. Seems confusing at first. Go to your master's swim workout and you'll see this coaches shorthand posted on a workout board.

One of the best ways to understand intervals is to diagram it as follows:

The interval training system has been supported by a tremendous amount of research to validate the premise that by raising and lowering your heart rate or workloads during a single workout, multiple zone benefits occur. Among the most basic of these benefits are:

• *Increased endurance ability or aerobic capacity, which is measured by the amount of oxygen that you can use (VO$_2$ max).*

• *Increased total number of calories burned if you increase your intensity.*

• *Increased fun, because you add variety to your workout.*

• *Increased focus on your training because of the need to watch for time and intensity variations, which seems to make the time go by faster.*

But, there is even more benefit to you depending on the type of interval training that you might do.

There are four different types of intervals, defined by their duration: short or sprint intervals, middle-distance intervals, long intervals, and endurance intervals. The four different interval types each affect differ-ent energy systems. Energy systems are the means by which the body transports and converts various fuels into energy. That's the primary point of doing intervals: to train the energy systems to both utilize spe-cific fuels and deliver nutrients to your muscles more efficiently and to improve lactate tolerance. You are actually training your fuel system as much if not more than the specific muscles.

To understand the different types of intervals, here's a more complete explanation.

Sprint and Middle-Distance Intervals benefits:

• *Increased anaerobic enzyme activity*

• *Increased lactate tolerance (pH levels)*

• *Increased specific muscle strength in the specific muscles used*

• *Increased power of fast-twitch muscle fibers (Type II)*

• *Increased phosphagen utilization (ATP-PC)*

Long and Endurance Intervals benefits:

• *Increased anaerobic threshold heart rate*

• *Increased amount of time spent at higher percentages of VO_2 max*

• *Increased lactate threshold and tolerance*

• *Increased number of mitochondria (density of mitochondria)*

• *Increased oxygen transport to and through the membranes*

• *Increased amount of oxidative enzyme activity*

• *Increased glycogen sparing ability*

There are four more important pieces to high performance interval-based training: 1) how many reps or total number of intervals, 2) how much time for rest between intervals, 3) the type of rest in-between reps, and 4) the work-to-rest ratio in each interval. When you have these pieces you can create a variety of interval workouts to match your goals. The table below illustrates the typical characteristics of the respective types of intervals.

ZONES AND INTERVALS				
Type of Interval	**Heart Zone**	**Energy Systems Affected**	**Time in Zone (TIZ)**	**Name of Interval**
Short	Max HR Number	ATP-PC (phosphagen)	<10 seconds	Wind Sprints
Middle	Upper Z5 Red Line	Glycolysis (lactic acid)	10 sec–1 minute	Red Line Intervals
Long	Lower Z5 Red Line	Mitochondrial (function)	1–5 minutes	Strength intervals
Endurance	Z3-Z5	Oxidative (enzymes)	5–15 minutes	Cardio intervals

There are two types of rest: complete and active. After the interval is over, you take a break or rest interval to allow time for your heart rate to drop to a lower zone. This is called a "recovery period" or recovery interval, and it allows your body to recover from the intensity of the interval, to shuttle away some lactic acid, and to resupply the muscles with fuel. Complete rest means that you slow to a stop, while active rest means that you slow down but you continue to move - that would be a walk or jog if you were running. Active rest for a cyclist means to shift down to lower gears and spin easy. Active rest to a swimmer means to continue to swim but using a different stroke for recovery and slow.

Here's an example. Let's say you want to do a long interval workout day. You are a swimmer and usually you like to swim continuously for the amount of time you have - say 30 minutes. You're ready for a change and want to exercise a different energy system with high performance heart zones intervals. Today you want to take that same amount of time, 30 minutes, but this time you are going to break it into five different parts. Your first five minutes is a warm-up of mixed strokes. You then start four sets of five-minute intervals by increasing the intensity of your pace by about 5-10 beats per minute, with a 3-minute active rest during the break between the two intervals. After completing the second of the two high-intensity intervals you take your warm down swim. One of the best ways to understand intervals is to diagram it as follows:

Type of Interval	# of reps	Number of Sets	How Much Rest	Type of Rest	Work-to Rest Ratio
Short	4-5	20–25	5 sec–1.5 min	Complete	1 : 3
Middle	3-4	8–10+	20 sec–2 min	Active	1 : 2
Long	2-5	6–10+	1 min–5 min	Active	1 : 1
Endurance	1-2	2–6+	2 min–10 min	Active	2 : 1

You might ask what additional benefit you gain for the trade-off in complexity with long interval training. The great news is that you are getting new benefits with each of the heart rate zones you're now ex-ercising in. The new zones challenge different energy systems and, sure enough, the body responds to your new regimen with adaptation – the specific energy system or muscle fibers involved change and improve their fuel utilization, becoming stronger and more efficient to meet the workload imposed upon them. In other words, you can train at higher workloads and perform better, and *you* can race faster.

Looking at each of the four different intervals respectively, here's what you are trying to accomplish:

CONTINUOUS INTERVAL   VS.   LONG INTERVAL

1 set x 20 minutes

$$\text{Heart Rate} = 70\% \text{ Maximum Heart Rate}$$

Intervals	Activity	Time	Heart Rate	Heart Zone
1	Warm Up	5 min	50%-70% Maximum Heart Rate	Z1-Z3
1	Swim	5 min	85% Maximum Heart Rate	Z4
1	Active Rest	3 min	60% Maximum Heart Rate	Z2
1	Swim	5 min	85% Maximum Heart Rate	Z4
1	Warm Down	2 min	60% Maximum Heart Rate	Z2
5 intervals			20 min.	

• **Endurance Intervals.** These are the very long repeat workouts at lower percentages of your maximum heart rate. A good example would be cross-country ski intervals – loop format. If your loop is 1–2 km, then your cardio-interval might be 5 sets at 80%-85% of maximum heart rate with a 2-4-minute active rest recovery between loops. This workout simulates racing conditions and results in improvement in your oxygen uptake. If you are a marathoner, this is key interval workout for you if you want to improve your time. The table below schematically illustrates endurance intervals.

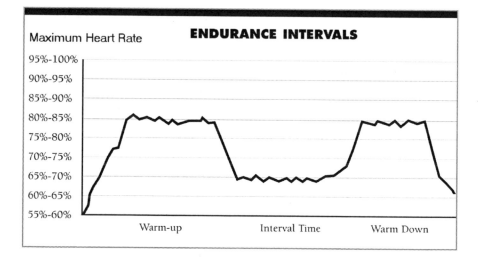

ENDURANCE INTERVALS

Maximum Heart Rate

95%-100% | 90%-95% | 85%-90% | 80%-85% | 75%-80% | 70%-75% | 65%-70% | 60%-65% | 55%-60%

Warm-up   Interval Time   Warm Down

• **Long Intervals.** These are long intervals at slightly faster pace than your race pace or at heart rates about 5 bpm above your low threshold heart rate. The purpose is to challenge your mitochondria, the energy factories in your muscle cells, to continue to produce energy at very high rates of demand. Typically, the effort interval is between a minute and five minutes and the rest interval 1-3 minutes. Because the intensity of the interval is slightly above your first threshold heart rate, you are working in an oxygen debt condition and must allow enough rest to repay this oxygen loan. If you are a 10K athlete, this will probably be your most important interval session. The table below demonstrates interval training sessions.

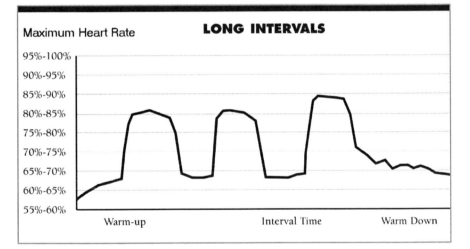

• **Middle Intervals.** These are the intervals for the middle-distance sprint athletes like the 100-meter swimmers and the 400-meter runners. The reason that these intervals are specific to these athletes is that they have the greatest need to improve their anaerobic glycolytic energy system - their ability to tolerate high levels of lactic acid. To develop this ability, middle intervals are a must. Middle distance athletes' training must be event specific, and their intervals can last from 10 seconds to one minute, with the recovery interval twice the length of the effort interval. This is a fast interval and you might well see your maximum heart rate on your heart rate monitor in the last few seconds. Because heart rate monitors work by averaging heart rates every 3-5 seconds depending on the model, your heart rate is actually faster than the monitor reads because of the lag time involved. The active recovery period is important. Continuing to move during the recovery helps with the removal of the lactic acid from the muscle tissues. This lactic acid is transported from the working muscles to the liver and other organs. At the liver, it is resynthesized into glucose, which reenters the blood stream and is transported back to the working muscles for fuel. This is called the "Cori cycle" and provides a benefit to middle-distance athletes who rely primarily on glucose for their energy. The following table shows you the pattern of a middle interval.

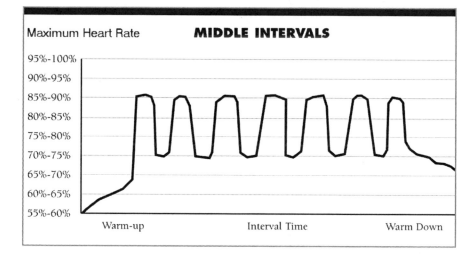

• **Short Intervals.** For sprint-distance athletes, the primary adaptation that needs to occur is to enhance their bodies' abilities to provide immediate bursts of quick energy derived from the creatine phosphate (CP) system (anaerobic phosphagen). You only have enough CP stored for about 10 seconds of high intensity exercise. Therefore, for these interval sets, all the effort intervals need to be no more than 10 seconds in length with about three times that amount of time for recovery. Recovery needs to be complete rest, with little to no movement, to allow for the resynthesis of intramuscular phosphates (such as ATP and creatine phosphate). This system recovers quicker when you stop, typically requiring about 30 seconds. These are all out sprint intervals - throw your heart rate monitor to the winds. In a 10-second interval you are totally driving sport-specific muscles and not your heart. However, remember that your heart is a "work now/pay now" muscle, so it is probably reaching close to maximum even though your heart rate monitor may not be presenting the data this way. Your goal is to build up to 20-25 repeats of this interval but start with about 10. It is extremely taxing and *not* for those just starting to learn interval training.

For the newly-converted interval trainers, start with the long or endurance intervals. They are more enjoyable and cover much lower heart rate numbers. You might even begin with a "fartlek," because they are as much for fun as for changing heart rate intensity. "Fartlek" is a Scandinavian term for "speed play," and it is just that: it playfully increases and decreases your heart's and your body's speed to obtain some of the benefits of intervals but with more fun attached.

A good example of a fartlek workout is the telephone pole fartlek. After you warm up, do a 10-20 bpm pick-up to the next pole and then slow back down to the following pole for recovery and repeat.

If you don't have telephone poles, then use mailboxes, fence posts, or sign posts.

As you get more accustomed to intervals, try the shorter ones and feel the differences. Each of the four intervals taxes a different energy system. Remember that, and you'll feel the experience accordingly.

Intervals can be helpful for almost all individuals who are training. For those who are part of a special population such as the physically challenged or rehabilitation patients, interval exercise can help raise your aerobic fitness levels without the stress on your systems of steady-state high intensity. The latest research shows that several, shorter intervals can result in some of the same adaptations as fewer, longer intervals. You don't even have to do them back-to-back. It's been shown that five minutes a day, three to six times a day is as good a work-out as one session of 15-30 minutes.

If a single workout or a string of them is missed, don't go back and try to make any of them up. If you miss some, and we all do, it's okay. You may need to rework your training schedule because, if it doesn't fit your time and your lifestyle schedule, it won't work for you. Busy people all struggle to juggle their limited time, but it can fit if you will make it fit. You can wake early and work out during eating periods and eat during working periods; you can even have a personal life by inviting your partner to train with you. It's that simple - make your training tree a part of your lifestyle.

THE 12 RULES OF HEART ZONES TRAINING FOR PERFORMANCE

As you progress in HZT, the Heart Zones Training system, there are a few standards or rules that need to be heeded. Following these guidelines will make an especially big difference as you climb onto the peaking and racing branches of your training.

RULE 1. 24-Hour Rule. If you are cross-training, you can do a Z5 or upper Z4 workout every 24 hours if it involves a different muscle group.

RULE 2. 48-Hour Rule. After a Red Line or upper Z4 work-out, you need to take a 48-hour break before you can train again in this specific activity. The reason is that the specific muscle recovery process requires 48 hours for replenishment.

RULE 3. 10% Rule. A single day's Red Line workout should not exceed 10% of the total zone time for the week.

RULE 4. 50% Rule. The total Z4 and Z5 workout time should not exceed 25%-50% of your total training time.

RULE 5. Rate Not Pace. It's more important to know your heart rate than your velocity or pace. That is, it is better to know at what percentage of your maximum heart rate you are training than your speed.

RULE 6. At-About-Around. If the goal (and the true definition of cardiovascular fitness) is to raise your low and high threshold heart rates as close as possible to your maximum heart rate, then high performance trainers who have reached the speed branch on the training tree need to spend 20-25% of their weekly time at-about-around their threshold heart rate. Remember, this is a moving heart rate number; as you get fitter it moves toward your maximum heart rate, and one of the best ways to raise your threshold is to train as close as possible to it.

> **Rules and Guidelines.**
> *These rules are meant to be your guide and not the law – staying within them is safe but they are only guidelines.*

RULE 7. Heart Sparing. Your upper heart rate limits are very stressful on *every* system in your body - over-training is frequently the result of spending too much time in the upper two zones. It's with a blend of the upper and lower zones and by consciously calculating how much time you train in the upper zones that you practice good heart-sparing training.

RULE 8. Zones Are Stress. The body learns to adapt to physical stresses and positively or negatively adapt to them. The three physiological systems stressed are muscles, energy, and cardiovascular.

RULE 9. Specific heart rate numbers. The narrower you can shrink the zones, the more precise your training. One way to do this is to establish specific individual heart rates which are key training indexes to use in ultra high performance training. Example: MSS or maximum steady state heart rate number or T_2, the high threshold heart rate number (see Chapter 18 for more on the HZ Threshold Training System.

RULE 10. The 5-Beat Rule. If your morning resting heart rate, before you get out of bed, is 5 beats above your normal average, drop your training for the day by at least one zone or take a complete rest day. An incremental increased resting heart rate is an excellent indicator of over-stressing your body's systems and is a warning sign or a wake-up signal to back off.

RULE 11. Highest Sustainable Heart Rate. One of the many secrets of heart rate racing is to maintain the highest heart rate number that you can sustain over the entire time period of the event. Your highest or maximum sustainable or steady state heart rate, your MSS is an individual heart rate number; for high-performance athletes, it's a number you pick based on time-trials and estimates. It is a heart rate number that you have trained at and know intimately because it is that borderline heart rate that could take you to either side: success or blowup. *Train and know well your highest sustainable heart rate before the race.* Time trial this heart rate number. For races longer than 20 minutes in duration, it is probably below your anaerobic threshold heart rate depending on environmental factors.

RULE 12. As training intensity increases, training volume decreases. Training intensity identifies the quality of exercise effort and is related inversely to volume (distance or time). If you are training more time in the higher zones then you need to decrease the quantity of training done during the specific workout session or training volume.

IT'S THE LINK

The only real way to know if high-performance Heart Zones Training works is to follow it and then take it to the starting line with you. That's what I did when I set my goal to win the master's division of the 1991 Ironman Triathlon. After weekly MSS heart rate time trials, I set my racing heart rates within very, very narrow windows: 150-155 bpm on the bike (for a 6-hour ride) and at 172 bpm on the 26.2-mile run (for a 3.5 hour marathon pace).

In this ultra-distance triathlon in Hawaii, there are two factors to beware of: cumulative fatigue and environmental extremes (extreme heat with high humidity). I factored both of these conditions into my decision and set my MSS heart rates accordingly. The race then became one between me and my heart rate monitor - not the competition.

As I rode my bike on the out-and-back race course, I was passed by hundreds of cyclists (there were 1,500 athletes in the race). I didn't allow that to affect my plan, although it always takes its toll emotionally. Rather, I stared at my friend the monitor for the entire ride, always keeping my heart rate within the narrow window of 150-155 bpm. On the uphills, I had to slow; on the down hills I had to work hard to stay within my heart zone window. On the return leg of the bike course, I passed the hundreds of cyclists who'd previously whipped by me as I steadily followed my heart rate and avoided the debilitation of extreme fatigue from racing in a zone higher than I could sustain.

I started the run and locked into my 172 bpm racing heart rate. It was comfortable, but my legs were tired.

Someone from the crowd yelled out that I was in fifth place and that the lead woman had 27 minutes on me. Calculating the 26 miles in a marathon, I figured that I would have to outrun her by a minute a mile - that would be difficult since I had raced her before and her primary event was marathons. I got depressed. I looked down at my monitor and, though I felt like I was exerting myself as much as before, my emotions took their toll. It read only 153 bpm.

What are you supposed to do in this situation? When you are racing and you go into a down period during the race and start to lose hope - what do you do? The answer is always the same. Reach down to that place deep inside yourself and find the internal power and strength to go back to your race plan. I worked out the effect of the news of fifth place and 27 minutes and went back to 172 bpm. I believed at that point that my race plan would work.

At the halfway point, someone shouted out that I was in second place and she had a 15-minute lead. When you are physically tired, it's very difficult to calculate numbers but this math was simple - I was catching her but not fast enough to cross the finish line ahead of her. I looked down at my wrist and the monitor that should have been locked in at

172 bpm now read 145 bpm. Depression was getting my heart rate down again. I had slowed my pace.

At this point, all high-performance athletes know exactly what to do. You can either toss your race plan to the wind and go for it, or you stick to it. Those who win always stick to the game plan. But cumulative fatigue was setting in as fast as the heat and the hours of high heart rate and doubt. This was a race of the mind as much as of the heart.

At mile 22 on the marathon course, I spotted her. Within minutes I was by her side, and I said something meaningless as I ran past her. As I pulled ahead, I didn't look back, but I did look down at my heart rate reading - 185 bpm, or 96% of my running maximum heart rate. That's dangerous ground, but that's what happens when you're so excited by the moment and so exhausted from 10-plus hours of racing.

This created a new problem in the race plan. What do you do when your heart rate is 185 bpm and you're leading? At this point, all high-performance athletes do the exact same thing. It's at this moment when you are running mere moments away from victory that you toss your monitor to the wind and you run with your emotional *heart,* not on rate.

I crossed the finish line and won the race by 90 seconds, after 11 hours of racing, because I had a heart rate monitor and she didn't.

Workout # 11:

Sizzling Hot Workout

Introduction. This is a workout for those of you who want to get faster - a lot faster. As we have mentioned previously, to get faster you need to follow the "at-about-around" principle by training at-about-or-around your two threshold heart rates. You can get faster by spending more of your training time around T_1 and T_2 heart rates but avoid the "black hole", the intensity range between the two thresholds..

Workout Plan. This 30-minute interval workout is called "Sizzling Hot" because it's almost all in your Red Line Zone (90-100 percent of maximum heart rate) and 20 minutes are spent above your first or low threshold heart rate. The Red Line Zone is a very high intensity zone so you can't stay there long and a rest period is needed after each interval.

You need to be training on a regular program before you attempt any sizzling hot interval workouts. The workout is commonly called a "ladder" but rather than being based on time or distance, the steps of this ladder are heart rate numbers.

To do this workout you will need to know your first or low threshold number, your T_1 heart rate number. This workout can also serve as a field test for your T_1. The workout consists of two times 20 minutes at the fastest you can go, with a 5 minute active rest between the two endurance intervals.

Set your cardiac tool, your monitor, so it calculates your average heart rate number for each 20 minute test. After warming up, run or ride your first 20 minute interval test then note the average heart rate. Take an active rest for at least five minutes then do another 20 minutes as hard as you can go. The average heart rate of the second test should be within five beats of the first test. Your estimated, your ballpark T_1 heart rate approximately 5 bpm below the average of your two field tests. Now that you know you're low threshold heart rate, here's the sizzling workout as shown in the chart.

WORKOUT			
Interval	Intensity	Exercise Time	Rest Time
#1 Threshold Heart Rate + 2 bpm		8 minutes	2 minutes
#2 Threshold Heart Rate + 4 bpm		6 minutes	3 minutes
#3 Threshold Heart Rate + 6 bpm		4 minutes	3 minutes
#4 Threshold Heart Rate + 8 bpm		2 minutes	2 minutes

Comment. It is important to look at the work to rest ratio when doing high intensity, long intervals. Overall, this workout consists of 2:1 work to rest ratio. As the workout intensity increases, the work interval, the exercise time, decreases.

Again, this is a workout where you are putting the pedal to the floor at near full forward speed.

Be careful, it will get you fitter and faster, but it's also a workout which requires a day of sport-specific rest for recovery. Pay attention to your resting heart rate the next day to make sure you haven't over-stressed the system. Just as each of our "trainability" or rate of getting fit is different, so our recoverability is individual. You may require more or less inter-recovery time, or the time between workout sessions to recover fitter than the workout before. That is the very definition of positive adaptation.

Chapter 16

Sex And The Heart Zones

Why would anyone want to find out what their heart rates are during sex? What's more, why would anyone want to talk about it?

Sex may be a touchy subject (pun intended!), but for some people it's a serious one. The topic comes up routinely for cardiac rehabilitation patients - any perceived marked elevation of heart rate for these folks can be a cause for fear and anxiety, and you can just imagine how that contributes to their sexual experience and peace of mind.

For others of us, the sex-heart rate relationship may not be as weighty a topic, but we still find it pretty interesting (I, for one, am tired of the fact that researchers seem to know more about the sexual habits of baboons than of humans). For many competitive athletes, who wear their heart rate monitors continuously, observing the effects of sex on their heart rates is something they couldn't help but notice.

When it comes down to the facts on the matter, however, the surprising thing is how far apart perception and reality are. Exercise isn't the only topic obscured by our paradigms.

Several months ago, at the invitation of my friend Lyle, a four-time Olympic biathlete, we took off for a Zone 4 Threshold zone workout running the hills in Portland, Oregon. On one particularly gnarly uphill I jumped on the topic, asking if, as a man, he had a mental perception as to what his heart rate was at the time of climax. Not a question one might ask of strangers, true, but Lyle isn't.

He responded that almost all of his cross-country skiing friends use heart rate monitors, some of them regularly sleeping with their chest straps and wrist monitors on, and that sex and heart rate zones is occasionally a topic of their discussion. Lyle said it is common for the men to express a certain frustration and astonishment at the low heart rate numbers their monitors record during sex. (Remember, these are competitive athletes; they like and are accustomed to seeing high numbers on their heart rate monitors. Lyle describes this as the "competitive heart rates" phenomenon, a common theme among competitive individuals.) Lyle is quick to add that there appears to be no correlation, and, if anything, a reverse correlation between high heart rates during sex and sexual performance. After all says Lyle, "the heart rate does go high on a long, slow distance workout."

If you're bold, you too, could try asking a close friend who is comfortable with the topic to just guess at the average heart rate for men and women during intercourse. I've found that the result is always the same: the men predict very high heart rate numbers, and the women chuckle and chide them, usually predicting low numbers.

The fact is, we know more about the effects of exercise on athletes and astronauts than we do about the effect of *sexual* exercise on people in their bedrooms. There is even less information available about sexual activity in people who have experienced heart disease. That's because it's not easy to study humans and sexual activity without running into all kinds of obstacles – psychological, physiological, and ethical. From the published research studies, the average heart rate for men in the "on top" position is 117 beats per minute for about 10-20 seconds of orgasm.

Now, you probably want to know why it's so low. The reason that average heart rates are so low is probably as much a matter of position and the muscles involved as individuals' perception of energy expenditure or the amount of perspiration released. During sexual activity, people are usually in a horizontal position, and they are not using the large muscle groups that are involved in cross-country skiing, swimming, or walking. They are also usually not, in metabolic terms, in a "steady state" of exertion, especially during the very brief, peak heart-rate period of orgasm.

FACTS AND FIGURES

Before quoting additional research, there are a few other facts that should be noted. First, it's always difficult to quantify sexual activity because of the emotional factors that can distort the physiological reactions and a cause a high degree of variation. Second, there is much less research data about the sex-heart rate connection in women than in men, because while the male sexual response is readily apparent, the female response isn't. Third, it is known that age plays a role in sexual response as well, but perhaps due to the small scale of most sex-heart rate studies, age data is not always taken into account. Fourth, there are *many* other factors that can affect the rate of sexual response, including depression (which is more common among those with heart disease), prescription or illicit drug use, or alcohol use. Keep in mind, too, the variability among people's resting heart rates - which can be as low as 30 beats per minute in the extremely fit and over 100 beats per minute in the sedentary low fit-and their maximum heart rates; this same variability will hold true for their average heart rates at the peak of sexual stimulation.

The last facts you should keep in mind are that the physiological response to sexual activity can be divided into four phases: (1) arousal/foreplay, (2) plateau, (3) orgasm, and (4) resolution. In the healthy population, the response to sexual intercourse is an increase in heart rate, blood pressure and respiratory rate. In general, this increase is gradual during arousal, increases rapidly in the minute preceding orgasm, peaks briefly during orgasm, and then rapidly declines to resting level within two or three minutes.

• In 1966, Masters and Johnson reported heart rates at orgasm in a range of 110-189 bpm. However, they didn't state the average values, how many people were measured, the age of the subjects, or any other variables.

• Hellerstein and Friedman, in 1970, using a portable electrocardiogram (ECG), reported a mean peak heart rate at orgasm of 117 bpm (range of 90-144 bpm). They recorded an average heart rate of 87 bpm two minutes before, 110 bpm one minute before, 97 bpm one minute after, and 85 bpm two minutes after orgasm. These researchers also measured VO₂ levels of their subjects to measure energy expenditure during sexual activity. They found that the highest oxygen intakes were 16 ml/kg/min. and the two-minutes-before and two-minutes-after values were 12 ml/kg/min. This energy expenditure is the same as walking a 15-minute per mile pace on flat terrain and for all but the most exceptional men - may amount to the equivalent energy expended in walking only several blocks at this pace.

• Jackson, using a ECG on the same 14 patients before and after taking beta-blockers (medication that prevents high heart rates), noted the average peak heart rate was 124 bpm before and 122 bpm after the medication was administered.

• Nemec used a portable ECG recorder and automatic ultrasonic recorder to study the heart rate and blood pressure responses of 10 men (ages 24-40 years) during four episodes of sexual intercourse with their wives. Two sessions were with the man on top and two sessions were with the man on bottom. Both positions were tested because physicians commonly counsel their cardiac rehabilitation patients to assume a more passive (on bottom) position to avoid overexertion. There was no significant difference between the two positions. The average heart rates for the men were 117 bpm man-on-top, and 114 bpm in the man-on-bottom position. These findings are illustrated in the figure on the following page.

• Stein took a group of 16 men aged 46-54 years and trained them for 16 weeks using a cycle ergometer, beginning 12 to 15 weeks after their first MI (myocardial infarction - a heart attack). Coital heart rate was measured twice before and twice after the training using a portable ECG recorder. Peak heart rate was 127 bpm before the training, and 120 bpm after training. In the control group of 6 men who did not train, peak heart rate remained statistically unchanged at 128 bpm.

• B.F. Skinner, in his summary of dozens of research studies, put it this way, "Looking at all of the studies on middle-aged men with or without MI, it is obvious that peak heart rate rarely exceeds 130-140 bpm. The relatively short period of peak intensity suggests that sexual intercourse in this group of men is not a strenuous activity."

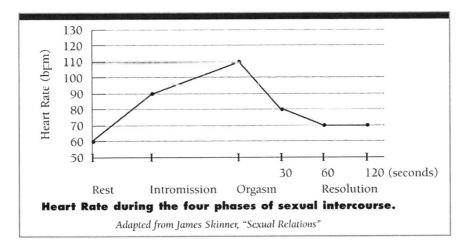

Heart Rate during the four phases of sexual intercourse.

Adapted from James Skinner, "Sexual Relations"

As we mentioned before, very little research has been conducted on women. This is unfortunate, but what is available includes the following:

• Bartlett studied young women and found that heart rate during coitus was not very different from that of their male partners.

• Garcia-Barreto studied 13 men and 10 women who had previously experienced heart attacks. Using ECG monitoring, Garcia-Barreto found no significant differences between male and female patients at the time of orgasm after their heart complications, with men averaging 111 bpm and women, 104 bpm.

SEX IN SICKNESS AND IN HEALTH

Death from heart attacks during sexual activity seems to be another one of those myths that needs busting.

• Ueno, who reported on 5,559 sudden deaths in Japan, found that only 34 people (less than 1%) were engaged in sexual activity at the time of death. Of those, 80% were committing extramarital sex, and most were with partners 20 years younger, eating rich food, and drinking alcohol within hours before their deaths.

• Scheingold and Wagner suggests there might be an issue of familiarity with your partner. In their research, men having sex with a new partner had significantly higher heart rates and blood pressure values.

• Johnston reported on 10 cardiac patients who had sexual intercourse with someone other than their regular partners. Two of these patients felt that their angina or chest pain was more severe during intercourse with the new person.

It appears from these studies that there is a low incidence of death related to coitus at home with a spouse. It also appears that being a man away from home having sex with a younger woman, drinking and eating in excess, combined with the psychological pressures of guilt, possible fear of impotence and being caught, may have just been too much stress - it did them in.

We conclude that sex does not appear to be a high-risk activity for the majority of the population from a cardiovascular viewpoint.

For post-coronary patients, it appears that most should be able to perform satisfactorily sexually and that the psychological and emotional effects of a heart condition seem to be more significant than the physiological effects. It might be wise though, for someone with cardiovascular limitations who under-takes a sexual relationship with a new person to be told of the possibility of increased heart rate response.

The bottom line is that the facts suggest sex is a Healthy Heart zone activity, and rarely does it take you up even to the Temperate zone! If your perception is that you are red lining when you are in bed with your partner, slip on a chest strap and measure your heart rate yourself. But, be prepared for a Healthy Heart zone workout of less than 20 minutes in duration, which doesn't meet the ACSM guidelines for even minimum exercise intensity or time.

Most of all, have fun testing your own individual heart rate responses. In your testing experience, if you have data to share that would enhance the current available research, by all means fax or mail this information to me, and I'll spread the word with or without your name-your choice.

After lecturing to a group from the Specialized bike company on the material in this chapter, I made the same offer. One of the leaders in the group, who obviously listened intently and wanted his own research data, faxed me the next day a print-out from his heart rate monitor after he had downloaded just such an experience. He wrote in large letters "Woman on Top" and circled the highest heart rate number. Sure enough, the researchers were right - 110 bpm was his highest value.

Workout #12:

Rate Not Pace Workout

Purpose. The purpose of this workout is to learn the relationship between pace or speed and heart rate.

Introduction. Every time I hear timers calling out my minute per- mile pace when I run, I use their cue to remind me that I need to listen to my heart rate monitor more than I listen to them. What I recommend is that you use all of the data that you can to assess and monitor your training and racing. Foremost, use your heart rate tools but add to them speed-and-distance monitors, metabolic devices, and power meters. And, as an aside, today you can connect different brands and different training tools together using the Dynastream ANT+ protocol - try it.

What happens to your pace when the temperature increases 15 degrees, when you hit the hills on the course, when there is a headwind, if you miss the aid station or if your blood glucose levels drop? Your heart rate monitor will quantify your physiological responses to these various racing stresses in real time, while the best the race clock can do is give you an elapsed time from which you can determine your after-the-fact average pace.

I have been using my heart monitor for the past 25 years and I am still surprised by the difference between what I feel about my pace or rate and the actual pace that I achieve. My recommendation is that you train with all training devices especially time and heart rate. Here's a great workout to do just that.

Workout. Find a measured course with mile markers. After a warm-up, do five one-mile repeats (5 x 1). Run at a steady pace with no accelerations. Each mile should be 30 seconds faster than the pace before and take at least two minutes active rest between each repeat. Always warm down at the end of the workout.

After the workout, average your heart rate for each of the one mile intervals by noting it for the last half mile or measuring it if you have this

SAMPLE WORKOUT LOG

MILE PACE RUNNING	AVERAGE HR	TRAINING ZONES
9 min/mile	145 bpm	Middle Aerobic Zone
8.5 min/mile	151 bpm	Upper Aerobic Zone
8 min/mile	158 bpm	Lower Threshold Zone
7.5 min/mile	163 bpm	Middle Threshold Zone
7 min/mil	172 bpm	Upper Threshold Zone

feature in your heart watch. Also note the corresponding training zone for your maximum heart rate and your pace.

An example of what you need to record is shown below.

Conclusion. You can now use the numbers from your "Rate Not Pace" workout to better understand the training zones they represent. When someone says to me, "Let's go for a five-mile run at about 8 minutes per mile pace," I always retort, "What about a five-miler in my lower Threshold Zone or about 160 bpm rate, not pace?"

Do this workout once a month because as your fitness improves, your average heart rate will drop. In other words, it will take less effort to run the same pace.

Chapter 17

Emotional Fitness Training

BIOFEEDBACK

One of the fastest growing segments in sports performance is psychobiology, the study of mind-body relationships. One way of interpreting studies of psychobiology is to look at information gathered from biofeedback.

Getting feedback is developed by learning how to get the essential information needed to keep your efforts on track. Feedback essentially means the exchange of data about how one part of a system is working with the understanding that one part affects all others in the system. This exchange of information is like circulation, the lifeblood of your performance. Without feedback, we are in the dark as to how well we are doing. That's just what heart rate measurement is; it's the biofeedback or the information that you need to have as to how much stress you are experiencing in response to a condition.

THE TWO MINDS

When the author Antonine de Saint-Exupery in *The Little Prince* wrote, "It is with the heart that one sees rightly; what is essential is invisible to the eye," he was saying that it's not just the mind's eye that is wise, it's the heart, the second mind, that is sometimes smarter. The heart muscle has become known as the seat of emotions. As such, if we can measure its activity we can measure our deepest feelings, our passions and longings and use them as a guide. When and why do we choose heart over head?

Sociobiologists have indicated that evolutionarily emotions have developed as a central role in our human psyche. Our emotions, they say, guide us in flight or fight decisions that can save our lives in times of danger. In terms of evolutionary history, these types of emotions have become necessary for their survival value and have become permanently a part of the reaction of the heart to stress and to relaxation.

As such, emotions then prepare the body for different kinds of responses. The four major categories of the hundreds of different kinds of emotions that can be measured by a heart rate response are important in emotional fitness training:

* **Anger.** Heart rate increases and a rush of hormones, such as adrenaline, generates a pulse of energy strong enough for vigorous action. Blood flows to the hands in anger. Types of anger are fury, outrage, resentment, wrath, exasperation, indignation, acrimony, animosity, annoyance, irritability, hostility, and at the extreme, pathological hatred and violence.

* **Fear.** At the time that it hits, the body freezes for a moment and then circuits in the brain's emotional centers initiate a flood of hormones that put the body on a general alert, ready for action. Often you can feel your heart pounding in your chest as it speeds up. Blood pressure increases as blood flows to the large skeletal muscles, such as in the legs, making it easier to flee and making the face color ashen as blood is shunted away from it (sometimes creating the feeling that the "blood runs cold"). Other physiological responses to fear include heart rate increases, slow breathing, facial expressions, edginess. Types of fear include anxiety, apprehension, nervousness, concern, consternation, weariness, qualm, edginess, fright, terror, dread, and as a psycho-pathology, phobia and panic.

* **Happiness.** The brain center inhibits negative feelings and increases energy as it quiets worrisome thoughts. The physiological change is that of quiescence which results in the body recovering more quickly from the biological arousal of upsetting emotions. Generally, heart rate drops as a body generally responds restfully. Types of happiness may include enjoyment, relief, joy, contentment, bliss, delight, amusement, pride,

sensual pleasure, thrill, rapture, gratification, satisfaction, euphoria, whimsy, ecstasy, and at the extreme, mania.

* Love. This emotion is the physiological opposite of the "fight-or-flight" response shared by fear and anger. The nervous system responds with a "relaxation response" which consists of a set of body reactions that generate a general state of calm and contentment with the feeling of tenderness. Emotional terms that share love include acceptance, friendliness, trust, kindness, affinity, devotion, adoration, infatuation, agape.

Basically, there are two different ways of knowing: knowing with the heart which is the emotional mind impulsive and intuitive and knowing with the rational mind, the one that is thoughtful and powerful. In folk distinction there is a dichotomy between the "heart" and the "head." Knowing something is right "in your heart" and knowing it is right "in your mind" are two different ways of knowing. These two minds, the emotional and the rational, principally operate in close harmony. Even though they are semi-independent, there is a changing ratio of rational-to-emotional control over decisions. Feelings are essential to thought, thought is essential to feelings. But there are some emotions such as passion which, when it surges, tips the balance and the emotional mind overtakes the rational mind. It can be so strong that "emotional hijacking" occurs.

Emotional hijacking is an emotional explosion which can range from when you feel like you "lost it" or blew up at someone to a degree of severity that you were so possessed by your emotions that you can't even remember what came over you. This is a form of neural hijacking.

So psychobiologists refer to this condition as "flooding" and the degree of it is measured in 10 beat heart rate increments above your ambient heart rate. If you are experiencing flooding, and the heart rate reaches 100 bpm as it easily does when in rage or tears when your endocrine system is pumping adrenaline and other hormones that alert your physiology to the severity of the distress. The exact moment of an emotional hijacking is apparent from a heart rate jump often to as great as 30 bpm within the space of a heartbeat. Muscles tense; it can seem hard to breathe. At full hijacking there is a swamp of toxic feelings that are inescapable.

Knowing that flooding begins at 10 bpm, use your heart rate monitor to measure your emotional responses to different situations. Adjust for the situation. Call a time-out or take a 10 minute break or change the pace of the game. This is called playing to your emotional IQ rather than your intellectual IQ. They are two different quotients and they are both involved in performance and achievement. That's what sport hearts do.

ANTICIPATORY HEART RATE STATE

For all performance, we can determine a state of your rational mind and a state of your emotional mind. Just in advance of an event, we can set an anticipatory state of readiness. This is often called the "ideal state of excitability," and it can be measured by using heart rate and measuring what is called "anticipatory heart rate." The energy elicited from this state of excitability can be harnessed and become a positive or a negative motivator. If the anxiety gets too high or if the excitement is too low, you'll see a diminished performance. The classic research in this area of performance describes the relationship between excitement and performance in terms of an upside-down U. At the top of the inverted U is the optimal relationship between anticipatory anxiety and performance. But, too little excitement - the first side of the U - results in apathy or too low a motivational excitement, while too much anxiety - the other side of the U - sabotages our performance. Look at the graph that follows to understand the relationship between physical performance and emotional pre-event excitability.

One of the measurement tools used by sports psychologists to predict an ideal performance state is heart rate. This anticipatory heart rate varies among sports and individuals, depending on the demands of the activity and level of excitement. For you to determine your pre-event ideal anticipatory heart rate, you will need to do your own self-analysis and in part, note your individual responses in different situations and begin to assess your patterns of readiness.

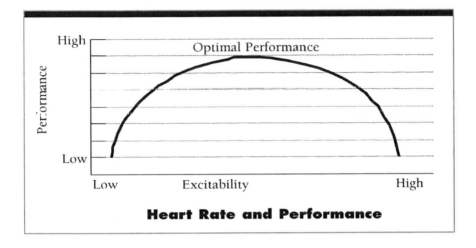

Heart Rate and Performance

A good example of this psychobiological relationship is shown in the results from studies completed on elite level shooters - pistol and rifle. Heart rate response was measured in a number of ways such as where the shot occurred in the cardiac cycle, cardiac deceleration, respiration, electroencephalographic (EEG) recordings and other measures. The results (Daniel Landers, *Psychophysiological Assessment and Biofeedback)* reveal the importance of the mind-body connection with regards to heart rate.

In their study, the average heart rate for the shooters before they shot was 73.3 bpm. Average heart rate during shooting was 86.3 bpm or a 13 bpm increase. Heart rate increases in a sports activity which has limited increases in cardiac requirements because of the arousal level of the shooter. Those in the study (sample size 62, male and female rifle/pistol shooters) whose heart rate dropped below resting or increased more than 50 beats above resting during their shooting period, scored the worst. The best shooters were those whose heart rate increased between 8-50 bpm. This means that for most shooters, there is an individualized optimal performance state that can be measured by heart rate monitoring.

When presented in graph form, the research showed that the inverted U relationship between heart rate and performance optimized at a heart rate of 92.6. This heart rate - 92.6 bpm – was the best indicator of shooting performance. From this graph, you can see that shooters perform better with heart rate elevated to an optimal level. It's important to know that the optimal heart rate for each individual shooter varies. Knowing these ideal performance heart rate ranges can be useful in providing feedback to any athlete. As a side note, it was thought by many shooters that the most desirable time to fire the pistol/rifle was between heartbeats. In fact, the researchers showed that there was no consistency in pulling the trigger in relationship to the cardiac cycle.

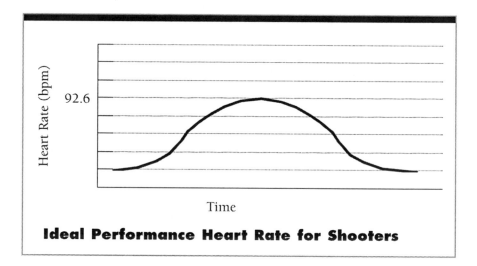

Ideal Performance Heart Rate for Shooters

ANGER AND HEART FUNCTION

Of all of the different emotions measured, anger was the only one which resulted in a drop in cardiac efficiency. That is, heart rate increases but stroke volume decreases. From dozens of studies to date, all the findings demonstrate the power of anger to damage the heart. Anger leads to higher cardiac risk for those who display it. It appears that anger and hostility may be one of the causes of the early development of coronary artery disease and that it may intensify the problem once heart disease has begun.

Physiologically, the stress from each episode of anger results in increasing heart rate and blood pressure. When these episodes become chronic whether the anger is expressed or not, then cardiac risk is dramatically increased. The good news is that chronic anger need not be a death sentence. You can change habits, and hostility is one habit that can change with help. The antidote to anger and hostility is to develop a trusting heart. With the right training and using a heart rate monitor as a biofeedback tool, hostility can be diminished. As people realize that anger can lead to an early grave, monitoring anger becomes more critically important.

Unburdening a troubled, a heavy, an angry, a depressed heart appears to be good medicine.

MONITORING YOUR EMOTIONAL FITNESS

Your coach and friend, the heart rate monitor, is the best tool we have available today to help you learn how to read and control your emotions. A smart heart uses this tool because its emotional intelligence (EQ) is as much if not more important than mental intelligence (IQ). Emotional intelligence comes from mastery of your emotional intellect.

As author and psychologist James Loehr writes in *The Mental Game*, "If you are aware of the times when your fighting spirit is apt to desert you, and if you can harness your intensity and confidence, you'll have a distinct advantage over the player who allows his (her) emotions to manipulate him (her)." Intensity and harnessing the power of intensity can lead to accomplishing your goals and it can be measured by using your monitor to assess your physiological response to the moment.

Let's use an example of strong EQ talent. Say you are running in a 10K race and your best friend catches you and passes you. You thought you were in better shape than your friend but maybe it's not your day; your biorhythms are down. Then you experience the "letdown" phenomenon of mentally and physically letting your competitors pull away from you as you suffer defeat, personal and actual. If we plotted your heart rate response during this scene, we probably would see a dramatic drop in your heart rate, or under arousal, after you were beaten by your emotional response.

Letting down in a competition of any kind is a mental state of under activation or low arousal response. That is, you are not sufficiently aroused to perform at your best. In Heart Zones Training terms, it's loss of heart rate intensity and can be measured by a lowering of heart rate, blood pressure, and other biochemical changes. In fact, you are not performing as well because you are not producing enough mental energy to do so. You suddenly don't try as hard, you lack that motivation or fight response, and the result is impaired performance.

It's frequently seen in the game of tennis. Watch as a player is ahead and all of a sudden their momentum falters. It seems as if they run out of steam and lose consistently. This sudden drop of performance or state of under activation can be traced in this example to a number of factors. According to Loehr, "Some players are incredible fighters. They're always coming at you whether ahead or behind, playing well or poorly, they're like bloodhounds on a hot scent. Adverse conditions, bad luck, and unfair calls rarely dampen their spirit. They consistently overcome these obstacles with two emotional responses: they become challenged and remarkably persistent." This is one of the smart heart's successful styles.

The emotional response opposite to under arousal is over activation. In this case of high nervousness, the athlete is trying too hard, is too excited or too angry or, if we used a car engine as an analogy, their rpms are too high. At the start of a race you'll frequently see a runner take off like a rabbit, only to later fade because they "went out too fast." Indeed, they did that probably because their arousal was so high and their perceived speed or intensity was low. Monitoring heart rate can abate that rabbit phenomenon. When your heart rate numbers drop uncharacteristically during or after a game or event, you are usually experiencing the letdown phenomenon. When heart rate numbers which stay uncharacteristically high during a recovery period are not attributable to exertion, they indicate over arousal.

At mile 23 in the marathon of one of the hardest races in the world, the Ironman Triathlon, I caught and passed my nemesis, the woman who was in first place in the master's division. I looked at my monitor, and after 10 hours of racing, it was at that moment of intense arousal reading 186 bpm (my maximum running heart rate is 192 bpm). I had two miles to go to the finish line and I couldn't afford to "letdown" or I'd lose. I raced with all heart and total fatigue for those last miles. For one of the few times in my life, I experienced what is the highest feeling in an athlete's life, the "ideal performance state," and though it was an extreme level of exertion, it was effortless. I was zoned, I was maxed out, I was hazed-tranced-psyched-pumped-tranced. I was in complete and exhilarating flow. I won the race, and crossing that finish line and looking up at the finish clock is a feeling and moment that is frozen in time for me. I felt a profound inner stillness and well-being. It was joy, power, control in one. Clearly, my mental state at this moment was my zenith and dramatically different from the mental state of poor performance. At that moment when I passed her, I have to confess I threw away my heart rate monitor (well, it was so high at 186 bpm anyway) and I ran to win. I ran these last few miles and I ran because it was effortless. This was one of my peak athletic moments, this was truly the ideal performance state.

EMOTIONAL AND PHYSICAL FITNESS ZONES

To trigger this ideal performance state is not the result of athletically playing well; rather you play well because you are in the zone. This is an important distinction. Zoning is a state of emotional balance. When your emotions change, your biochemistry changes. When your biochemistry changes, so changes your performance. It's when the chemistry and the mind are in balance, when there is a rich mixture of the mind and the body that you achieve maximal performance. The zone is actually a fine-tuned place, it's not a chemically induced trance state. And it's controlled by you. You create the state of mind-body where your emotional and mental climate is maximized. As you practice this technique, watch the changes in your heart rate's response to our different mind-body situations. Zoning is a learned state and there are a few ways to practice getting into your ideal performance zone:

• *Positive Mind-Emotion State.* Listen to your positive inner self-talk, think positively, talk positively, look for the good and strong in yourself and your performance. This positive emotional methodology will increase your body's chemistry to provide the emotional and spiritual fuel for performance. Replace anger with challenge, fear with desire, frustration with determination, and each time you will be learning how to program your mental zone.

• *Enhanced Self Awareness.* Fine tune your awareness by feeling the mental and emotional state when you are successful. What is your mental and emotional climate during your best athletic moments? When you get into the flow, what does it feel like and how did you get there? Learning how to become more self aware leads to opening the pathways to more self awareness.

• *Combining Mental Zone and Physical Zone.* As you learn the never-ending process of zoning, observe the differences between when you are only mentally or only physically in the performance state. It's by the combination of the two that you reach your highest state. The blocks to physical zoning can be anything from overtraining, to dietary problems, lack of real sleep, and muscle imbalance, while the blocks to mental zoning can be emotions, concentration, or self esteem. Unless the blocks are released, unless the two, EQ and IQ can merge, only then can you achieve optimally.

• *Positive Visualization.* Creating a positive image of your actions and feelings leads to their outcome. If you are a triathlete, visualizing passing riders on their bikes is positive visualization. Visualizing not being passed on the bike, or not going down on your bike, or not having a mechanical breakdown is negative visualization. What you most fear too often becomes true because your mind cannot tell the difference easily between a real visual cue and an imagined one. Clearly, if you are not winning or achieving your goal, something is breaking down. Understanding these breakdowns is the first step to improvement. That's how you turn a breakdown into a breakthrough.

ATHLETIC STRESS

Exercise deals with both of the three kinds of basic stress: emotional, metabolic, and physical. They can each be measured by their biochemical responses. A heart rate monitor is a personal power tool because it can assess biochemical changes. Stress can also be classified as external and internal. Heat, altitude, lack of sleep, nutrient changes are all types of external stress. Anger, anxiety, fear, happiness are a few of the internal stresses that we encounter.

Managed stress in the right amount is healthy for us. That's because the body adapts to positive stress by getting stronger and fitter, to negative stress by getting weaker and de-conditioned. This process is called "adaptation" and it's why we expose the body to exercise stress - to enhance its ability to do work. If we apply too much exercise stress, the adaptation that occurs is called "overtraining" and if we apply not enough stress, then we are under training the body and mind.

Sports training is a form of physical and emotional stress in a controlled dose which leads to improvements in our strength, flexibility and cardiovascular capacity. Races, tournaments, and meets are all examples of emotional stress, which managed and controlled, leads to improvements in our mental strength, flexibility, and fitness.

Perception of an event is a key to the dimension of the stress. If you perceive something as threatening, then it will be an increased stressor. If you perceive the same event as enjoyable, then it will be less stressful. Exposure to high amounts of stress leads to burnout. Racing too much can lead to temporary mental burnout, while training in too high a zone for too much time in zone can lead to a temporary physical burnout. Too much time in the athletic pressure cooker - too much training and racing – can lead to permanent burnout.

Recovery is a key antidote to stress. Recovery is that time when we are relaxed and rid of the stressors. There are both mental and physical components to recovery and both types are required for full recovery. Recovery can be easily measured using heart rate technology and logging your exercises. When rapid heart rate recovery occurs, both mental and physical stress is at its lowest. Active recovery means that the physical stress of high intensity is removed but the person remains active and does not sit or lie down for recovery.

How fast you recover is an indicator of stress reduction competence. For example, when I swim in my Red Line zone (maximum heart rate swim 170 bpm) and do repeat intervals at 155 bpm, if I completely rest between intervals I usually see my heart rate drop a beat per second. If I notice after 30 seconds that my heart rate has only dropped 20 beats, I know that this is not a characteristic recovery rate and that I am not recovering as fully as normal. I then adjust my workout to lower the stress level.

Similarly, if I see that my morning resting heart rate is more than about 5 bpm higher than its characteristic value, I know I am over-stressed and I change my entire day's activities. This resting measurement is telling me that I am in a higher than normal stressed condition which is a response to some biochemical activity within me. When I ignore this information, inevitably my day goes poorly with high expectations that are not met, with the onset of a problem whether mental or physical, and without my normal energy level.

Just as there are chemical changes in the muscle tissue which causes a muscle to contract, known as the Kreb's cycle, so there are chemical changes that happen from the mind sending transmitters which result in the emotions changing. Credit for this discovery goes in large part to Chadace Pert, formerly chief of brain biochemistry at the National Institute of Mental Health. After years of research, she discovered "neuropeptides", which are small protein-like chemicals housed in the brain's limbic system and are the transmitters of emotions and feelings. The limbic system which has long been known as the emotional center within the brain, controls the chemicals- neurohormones such as cat-echolamines - that cause emotional change.

These chemicals are the mind's response to stress and relaxation. To increase your ability to recover from stress, improvement in neuro-hormonal function is necessary. This is accomplished most healthily by living a life of balanced stress and recovery, by expending and recapturing personal energy. This process is one example of "oscillation" or wave theory.

Emotional fitness training is a way to listen to your heart by becoming aware of your emotional state and learning to consciously shift to a healthier zone if you happen to be in a toxic zone. Just as the body is designed to heal itself, the emotions can be used to guide us from a condition of stress and disease to a state of peace, health, and compassion.

There are five emotional fitness zones. As they are being described, take some time with each one to notice which of these is most familiar to you, and where you tend to spend your time.

EMOTIONAL ZONES® / HEART ZONES® TRAINING

THRESHOLD ZONES

DESCRIPTIONS

5c LETHAL ZONE
AVOID THIS ZONE FOR FEAR OF YOUR HEALTH AND SAFETY. IT MAY BE LIFE THREATENING.

5b TOXIC ZONE
OUT OF CONTROL. ACTIONS ARE AGGRESSIVE, VIOLENT, SOMETIMES HYSTERICAL. AVOID THE TOXIC ZONE.

5a DISTRESS ZONE
ENERGY ZAP STATE. CHARACTERIZED BY WORRY, ANGER, DEPRESSION, AND ANXIETY.

EMOTIONAL THRESHOLD LINE

4 PERFORMANCE ZONE
FOCUS. CONCENTRATION. IN THE "FLOW". VERY, VERY HIGH ENERGY. CREATIVE.

3 PRODUCTIVE ZONE
ACCOMPLISH TASKS. GET THINGS DONE. FEELING POSITIVE. DYNAMIC.

2 INDUSTRIOUS ZONE
DILIGENT. ACTIVE. WORKING HARD. ASSIDUOUS. ATTENTIVE. PERSEVERING.

1 SAFE ZONE
REVITALIZING. RENEWING. RECHARGING YOUR EMOTIONAL ENERGY. RESTORATIVE.

Zone 1. Safe Zone

The safe zone gives us energy. It is where we go to re-charge our batteries, to calm ourselves, to get peaceful, to re-focus our energy. The safe zone is very personal and it is important for you to design your own safe place. For some, Zone 1 will have a prayerful or meditative focus. For others, certain music or sounds of nature will create a peaceful inner feeling. A visual memory of a beautiful place or a remembrance of a special moment or thoughts of compassion toward a loved one may put your heart at peace. Just as exercise training is one of the best things for your physical heart, a well-developed Safe Zone is the greatest gift that you give to your emotional heart.

Zone 2. Productive Zone

The productive zone is a range of feelings in which may spend much of your time at home, work or play. In this zone, you are getting things done and feeling pretty good. You are relatively peaceful and focused, going about your day-to-day responsibilities. In Zone 2 you have access to both your emotions and your thoughts.

Zone 3. Performance Zone

The Performance Zone has all of the features of Zone 2 except it is characterized by greater focus, concentration, positive intensity and accomplishment. You would probably be in Zone 3 when you are doing something you really love, whether it be work, play or relationships.

Zone 4. Distress Zone

Zone four drains us of energy. The Distress Zone is a state where the bad stuff starts to happen. It is characterized by feelings of fear, worry, anger, anxiety, depression, overwhelm, guilt, and helplessness. This is where the stress response is triggered and physiological changes begin to affect heart rate, blood chemistry, and activity in all the cells and organs within the body. The ability to think clearly declines and the emotions begin to take over. In Zone 4 we become much less productive in our work and much more destructive in our relationships.

Zone 5. Red Zone

The Red Zone is a place you never want to go. This is out of control behavior, raw emotion with no rational thought. It is characterized by aggression, violence, and hysteria. This is where abusive and destructive behavior happens. It is highly toxic to the person in Zone 5, as well as anyone else nearby. The field of psychoneuroimmunology (psycho = mind, neuro = body's nervous systems, immunology = the body's natural ability to defend and heal itself) teaches us about the connection between our thoughts and what happens in our bodies. Our emotions and perceptions of what is happening in our world cause our heart and our brain to send messages that stimulate physiological responses. Our emotional states trigger reactions in our body that affect heart rate, blood chemistry, and the activity of every cell in the body. Our immunity is compromised when we are under stress. Fatigue and stress-related complaints account for a high percentage of all visits to primary care physicians. Remember, stress is our perception of an external

Dr. Dan Rudd, author of *Health in a Heartbeat*, at one of his workshops teaching the Emotional Heart Zones.

situation that brings about an internal response, and stress is a huge energy drain. While all of us experience a range of emotions, most people have a specialty, a familiar set of feelings that follow them around like a shadow, or certain situations that regularly set them off. Some people get real good at fear and worry, finding something to worry about in almost any situation. Others are addicted to rage, and can be triggered instantly at home or work if things do not go the way they think they should. Some folks seem to have a positive outlook, even in stressful situations, looking for the good in whatever is happening.

Some think that stress kills us. It may. However, high doses of stress can be helpful and provide for adaptation to occur if there is a sufficient wave of recovery to accommodate it. Stress won't break you unless you fail to plan for sufficient recovery. High linear stress, for example, in the form of a high ambient or resting heart rate or feeling like you are in a high pressure environment continuously can be lethal. The human being is one of the most awesome cyber-machines to ever stalk the planet. Martial arts master and exercise theorist George Leonard, perhaps put it best when he wrote that we are all mostly unrealized potential. When we thrill to an event like the Olympics, we're not responding to whose training regimen was the best or which country had the best nutritionist. Instead, we resonate to people who grasp a small part of that potential and *reach*. It is the reach that's important.

If you are interested in more information about emotional fitness training, contact Dan Rudd, Ph.D. He presents seminars and workshops which teaches the application of emotional fitness training.

Workout #15:

The Body-Mind Session

Introduction. The heart muscle has a dual role: to be a blood pump and to be the mental inspiration pump. With the emphasis today on the mind-body connection or psychobiology, one can easily see that the heart is a double muscle. It provides for both work capacity and for mental desire. Here's a workout that challenges both of the heart's primary capacities - a mind-body connector.

Purpose. To measure your ability to accurately predict heart rates during varying paces.

Workout Plan. Set your heart rate monitor so the alarm sounds every 10 minutes. You will have to use your wrist watch if your model does not have this feature. Calculate and post 70 percent of your max heart rate (maximum heart rate) and each five percent increase up to 90 percent. If you don't know your max, take a test. For a maximum heart rate of 195 beats per minute (bpm) these values would be 137, 146, 156, 165 and 175 bpm.

Workout. Warm-up for however long is appropriate for your selected activity, then begin your workout and start the alarm function on your watch or monitor. Without looking at your monitor, workout for 10 minutes at what you think or perceive to be 70 percent of your maximum heart rate. Exert a steady-state effort for the entire 10 minutes.

When the alarm sounds, look at the monitor and make a mental or physical note of the heart rate. Step up the interval (this is a 10-minute ladder) to what you think is 75 percent of max for 10 minutes without looking at the monitor. When the alarm sounds, note the actual heart rate and keep a mental record of it. If you can do the math, note your error.

Follow the same procedure for 80 percent, and 85 percent if you can maintain it. If this pace is above your anaerobic threshold heart rate, you probably cannot withstand it. Warm down, then compare your perceived effort with your actual heart rate. The error may be so great that you may never train without a monitor again.

Outcome. If you are more than five beats off, you need to train your mind more than your body to truly and undeniably know (and I use the word "know" as in having knowledge) your heart rate intensity.

Repeatedly to ad nauseam, I hear people say, "I don't need a heart rate monitor because I know my heart rate whenever I train." This is athletic elitism and arrogance at its most obvious. After completing this workout, I "know" that you will agree that my friend and Olympic Biathlete Lyle Nelson is right when he writes, "It takes a lot of heart (blood pumping capacity) and a lot of "heart" (confidence and inspiration) to achieve your best-possible performance. It's only with the heart rate monitor that you can achieve both. I "know" and I "feel". This is the mind-body connection."

Chapter 18

The Threshold Training System

When I first began serious training with a heart rate monitor, around 1982, I was one of the earliest adopters of a new genre of equipment for sports performance called personal training tools. At that time, few competitive athletes had a heart rate monitor, and if they did, even fewer knew what the numbers meant or how to use it to improve our fitness. At that time, almost thirty years ago, there was no such thing as training or heart rate zones. There was no other consumer-accessible technology — such as lactate analyzer, metabolic cart, GPS-monitors, or power meter — because such equipment was only available in the labs. These powerful measurement and monitoring tools were locked up to most, used principally for research. Most of all, there was little to no understanding of what to do with that equipment, nor how to create programs or applications to help people get healthier or, for those of us that are competitive, to help athletes reach the finishers' podium. And now that first instrument, the heart rate monitor, is celebrating it's third decade birthday, with millions of users around the world using it as one of their key training tools.

As a matter of history, that first heart rate monitor that I acquired in the early 1980's was hard-wired to a small box that I wore on my chest without a watch — the heart rate data was shown with a small display on the top. Several years later, I purchased my second heart rate monitor for $400, which was a lot of money for a personal training tool that I knew little about. It was one of the first wireless heart rate monitors, the Polar Vantage XL. My journey as an applied exercise physiologist specializing in personal training tools was then in its infancy. And that journey grew into my authoring the first book on training with a cardiac monitor in 1992 titled *The Heart Rate Monitor Book*. It became a best-seller.

That's the genesis of heart rate training and why I created the world's first heart rate training system and wrote the first book about it — because there was nothing available for athletes, like myself and others, who knew that applying science to training paid off in prize money, trophies, sponsorship, and wins. I have dedicated the last three decades to creating programs using personal training tools — power meters, metabolic carts, speed-and-distance monitors, and heart rate watches. Each of these programs are designed to help children and adults lose weight, lower their stress, get fitter, and to help individuals perform at their best. HZT is practiced in school PE classes, corporate wellness programs, medical practices as the standard exercise health prescription. And, that first program was built on setting training zones based on maximum heart rate. But, there are other ways - let's explore them now.

TRAINING WITH A HEART RATE MONITOR BEGINS WITH AN ANCHOR POINT

An anchor point is a value or position that you can attach to. One of the reasons to affix training intensities to an anchor point is to set your training zones by "anchoring" them on a physiological or mechanical indicator. Biomarkers, indicators of where physiological changes occur, are standard anchor points for setting training intensities, or zones. These physiological markers occur as exercise intensity increases and the body compensates for the harder work by recruiting more working muscles, increasing and changing breathing responses, making changes in thermal responses (releasing heat, sweating), and metabolizing different fuels (substrates). Each of these different ways of detecting and measuring markers can be associated with, or coupled to, a heart response — in this case, a heart rate number in beats per minute.

As in sailing, when you toss out an anchor without knowing how deep the water is, you sure better have a lot of rope. Is the water depth 10 feet or 1 mile? Do you need 10 feet of rope or 5,280 feet of rope to attach to your anchor to secure your boat? Similarly, in training, if you don't know your primary anchor numbers, your training might freely float with nothing to secure it to and nothing to use to make modifications to it.

anchor points depends on a different measurement tools and typically uses some complimentary analysis of the data that is collected. Each of these sports instruments — power meters, heart rate monitors, metabolic carts, and other devices that can sense and measure your physiological changes — are providing data that as athletes, coaches, and educators we can use to interpret and then create training plans and programs. Once you have measured or estimated your anchor number and you have programmed that number into a heart rate monitor or other power tools, then you know with every stroke or step your zones and other robust information like training load and training stress.

Those four key biomarkers are:

• *Lactate Threshold:* Lactic acid concentrations in millimoles of blood lactate. Lactic acid is one of the products of anaerobic carbohydrate metabolism in the cells.
• *Ventilatory Threshold:* Ventilatory changes with changes in the ratio of oxygen to carbon dioxide to total inspired and expired air.
• VO$_2$ Max: Maximum oxygen consumption or milliliters of oxygen consumed. Maximum oxygen consumption is the highest volume of oxygen (VO$_2$) recorded during maximal exercise.
• *Maximum heart rate:* The highest number of beats per minute that you can produce with genetic limitations.

Of these four markers above, which is the best physiological marker for you to use for anchoring your personal zones and training methodology? And how do you accurately measure that anchor point to set your different training intensity levels? The answer is: it depends.

It depends on your goals. It depends on your experiences. It depends on how much you know about training and how much you want to know about training. It depends on what personal or professional training tools you have or are willing to invest in. It depends on whether your objective is to get and stay fit or whether you are going for the gold. It depends on what equipment and facilities you have access to. It depends on which anchor point resonates with your style of training. And, maybe most of all, it depends on what training system you believe in.

Scientifically-based cardiovascular training systems or methodologies like HZT, Heart Zones Training give athletes maps to follow. Following a legitimate training program based on scientific research produces results. Some coaches keep their methodologies a secret, believing that if they let others become familiar with it, other coaches will steal their system and produce better athletes. Other coaches, like myself, believe in sharing our skills, our expertise, and our training programs and plans in hopes that by doing so, everyone does better.

Back to the four big biomarkers. If you have access to an exercise lab, which few of us have, then you can take a metabolic test and get all four of biomarkers measured, the zenith. If you don't have that luxury, then you are left with one choice - field tests. Get access to as many different tools that you can - GPS for speed-distance, heart rate monitors for physiological responses, watt meters for measuring accurately caloric expenditure and energy output. How to do the field tests to measure the biomarkers is latter in this chapter.

Deciding on which training system, tools, and anchor point for training zones to use is a decision for you to make or for you and a certified coach, like a Heart Zones CC, Certified Coach, to suggest. Before you decide on the training system that resonates with you, let's go through each of the biomarkers so that you can choose one that best fits you.

THE FOUR ANCHORS

There are four markers that are commonly used to anchor your training zones. There is no *one* way to train but many different methodologies. HZT is based on using these biomarkers, their companion training tools, and a system that measures, monitors, and manages, the 3Ms of training.

Anchor Point #1. Lactate Threshold Marker

There are two distinct lactate threshold - the first, LT_1 and the second LT_2 or the low and the high. They are measured using a blood lactate analyzer which uses a small blood sample to determine the concentration of lactic acid in your bloodstream. By measuring lactate at different exercise intensities, you can assess your individual lactate response to exercise and other stresses. The lactate analyzer allows you to monitor the quantity and rate of lactate production at various levels of speed, oxygen consumption, or power output.

The first lactate threshold, LT_1, occurs at the heart rate or intensity number when lactate first begins to rise above the steady-state base-line level. The second lactate threshold, LT_2, occurs at the intensity level when lactate is one millimole per liter above your baseline level *or* one millimole above the maximal steady state.

Look at the following diagram to see that as exercise intensity (speed, heart rate, stress) increases, lactate is stable until a certain point when blood lactate level begins to rise. That inflection point when it initially begins to rise is the low threshold, LT_1. As the exercise effort becomes

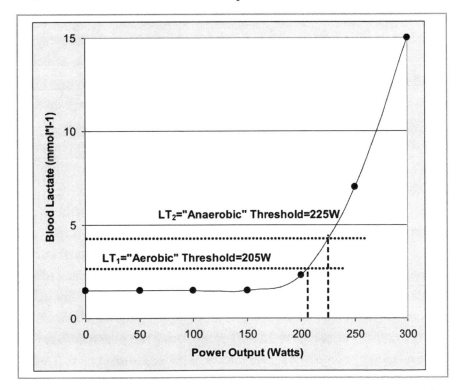

more intense, the second threshold is reached. Use the heart rate, power output, pace or speed when LT_2 to measure this biomarker.

Analyzing blood lactate is an invasive test. Your blood is sampled by a pin prick to draw a small amounts of blood, usually from your fingertip or your earlobe that is used for the analysis.

Anchor Point #2. Maximum Oxygen Consumption/VO_2 max Marker

A metabolic cart, also called a respiratory gas analyzer or VO_2 cart, is used to measure the amount of oxygen in milliliters of oxygen that you can consume at rest and during exercise. This biomarker is measured based on your body weight and time and is stated in oxygen per kilogram of body weight per minute (ml/kg/min).

The maximum amount of oxygen consumed at an all-out effort is called maximum oxygen consumption, or VO_2 max. This is a measurement of your aerobic capacity and is considered by many exercise scientists as the "gold standard" in fitness testing. It is a popular assessment because it is a non-invasive and an accurate way to measure the amount of oxygen consumed and utilized by the athlete. As a fitness assessment, measuring VO_2 max has been a common test since the turn of the last century, in the 1900s. At that time, expired oxygen and carbon dioxide were captured and measured in big bags called Douglas bags. Today, your aerobic capacity can be measured with small, portable devices that personal trainers, coaches, and certified metabolic specialists use.

Your aerobic capacity is dynamic because it changes as you gain or lose cardio-fitness. Let's use an example of an unfit woman with a measurement of her maximum volume of oxygen, her VO_2 max of 20 ml/kg/min. This number is the anchor point for her to set her training zones. In this example, she would train in a Zone 3 that is 70%-80% of her VO_2 max, or 14–16 ml/kg/min. As she gets more fit, her VO_2 max changes and her capacity improves to 30 ml/kg/min. Using her new maximum oxygen consumption number, she then re-sets her new Zone 3 to 21–24 ml/kg/min.

The higher your maximum oxygen consumption, the better your performance. Because your VO_2 max is dynamic, it is necessary to periodically test it in a fitness or exercise laboratory, to recalculate VO_2 max and then anchor training zones using the new value.

Anchor Point #3. Maximum Heart Rate Marker

Maximum heart rate is the highest frequency that your heart can beat in one minute. A heart rate monitor is all you need to measure maximum heart rate. Maximum heart rate is one of the easiest anchor points to assess because it is more or less static, changing over time as slowly as a glacier in the fit population. It doesn't change with fitness and only decreases ever so slowly with age, most likely with age-related loss of fitness. In Chapter 6, The Five Heart Training Zones, you read a complete description of who, what, how, and why to use maximum heart rate as the anchor point for setting training zones.

One of the reasons to consider using a different anchor point according to Carl Foster, "Using a percentage of heart-rate maximum (HRmax) (70 to 90%) is probably the most widely used approach for programming and monitoring exercise intensity. There is a very large body of evidence supporting this approach. Specific values of percentages of maximum heart rate are not necessarily equivalent intensities in different individuals. Thus, the use of percentages of maximum heart rate may be less than optimal.[1]"

Anchor Point #4. Ventilatory Threshold Markers - T_1 and T_2

There are two distinct ventilatory thresholds, the first and the second. Low ventilatory threshold, the first one, occurs at that cardio-intensity when there is first an increase the amount of breathing required, a shift in the breathing pattern. The most accurate way to assess each of the two ventilatory thresholds is to use a metabolic cart which measures inspired and expired air, aka ventilation. As we breathe in

---

[1] Cardiorespiratory Training: Programming and Progressions. Foster, Carl. page 14.

oxygen (O_2), it is absorbed to support the working muscles and the respiration of all cells in the body. The muscles and other cells then release carbon dioxide (CO_2) as the by-product of energy production, muscle contractions and metabolism. When exercising, the amount of oxygen required increases and the production of carbon dioxide also increases. Because both of these increases in gas changes occur in different amounts and at different intensities, they serve as two primary physiological markers that can be used as anchor points. The low or first threshold, VT_1, is marked by an increase in both the volume of oxygen consumed (VO_2) and total inspired and expired air (VE, or ventilatory equivalent) while the amount of carbon dioxide expired remains constant.

A second threshold, VT_2 occurs when the amount of air that we breathe shifts again, but this time there is an increase in carbon dioxide expired. This second threshold is called the high or second ventilatory threshold. There is no corresponding increase in oxygen consumed at the second threshold. This second shift becomes the marker for VT_2. These two shifts in ventilation, VT_1 and VT_2, are used as convenient biomarkers for anchoring training zones as well as assessing changes in fitness.

THE NEW THRESHOLD TRAINING

The measurement of different thresholds that occur with different levels of exercise intensity is not new, but training with it is. About 90 years ago, A.V. Hill, an exercise physiologist pioneer, first published the research to show the relationship between changes in lactate concentrations and ventilatory responses.[2] This was the first connection that the increases in lactate concentration were possibly remedied with an increase in oxygen consumption, the beginning of anaerobic carbohydrate metabolism. There is still considerable debate today whether cellular anaerobic metabolism in the working muscles is really the cause of lactate increases, yet there is near total agreement that exercise intensities associated with the ventilatory thresholds and the lactate thresholds can be used for training, analysis, and diagnostic purposes.

For our purposes, the out-of-fashion term "anaerobic threshold" is now simply called "threshold". Threshold is the term used commonly for the first or low threshold. It is a cross-over point between sustainable and non-sustainable exercise intensity. Whether measured using heart rate, power output, ventilation, lactate levels, or percentage of maximum oxygen consumption, the low threshold is the maximum lactate steady state, before lactate begins to rise. There is a great deal of controversy[3] that surrounds the term "anaerobic threshold" (AT).

The reason the term is in disfavor by researchers and applied exercise experts is that the term has a dozen or more confusing and conflicting definitions.

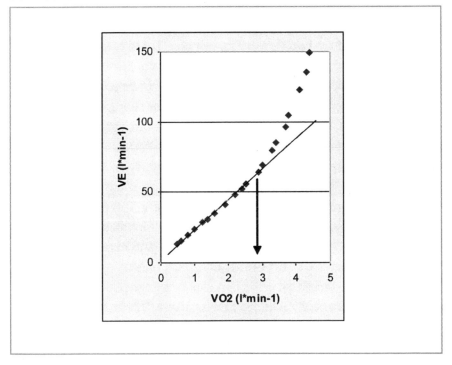

[2] Hill, A.V., Long, C.N.H., and Lupton, H. (1924). Muscular exercise, lactic acid and the supply and utilization of oxygen: Part VI. The oxygen debt at the end of exercise. Proceedings of the Royal Society of London, 97, pp. 127–137.

[3] Foster, C., Cotter, H.M.: Blood lactate, respiratory and heart rate markers on the capacity for sustained exercise. (Maud PJ, Foster C., editors) Physiological Assessment of Human Fitness, 2nd edition, Champaign, IL, Human Kinetics Press, 2005, pp. 66–67.

As an index or a way to relate performance in endurance events, threshold measurements are a more effective gauge than the gold standard measurement of VO_2 max. It more accurate to use threshold data to predict training-induced changes and compare endurance capacity than aerobic capacity. There is a lot of discussion by experts but insufficient research to show that training at the threshold intensity is best. Training at or below threshold levels keeps the individual from the negative effects of high intensity training, such as high lactate levels that disturb aerobic metabolism. Also, too much above-threshold training results in decreases in the total training time or distances that you can endure and enjoy.

TWO THRESHOLDS, NOT ONE THRESHOLD

In the early 1980s, researchers began to first publish studies reporting that indeed there are two thresholds, not one. These two thresholds have now been accepted by most scientists and are just being popularized today. These two thresholds are measured in two different ways: by monitoring changes in the blood lactate (LT) or changes in ventilation (VT). For lactate threshold, the first threshold is measured when the levels of lactate reach what is known as the "maximal lactate steady state," which is the highest sustainable concentration of lactate before it begins to rise. The second way to measure threshold is the body's ventilatory response to increases in exercise stress. This response is a shift in the first discontinuous increase in total air inhaled and exhaled. This first or low threshold occurs when you start to compensate for the increased exercise stress by first breathing harder.

The low lactate threshold is the first sign or evidence of increases in blood lactate concentration above resting levels. This intensity, coupled with power, oxygen uptake, pace or speed, or heart rate is the first lactate threshold, or LT_1. This is an effort that can be sustained for a long time, a high intensity steady state exercise. Examples of this effort are a marathon running pace for recreational runners or the pace when you can talk without undue strain. You might think of it as your highest conversational pace, you can still chat but you can feel your effort doing so.

This first threshold is also marked by a ventilatory response when there is a disproportionate increase in the amount of air that you breathe per minute compared to the amount of oxygen consumed (VO_2). The low or first threshold, formerly known as the "aerobic threshold", has a plethora of other names as well, which has led to confusion of exactly what is being measured. The first threshold for aerobically fit individuals is often around 80% of maximum heart rate.[4] This threshold is the highest work effort or load that can be sustained for about 20-30 minutes for the recreational athlete without a progressive increase in the blood lactate levels. For the elite cyclist, it is that intensity that can be sustained for about 60 minutes usually during a competitive event.

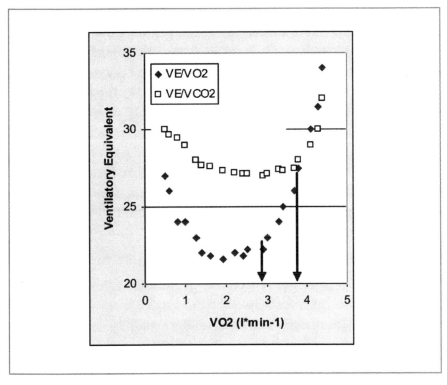

Regardless of how it is measured or coupled, the first lactate threshold LT_1 and the first ventilatory threshold VT_1 are substitutes for each other where the effort or intensity at VT_1 approximates LT_1. LT_1 is a surrogate marker for VT_1. Whether it is measured via blood or respiration, for a runner or cyclist, this biomarker is your sustainable exercise capacity. That is, your ability to continue exercising at the low threshold is mostly limited by the amount of muscle fuel, or glycogen, you have available.

The second threshold is also measured by changes in breathing and in blood lactate levels. The second lactate threshold, LT_2, is often called the maximal lactate steady state or RCT for respiratory compensation threshold. It is marked by a blood concentration of around 4.0 millimoles or one millimole above the maximal steady state level.

This second threshold is also marked by a second increase in the amount of total air that we breathe. This time there is an increase that is out of proportion to either oxygen consumption or carbon dioxide production. At this effort, conversation becomes more than just strained, but essentially extremely difficult for everyone.[5] This threshold often occurs at about 90% of maximum heart rate. For our purposes here, it is called the high threshold where VT_2 approximates LT_2. The high lactate threshold, LT_2, is a surrogate marker for VT_2 and VT_2 is similarly a surrogate or substitute marker for LT_2. For our purposes, this exercise intensity is called the second threshold or threshold two or T_2. Because of the confusion in terminology and the difficulty for many to comprehend these markers of physiological changes, the differences between high and low threshold are shown as follows:

The first or low threshold called T_1:

Maximal lactate steady state = LT_1 = range between 2.0–2.5 mM of lactate = sometimes confusingly called the aerobic threshold = VT_1 = approximately 80% of maximum heart rate or simply T_1

The second or high threshold called T_2:

Approximately 4.0 mM of blood lactate concentration = sometimes confusingly call the anaerobic threshold = respiratory compensation threshold = approximately 85% VO_2 max = individual anaerobic threshold = VT_2 = about 90% of maximum heart rate or simply T_2

Yes, there are slight differences between the measurement of low threshold using lactate versus ventilation but they are not substantial enough to quarrel over. And yes, there are small differences between the exercise intensity that best describes the high threshold but they are not large either. The second lactate threshold and the second ventilatory threshold happen at the highest intensity at which truly sustainable exercise is possible for under 8 minutes. T_2 is the highest intensity you can sustain without turning on the afterburners that lead quickly to exhaustion.

In other words, the heart rate, breathing, acidic levels of the blood, and effort are nominally different at each of these two measurements. To be precise, the low and high thresholds should be measured by drawing blood samples for lactate threshold (LT) or by using gas analyzers (VT). But in large part, the day-to-day variations in our own physiology from over or under training, from the effect of our nutrition, from gaining or missing sleep, and from the allostatic stress of our lives complicate these results. Generally, exercise scientists don't care about how thresholds are measured, but that they are measured, period.

THREE MUSKETEERS OF THRESHOLD TRAINING

Have you ever accomplished something but someone else gets the credit for it? Or have you ever accomplished something and no one gets the credit? Well, I don't want that to happen to the modern-day scientists who contributed to the development of the Heart Zones Threshold Training system, because there is credit that deserves to be dispensed. There are three stars, exercise scientists celebrities, who have not only helped to investigate threshold responses but have been champions for using the two biomarkers for athletic training. These are the researchers who toil in the labs, making some of us their so-called lab rats to uncover and discover how the human body really works.

The first musketeer is Karl Wasserman, MD, and author of *Cardiopulmonary Exercise Testing and Cardiovascular Health* (2002). Karl deserves most of the credit for his ground breaking investigations of the ventilatory thresholds and the identification of the close associations of lactate response to ventilatory response in the 1960s.

The second musketeer is actually a team of researchers who were first to explore the importance of measuring lactate by taking blood samples to assess changes in the pH caused by changes in exercise intensity, Skinner/McLellan and Kindermann. They identified the two lactate thresholds as biomarkers, publishing the early studies about this relationship.

My favorite musketeer of the three is Carl Foster, Ph. D. Carl who is credited for his exhaustive work in putting together training concepts and theories that lead to the creation of the Foster Threshold Talk Test, a field test for measuring both the low and high threshold numbers in one assessment. Carl, the past President of the American College of Sports Medicine, also deserves credit for his seminal work using the practical application of rating of perceived exertion, RPE. Carl Foster, currently at the University of Wisconsin-La Crosse, adapted the original Talk Test to create a new assessment, the Threshold Talk Test to field test threshold using RPE, ability to speak, and heart rate data. He now has several peer-reviewed published articles validating the test that you are about to experience.

Ready to take a field test to assess your low or T_1 and the high threshold or T_2 ? Popularly known as the "Talk Test" or Foster "Can You Speak Comfortably" threshold field test.

ONE TEST, TWO THRESHOLDS

There are a number of different field tests to estimate threshold heart rate numbers that couple heart rate with speeds at a certain distance; duration of time, especially in race competitions; and rate of perceived exertion (RPE). The purpose of taking just one test to measure threshold is that it is easy to administer, doesn't require anything but a heart rate monitor, and is backed with scientific research to validate the results. As a quick review, the following is a description of the low and high thresholds used for field testing purposes:

• *Low Threshold (T1):* This ventilatory, or breathing response or effort in speaking is associated with the last heart rate number when you acknowledge that speaking during the exercise is comfortable. This is the heart rate number that corresponds with the first threshold, T1. This intensity is the heart rate number coupled with the last stage when you answer "yes" to the question: Can you speak comfortably?

• *High Threshold (T2):* This second shift in the ventilatory response to exercise is the effort level when the individual can no longer speak comfortably at all. At this point in the field test, the individual no longer wants to or can speak easily or continuously.

There are advantages to using ventilatory or breathing responses as a way to measure the two threshold heart rate anchors using this test. According to Foster, "Testing for the low threshold has the advantage of still being in the safe zone, so you aren't going to start killing off the unfits during the test."

How accurate is this field test for the two thresholds compared to lab tests? According to Foster and his research, "It is within spitting distance of laboratory tests for the first ventilatory threshold." That spitting distance is close enough to lab accuracy for you to use to test and later re-test to measure your important biomarker, T_1.

PROTOCOL FOR THRESHOLD TEST: ASK THE QUESTION, "CAN YOU SPEAK COMFORTABLY?"

The Foster "Can You Speak Comfortably" Threshold Field Test uses a speech provoker which must be spoken out loud. The speech stimulator that Carl Foster found works the best is the "Pledge of

Allegiance," familiar to most Americans because it is learned in most elementary schools and because it is both short and long enough - a 31-word paragraph. If you prefer, you can use any other paragraph of similar length, as long as it is easy to remember and recite. Put the words of that paragraph on a cue card so that you—or the individual taking the test if you are administering it—can read it aloud. It's easiest to perform the test on a calibrated exercise cycle or treadmill because you can regulate the workload more accurately, but you can take the test on a running track, swimming in a pool,[6] or on an outdoor bike.

If you are self-administering the test, here's the basic how-to-give-it-to-yourself protocol. Put on your heart rate monitor and turn off the monitor's zone alarms (audible or visual). Make sure that you are familiar with this test protocol in advance. As in all cardio-exercise activities, begin with an adequate warm up before starting. Each exercise stage in the test is 2 minutes in duration. Using a count-up timer, at the end of each 1 minute and 30 seconds, begin to say aloud the Pledge of the Allegiance or similar paragraph at a moderate and even speech rate.

After finishing the recitation, ask and then write down the answer to the question "Can you speak comfortably?" There are only three acceptable responses:

• *Yes (+):* This means unequivocally, without doubt, you can speak comfortably.

• *Not sure (+/-):* This means maybe, possibly, doubtful.

• *No (-):* This means you cannot speak comfortably, no longer wanting to freely speak.

At the end of each two-minute exercise stage, write down the answer to the question "Can you speak comfortably?" by recording a plus sign (+) for a "yes," a plus and minus (+/-) for "not sure," and a minus sign (-) for "no" in the form shown. Then increase your heart rate by 10 bpm, exercise for 1.5 minutes, recite the Pledge of Allegiance or other paragraph, and then answer the question "Can you speak comfortably?" again. Continue to repeat these two-minute stages until you reach an effort where you begin to doubt whether you can speak comfortably and as easily, and you answer the question "not sure" and write down (+/-). You now have a choice to stop the test or continue. I recommend that you stop the test because what you need most is your heart rate number coupled to T_1. If you would like an estimate of the second or high threshold and you are fit and healthy, you can voluntarily continue the sequence until you say "No" but it is not necessary and should only be continued if you are fit and healthy.

The following is a step-by-step description of the Foster "Can You Speak Comfortably" Threshold Field test aka the talk test.

Step 1. Warm up adequately for at least 3–5 minutes.

Step 2. Each stage is 2 minutes. Starting at a heart rate of 110 bpm, increase effort or intensity by 10 bpm for each 2-minute stage.

Step 3. At 1.5 minutes into each exercise stage, recite the Pledge of Allegiance out loud.

Step 4. After recitation ask this one question: "Can you speak comfortably?"

Step 5. There are only three answers that you may select: yes (+) or uncertain (+/−) or no (−)

Step 6. Enter a sign that matches your answer in the table below after each 2-minute interval.

Step 7. Continue to increase the effort steadily until you answer 'uncertain." Stop the test.

Step 8. Cool down adequately.

Step 9. Circle the last positive "yes" or (+) heart rate number. That is your low threshold number.

Step 10. Use the Heart Zones Threshold Chart to set your five training zones.

• T_1 = The last "yes" or plus sign (+), called the "last positive" is your low threshold.

• T_2 = Your first negative (−), when you say "no," is your high threshold.

Time (minutes)	Heart Rate (bpm)	Yes (+) Not Sure (+ -) No (-)	Power (watts) if you have a meter	Stage (2 minute intervals)
0-5	110 bpm			0
5-7	120 bpm			1
7-9	130 bpm			2
9-11	140 bpm			3
11-13	150 bpm			4
13-15	160 bpm			5
15-17	170 bpm			6
17-19	180 bpm			7
19-21	190 bpm			8

The low threshold is the last heart rate number, the last stage, that you answer "yes." At this intensity level, you still elicit a positive response. You can recite the Pledge of Allegiance without undue stress on your breathing pattern. The heart rate number at the last measurement before the response "I am not sure" or "uncertain" is called the "last positive." This heart rate number is your T_1 or first threshold marker.

The threshold field test continues for another 2 minutes and 10-bpm increase and so forth until the individual answers the question "Can you speak comfortably?" with the answer "not sure." You are not sure whether you can talk comfortably. Saying the Pledge of Allegiance is more difficult than the last time you answered the question. This is above T_1 and you can choose to stop the test. You have all the data you need, your heart rate number at your low threshold, the last positive "yes."

The negative stage (−) is when you first cannot talk comfortably. This heart rate intensity is approximately 90% of maximum heart rate or a rating of perceived exertion of an eight or RPE 8. You cannot recite the Pledge of the Allegiance without difficulty or uncomfortable breathing. Ratcheting up the test to hit the high threshold number is not for beginners, unfit persons, or those returning to fitness activities.

According to Foster, there are a few tricks to making the threshold field test more accurate:

• Do the test at least two different times to reduce error. It can be done on the same day. Take at least a 10- to 20-minute break between the two tests.

• Use an easy-to-control piece of cardio-equipment such as a cycle ergometer or treadmill, for example. You can control speed and gradient increases more precisely than walking-jogging-running outside, where you must estimate your effort levels rather than using electronic dash-board information.

• Enlist a Heart Zones CPT, Certified Personal Trainer who has experience with the assessment and knows the protocol to facilitate the test in order to eliminate error.

• If you are a multi-sport athlete, do the test in each sport activity, because both threshold heart rates are sport specific.

WHAT'S REALLY GOING ON

So what is happening physiologically? Basically, as exercise intensity increases, ventilation increases in a linear manner until you reach a certain intensity level called the first "cross-over" point. At the cross-over intensity level, the ventilatory demands are greater than the ability of the oxygen delivery system to meet those demands. At this intensity level and heart rate number, ventilation increases exponentially rather than linearly. The cross-over point is nearly identical to the first lactate threshold intensity level. At the point that ventilation crosses over from linear to exponential increases is known a first ventilatory threshold (VT_1). As Carl Foster explains, "The discontinuity of linearity in either blood lactate accumulation or ventilatory patterns during incremental exercise represents a convenient marker of exercise training intensity."

WHERE IS T_2?

High threshold, T_2, is located somewhere Zone 5a and Zone 5b.That is, the second threshold is about or around or near the heart rate numbers that are 105% of your threshold heart rate. That means that there is about a 6-10 bpm separation between the low and the high threshold, between T_1 and T_2 . This difference, this range, is highly variable and unique to each person in large part based on their fuel or substrate utilization.

You can see from the Threshold Chart that the heart rate value at 105% of threshold divides two zones. T_2 is between the Lactate Clearance Zone 5a and the Maximum VO_2 Zone which is 5b. This separator, 105% of threshold is an estimate of T_2 and not laboratory-tested precise. To measure accurately your heart rate at T_2 , you need to participate in a metabolic assessment test described earlier in this chapter. Lab quality tests are easy to take today with the increase interest in physiological testing for performance. For those who are highly competitive in your sport, taking 2-4 metabolic assessments a year is recommended. That is because both vary with your fitness level and your training cycles. The goal is to move the two dynamic threshold numbers higher and higher toward your maximum heart rate.

THE THRESHOLD ZONES

Just like maximum heart rate training, threshold training uses the zones methodology of anchoring the zones on physiological biomarker. The five threshold zones are similar to the five maximum heart rate zones with some important differences. When exercise effort reaches T_1 intensity, the metabolic response to the high, hot, hard stress turns exponential. Below threshold, the heart rate response is linear, above the first threshold, it becomes exponential. Thata is after T_1 there is a major shift in your cardio-response and effort to compensate for the severe metabolic stress.

This shift from linear to exponential begins when heart rate first crosses over into Zone 5. To delineate these changes, Zone 5 is subdivided into three sub-zones: Zone 5a, Zone 5b, Zone 5c. All three of these sub-zones, the Zone 5 a, b, c, are very hard, high, hot zones. They are reserved for the brave at heart that love higher intensity and the wonderful benefits that are derived from the appropriate amount of time spent there.

There are different benefits that accrue from each of the threshold zones. Use the following Zone Description chart in your planning should assist your decision on TIZ, time in zones in order that get the most benefits out of each work out.

Zone Number	Zone Description
1	This is very low intensity, the comfort zone. Training in Zone 1 burns a low number of calories. Training in this zone provides some health benefits: lowers cholesterol, reduces stress, and improves your blood pressure.
2	This is an easy zone that you can maintain for long periods of time. Warm-up and cool-down in this zone. Do your recovery workouts in this zone. Enjoy light intensity walks, rides, skates, and runs because you just begin to break a sweat training in Zone 2.

Zone Number	Zone Description
3	This is a moderate intensity zone that provides aerobic improvement benefits: increases in the number of mitochondria, improves fat utilization, and burns more total calories than the lower zones. Cardiac muscle improvements occur resulting in increased capillary density and profusion.
4	This is the sub-first threshold zone that results in improvement in aerobic capacity or cardiovascular fitness improvements. Build up your concentration of aerobic enzymes by spending time in this high calorie burning zone.
T_1	**Low Threshold**
5a	This above T_1 zone is a valuable place to spend your cardio-workout time because it improves your ability to tolerate and clear lactate. The supra-T_1 zone are for those who want to get fast and faster at their sport-specific activity because it improves the energy systems that support speed.
T_2	**High Threshold**
5b	This high intensity zone is for those who want to increase their maximum volume of oxygen, max VO_2 or maximal aerobic capacity. Most can only stay in this zone for 2-8 minute intervals without being forced to recover from the intensity. Highly stressful but very important if you want to achieve your highest level of cardio-fitness.
5c	This zone is above the stratosphere training intensity and is reserved for the extremely fit individual. If you are training with a goal of fitness you do not need to spend time in this zone. You are very close to your maximum heart rate. You can only stay in this zone for a mater of seconds with 20 seconds being long. This is for ballistic training activities.

Refer now to the Threshold Zones Chart on the next page. Read horizontally across the headings on the top row. Those headings give you details, by zone, of each of the following: zone number, intensity, of threshold, benefits, workout types, load, wellness zones, intensity measurements.

This Threshold Zones chart is the heart of the Heart Zones Threshold Training system because it provides you with the information that you need to support training in different intensities, or zones, to get different results. If you want to lose weight, do high performance training, or use physiological biomarkers for your training, using the Heart Zones Threshold Training system is for you.

HOW TO CALCULATE TRAINING LOAD

You can measure or quantify training load, the amount of exercise, by using the time in zone calculation that spells the word LIFT where:

L = IFT *or*

Load = Intensity x Frequency x Time *or*

Training Load = Zone Number x Number of Workouts x Elapsed time

Using the LIFT formula is key to your training because it quantifies the amount of exercise not just the volume (time or distance) by adding the key component - exercise intensity or effort.

As you climb into higher threshold heart rate numbers the weight or the load of the experience shifts from a linear to an exponential cardiac and metabolic cost. That means that each minute above T_1 is no longer a linear but becomes curvilinear increase in load. In calculating training load for threshold use the weight or values that as the multiplier. That is, each minute in each zone for threshold training shifts from below T_1 to an exponential value above T_1.

Zone Number	Number of Heart Zones Training	Example of a 10 minute workout in each zone
5c	90	Impossible to sustain for > 1 minute
5b	30	300 points
High Threshold		
5a	10	100 points

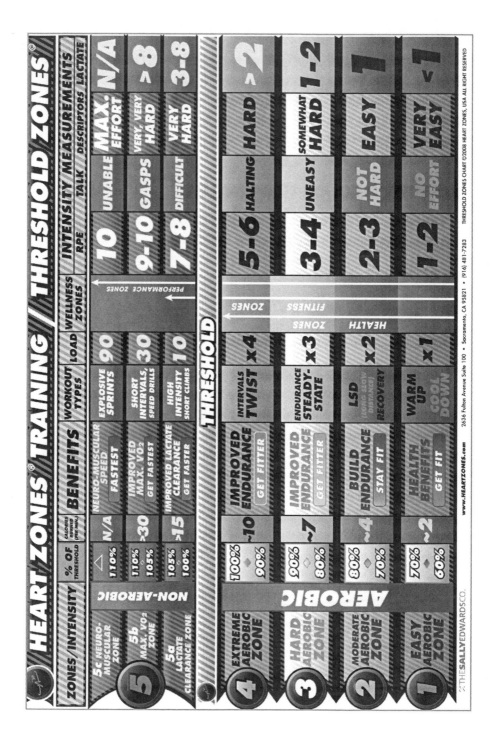

HEART ZONES® TRAINING // THRESHOLD ZONES

ZONES/INTENSITY		% OF THRESHOLD	CALORIES BURNED (PER MIN.)	BENEFITS	WORKOUT TYPES	LOAD	WELLNESS ZONES	INTENSITY MEASUREMENTS			
								RPE	TALK	DESCRIPTORS	LACTATE
5 5c NEURO-MUSCULAR ZONE	NON-AEROBIC	△110%	N/A	NEURO-MUSCULAR SPEED **FASTEST**	EXPLOSIVE SPRINTS	90	PERFORMANCE ZONES	10	UNABLE	MAX. EFFORT	N/A
5b MAX. VO₂ ZONE		110% 105%	>30	IMPROVED MAX. VO₂ **GET FASTEST**	SHORT INTERVALS, SPEED DRILLS	30		9-10	GASPS	VERY, VERY HARD	>8
5a LACTATE CLEARANCE ZONE		105% 100%	>15	IMPROVED LACTATE CLEARANCE **GET FASTER**	HIGH INTENSITY SHORT CLIMBS	10		7-8	DIFFICULT	VERY HARD	3-8
THRESHOLD											
4 EXTREME AEROBIC ZONE	AEROBIC	100% 90%	~10	IMPROVED ENDURANCE **GET FITTER**	INTERVALS TWIST	x4	PERFORMANCE ZONES	5-6	HALTING	HARD	>2
3 HARD AEROBIC ZONE		90% 80%	~7	IMPROVED ENDURANCE **GET FITTER**	ENDURANCE STEADY-STATE	x3	FITNESS ZONES	3-4	UNEASY	SOMEWHAT HARD	1-2
2 MODERATE AEROBIC ZONE		80% 70%	~4	BUILD ENDURANCE **STAY FIT**	LSD (LONG SLOW DISTANCE) RECOVERY	x2	HEALTH ZONES	2-3	NOT HARD	EASY	1
1 EASY AEROBIC ZONE		70% 60%	~2	HEALTH BENEFITS **GET FIT**	WARM UP COOL DOWN	x1		1-2	NO EFFORT	VERY EASY	<1

© THE SALLY EDWARDS CO. www.HEARTZONES.com 2636 Fulton Avenue Suite 100 • Sacramento, CA 95821 • (916) 481-7283 THRESHOLD ZONES CHART ©2008 HEART ZONES, USA ALL RIGHT RESERVED

Zone Number	Number of Heart Zones Training	Example of a 10 minute workout in each zone
Low Threshold		
4	4	40 points
3	3	30 points
2	2	20 points
1	1	10 points

GIVE THRESHOLD A SHOT - IT WORKS

There are a lot of different ways to train using training tools that make your workouts easier and more powerful. Threshold training has become popular particularly among cyclists and triathletes because of it's very nature. It is dynamic. It is based on metabolic changes more than central cardiac changes. It demands that you test and re-test. It is motivational because it shows the improvements in your fitness. It is simple way to train. Try it. Give it a chance. Take the gauntlet and charge into a new phase of your training - threshold training.

I can give you pages of reasons to change from any of the training systems you might have used in the past from the Heart Zones original maximum heart rate system, or our power cycling system, or using RPE for your training, the time-trial/pacing system. Rather, I'll challenge you to give threshold training a try and see for yourself. Few who try it return to the Heart Zones maximum heart rate system. Why? Find out for yourself - it's a major shift in how you train.

And, if you make the change to the Heart Zones Threshold Training system, I guarantee this, your fitness level will change. Your training program will change. And as a result, your performance will change. The axiom "All things change when we do" is never more true than by trying a different way to workout.

So program one or two threshold numbers into your monitor and start training using the system - but begin with a field or lab test to measure your two thresholds. Load those numbers into your heart rate monitor as a new zone. And train above and below T_1 and T_2. Strange things can happen training between the two Ts. It's called the Black Hole. Stay tuned there's more about the Black Hole comin' to you!

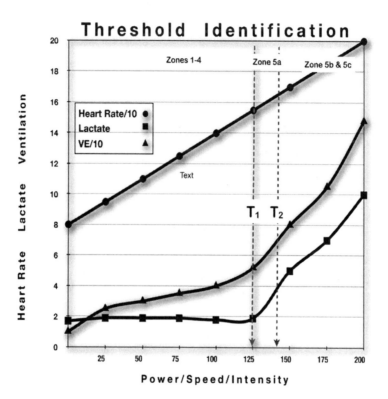

Chapter 19

Every Heart & Every Body

We sit across my conference table at the from each other, separated by gulfs of hardwood and culture. The four Japanese businessmen in their dark suits and white shirts smile politely, looking directly at my more informal team of three.

We've come to this conference table to try to effect an unlikely alliance, marrying our very American franchise of athletic footwear specialty stores to the very Japanese monolith of one of the semi-legendary billion-billion yen kegetsu conglomerates. Their business is the business of international commerce, the pouring of molten steel, the creation of silicon chip with an annual report that looks like a telephone book. After 17 years and co-founding Fleet Feet Sports, my company is tiny in comparison.

We've done our homework on these gentlemen, and frankly, we are more than a little puzzled. Finally, after polite small talk, I open the meeting in classic American directly-to-the-point style: "Why would a kegetsu be interested in having the Japanese rights to Fleet Feet Sports, a small American franchise athletic footwear company?"

There is a slight, perhaps not entirely comfortable, pause. Then the most senior representative, with carefully selected and placed words, explains that it is not necessarily the franchise opportunity that they covet. What they would like to import, rather, is our fitness values and active lifestyle. It would give their company great status, he continues, if they could bring to Japan a company like Fleet Feet Sports.

"Our society has historically been one of spectators," he says. "Those who watch and don't do. But we are trying to become a society of participants - those who do and want to become more. We would, ultimately, like to evolve into the highest state called 'be', that of being fit and strong, living our values by being who we are and living a fitness lifestyle."

Watch...do...be.

What this team of Japanese businessman wanted to buy from me was a way to export the fitness lifestyle, albeit through a sports shops brand that walked-the-talk. You see, those at Fleet Feet Sports, the company that I co-founded in 1976, was at the highest of the three evolutionary phases:

- Watchers - spectators who stand on the sidelines and cheer for others.

- Doers - active people who do so because they have to.

- Be'ers - the mostly highly evolved state of those who live the be active lifestyle.

Watch...do...be. Where are you on this evolutionary process? I ask because Heart Zones Training is a revolutionary new fitness, health, performance, and weight management system. It is the program that can help you translate your goals into reality and, ultimately, into the healthy and nurturing lifestyle. This isn't a "talk-show" miracle. We don't have pills that can make you be thinner, richer, smarter, and more attractive. Rather, here is something based on a solid scientific foundations that's guaranteed to work.

What we do have is a plan - a system - a methodology called HZT or Heart Zones Training, that can free you from watching (whether it's a video your eyes are glued to or this book) and lead you through doing to the highest stage, being. It doesn't matter where you place yourself on the continuum from couch potato to Olympian; Heart Zones Training is a personal fitness revolution that can and will work for you. The point of the story and Heart Zones Training is that we have a credible chance of reaching fulfillment, of living happiness if we can transcend into a lifestyle of health and fitness. "Being" in the watch...do... be sequence is when you accomplish that.

You've probably heard those word "evolution and revolution" before, attached to everything from exercise machines to chips and dip. The revolutionary secret behind Heart Zones Training is the soul of a new machine: the heart rate monitor. A heart rate monitor does exactly what it sounds like it should be doing - monitoring your physiological response to stress using the language of heart rate. Technology has evolved to the point where any of us can put a transmitter around our chests, then watch our hearts thump...thump...thump on the watch-like receiver on our wrists.

So, what's so revolutionary about this?

Just this: for the first time we have a solid link between our bodies and our minds, a reliable feedback loop that connects the brains with the brawn, so that we are truly in control of managing our wellbeing.

That's what *Heart Zones Training* is. Now just HZT.

Appendix 1.

Heart Zones Company and Products

Heart Zones USA is the premier provider of training services and programs for fitness enthusiasts, athletes, coaches, personal trainers, indoor cycling instructors, weight management consultants, and health/PE teachers. In 1992, the company developed the world's first heart-rate training system, the Heart Zones Training™ system. The company's branded and proprietary cardiovascular training system, Heart Zones Training, is practiced worldwide. Additionally, the company is the pre-eminent developer and patent-holder of new training systems coupled to new training technologies that meter, monitor, and manage fitness and sports performance cardio-training, emotional training, and metabolic health.

Founded by Triathlon Hall of Famer, best-selling author, celebrity coach, and legendary runner/triathlete Sally Edwards, Heart Zones USA has dedicated the last two decades to the research and application of the Heart Zones Training system.

Heart Zones USA is the world leader in training, education, and coaching services using a holistic approach to help individuals live an active healthy lifestyle. The company leads live and web events including seminars, workshops, certifications, and conferences to train fitness enthusiasts, health care workers, fitness professionals, teachers, and weight management specialists.

Offering a broad range of products and services to meet the unique needs of anyone practicing, coaching, or teaching cardiovascular training, Currently, Heart Zones Training is used in 10,000 schools in America, Canada, Asia, and Western Europe and has certified over 5,000 individuals and coaches in the branded and proprietary training system.

Appendix 2.

About the Author

Sally Edwards, MA, MBA is the creator of the Heart Zones Training™ system. She is one of America's leading fitness, health, and sports performance experts. The proprietary and branded training system includes the patented and copyrighted Threshold Training System, Power Watts Cycling, and Heart Rate Training.

Sally has authored more than 23 books on health and fitness including her latest work, *The Big Book of Running* with Carl Foster, PH. D. (2010). With six titles on heart rate training including the first, *The Heart Rate Monitor Book,* Sally is recognized worldwide as the leading authority on training with both the cardiac muscle as well as the tools that monitor, measure, and manage health programs using a heart rate monitor.

This professional triathlete is a 16-time Ironman finisher and master world record holder, a member of the Triathlon Hall of Fame, and National Spokeswoman for the Danskin Women Triathlon and the Trek Women Triathlon. She has finished over 130 all-women's races.

This professional runner has won races from a mile to a hundred miles. She set the course record at the Western States 100 Mile Endurance Run, the American River 50 Mile ultramarathon, ran in the historic 1984 Olympic Trials Marathon, and won the Iditashoe 100-mile Snowshoe Race.

Today, she uses her passion for getting America fit to lead a company and team of Master trainers and coaches to present seminars, certifications, and workshops around the world for fitness professionals, health and physical education teachers, athletes, and fitness enthusiasts on physical, emotional, and metabolic fitness. She is the CEO of The Sally Edwards Company, a professional motivational speaking company.

INDEX

Breinigsville, PA USA
15 December 2010
251456BV00002B/2/P